Women's Leadership in Marginal Religions

Women's Leadership in Marginal Religions:

Explorations Outside the Mainstream

Edited by
Catherine Wessinger

UNIVERSITY OF ILLINOIS PRESS
Urbana and Chicago

© 1993 by the Board of Trustees of the University of Illinois
Manufactured in the United States of America
1   2   3   4   5   C   P   5   4   3   2   1

This book is printed on acid-free paper.

Library of Congress Cataloging-in-Publication Data

Women's leadership in marginal religions : explorations outside the mainstream
/ edited by Catherine Wessinger
      p.   cm.
Includes Index.
    ISBN 0-252-02025-1 (hard).—ISBN 0-252-06332-5 (pbk.)
    1. Women and religion—United States—History.   2. United States—
Religion.   I. Wessinger, Catherine Lowman.
BL2525.088   1993
291.6′082—dc20   93-7350
                                                                         CIP

Contents

Acknowledgments

First of all, I wish to acknowledge the contributors to this volume. From the contributors, I have learned much that has greatly enhanced my ability to teach about women and religion. Of the contributors, primary thanks must go to Mary Farrell Bednarowski. This volume would not exist if she had not written her 1980 *Journal of the American Academy of Religion* article on women's leadership in nineteenth-century marginal religions in America, and if she had not been willing to let us use this article as a starting point. Through the course of this project, it has been a pleasure to discover in Mary Farrell Bednarowski not only a stimulating colleague but also a good friend. The manuscript as a whole has benefited from comments by Catherine Albanese, Stephen Stein, and Amanda Porterfield. Amanda Porterfield's comments along with conversations with Tom Robbins were particularly helpful in pushing me to address explicitly issues in the Introduction that were formerly implicit. I have received useful feedback on individual chapters from Tiina Allik, Ina Fandrich, Nancy Anderson, Alanda Wraye, Starhawk, Joy Dixon, Joy Mills, Julieta Ruppert, and Karma Lekshe Tsomo. Contributors Mary Farrell Bednarowski and Rosemary Radford Ruether were very helpful in giving me feedback on specific chapters. I appreciate Timothy Miller's assistance as a consultant on marginal religions. I thank Liz Dulany, associate director of the University of Illinois Press, and Rita D. Disroe, manuscript editor, for carefully steering the manuscript to publication.

Introduction

Going Beyond and Retaining Charisma: Women's Leadership in Marginal Religions

Catherine Wessinger

Charismatic women have played significant roles as religious leaders in America. The spiritual experiences and visions of Ann Lee (d. 1784) and her ecstatic modes of worship attracted a following, ultimately resulting in the ordered Shaker communities of celibate men and women that flourished in the early nineteenth century. Later in the nineteenth century, American women became famous as trance speakers and mediums after the Fox sisters' claims of communication with the dead sparked interest in Spiritualism. Mary Baker Eddy founded the Church of Christ, Scientist, based on her healing experience entailing her immediate perception of the truth contained in the gospels. The mysterious Russian noblewoman, Madame Helena Blavatsky, claimed to receive teachings directly from hidden Masters of the Wisdom, and these teachings became the primary scriptures of the Theosophical movement. In contemporary America, white Pentecostal women cite God's calling to justify their itinerant preaching or pastoral ministry. Due to their direct contact with the Holy Spirit and with their spiritual foremothers, African American women in New Orleans are ordained as ministers, bishops, and archbishops in the Spiritual churches there. The extraordinary nature of the leadership of all these women suggests that there is a need for women's religious leadership to be sanctioned by charisma, the direct experience of the sacred. But is it possible for women to go beyond charismatic legitimation of religious authority, and if so, how will that take place?

   In the study of the world's religions, a search for women as religious leaders inevitably leads to charismatic women who are saints, shamans, healers. However, recent scholarship has amply demonstrated that in mainstream religious traditions most women are marginalized. This marginalization determines women's options for leadership, access to education, and women's relation to institutional structures. In a highly patriarchal religion and culture,[1] women may be seen as incapable of achieving the ultimate religious goal. The theology and folklore may depict women as less than fully human and certainly not as equal to men.[2] In a patriarchal religion, women are not deemed capable of exercising religious leadership in the ways that are institutionally routinized in that religion. Occasionally, a charismatic woman may break through the patriarchal structures and establish for herself a sphere of freedom based on her direct communication with the sacred. This strategy accounts for the often noted connection between women's religious leadership and spirit possession.[3] The charismatic woman's experiences may be co-opted and contained by the structures of the patriarchal religion,[4] or she may succeed in founding her own religion, which is necessarily marginal to the mainstream patriarchal religion and culture. Since the inclusion of women in positions of leadership and authority can be taken as a primary indicator of full inclusion of women in a religious tradition, the marginalization of women in the religions leads to the following question: What factors are conducive to women's religious leadership that are not based primarily on charisma?

Women's Leadership in Marginal Religions: Explorations Outside the Mainstream, while examining the lives of a number of charismatic women founders, is primarily concerned to discover if there are factors supportive of the routine, noncharismatic religious leadership of women. After the passing of the charismatic woman founder of a marginal religion, religious leadership usually passes to men. What factors, if any, help to ensure the continued religious leadership of women? In the course of this inquiry, our scope is primarily marginal religions in nineteenth- and twentieth-century America. These marginal religions shed light on the theological and institutional factors that are likely to promote women's routine leadership.

Gender of Deity, the Fall, the Clergy, and the Roles of Women

In an article published in 1980 entitled "Outside the Mainstream: Women's Religion and Women Religious Leaders in Nineteenth-Century America,"[5] Mary Farrell Bednarowski argues that common factors can be found in religions with women in important leadership roles. Bednarowski, a historian of religions in America, was looking for women religious leaders, women who were not subordinated in their religion. In her search, she noted that standard works on religions in America omitted consideration of women's religious experiences and achievements. In the mainstream religions, women primarily were members of the congregations, while the ministers, leaders, and theologians were men. Bednarowski further noted that the few women who were mentioned in standard histories were leaders in dissenting religious groups.[6] After making a comparison of four such marginal groups that have their origin or experienced their heyday in the nineteenth century—Shakerism, Spiritualism, Christian Science, and Theosophy—Bednarowski proposed that "women achieved leadership positions and equal status with men" in religions possessing the following four characteristics:

1. a perception of the divine that de-emphasized the masculine either by means of a bisexual divinity or an impersonal, non-anthropomorphic divine principle;
2. a tempering or denial of the doctrine of the Fall;
3. a denial of the need for a traditional ordained clergy;
4. a view of marriage that did not stress the married state and motherhood as the proper sphere for woman and her only means of fulfillment.

In the light of the main emphases of the Judaeo-Christian tradition, it is apparent why, based on the empirical evidence discovered in these marginal religious groups, Bednarowski highlighted these four characteristics. Our western culture's emphasis on a God who is omnipotent, transcendent, and sometimes vengeful is seen by feminists as being played out in authoritarian and punitive religious structures. They consider this God to be modeled after the patriarchal head of the ancient family, in whom all rights were vested over the other family members and slaves.[7] This solely masculine image of God makes it nearly impossible for his believers to accept a woman in a priestly role. The film *Woman-Priest,*[8] which records the "irregular" ordination in 1974 of eleven Episcopalian women as priests, also records the protest of a male priest who proclaimed "God shall be called Father and so shall his priests!" In the Roman Catholic Church's "Declaration on the Question of the Admission of Women to the Ministerial Priesthood" (1976), the maleness of Jesus Christ becomes a bar to women being priests. This document describes the priest as acting in the person of Christ (*in persona Christi*) and "being his very image, when he pronounces the words of consecration." There must be a "natural resemblance" between the priest and Christ, and if the priest were a woman "it would be difficult to see in the minister the image of Christ."[9]

A historical examination of women in the Judaeo-Christian tradition shows that the traditional doctrine of the Fall, in which a woman is seen as the cause of the Fall and women generally are seen as more sinful than men, must either be reinterpreted or denied outright if women are to be considered equals and to exercise religious leadership equally with men.[10] My chapter in this volume on American women who turn to Hinduism and Buddhism suggests that it is not only the Judaeo-Christian tradition that has blamed the fallenness of the human condition on women. Rosemary Radford Ruether notes, that to counter this situation, some of the liturgies of the Women-Church movement reclaim and affirm Eve and the apple. As a feminist theologian, Ruether reinterprets sin as a condition where life-giving relationships of equivalence are turned into death-dealing relationships of dominance and subordination.

For women to function as religious leaders necessitates a broadened view of gender roles that does not stress marriage and motherhood to the exclusion of other activities and means of fulfillment for women. Even in the Christian monastic traditions, a woman is validated in her role as a celibate religious because she is the bride of Christ. In his 1988 statement "On the Dignity and Vocation of Women," Pope John Paul II affirms the equal dignity of women but is unable to imagine a woman in any other vocation besides those of mother or virgin.[11]

This book explores the issue of women's religious leadership in light of Bednarowski's four points in order to come to a more complete understanding of factors supportive of women's religious leadership, particularly leadership that is not supported by claims of extraordinary charisma.[12] These characteristics have for some time been affirmed by contemporary religious feminists as necessary for a religion in which women are equal. The essays in this book determine if this is actually the case by an empirical examination of the evidence. The four factors profiled by Bednarowski represent the starting point for our consideration of women's leadership in marginal religions, but the authors have not confined their inquiry to only these issues. In this investigation, we have been primarily concerned with groups that either have women and men in similar and equal roles, or groups in which the leadership of women predominates.

Marginal Religions

In examining women's leadership in marginal religions, it must be noted that there are many types of religious marginality. To a great extent, whether or not a religion is considered marginal depends on the perspective of the person or group making that judgment. R. Laurence Moore, in his *Religious Outsiders and the Making of Americans,* has pointed out that religious marginality is very fluid, and that religions regarded as marginal to American culture can possess typically American characteristics. Before

World War I, the American religious mainstream was regarded as Protestant, even though as early as the mid-nineteenth century, Roman Catholicism was the largest denomination in the United States. The editor has been guided by the definition of the American mainstream that was popularized after World War II, that of Protestantism-Catholicism-Judaism.[13] This assumption was operative retroactively even to those periods when Catholicism and Judaism were not considered part of the American mainstream. Even within this broad definition of the American mainstream, there can be found groups, for instance the Mormons, that are considered marginal even though they are numerically very large. There are many types of religious marginality, and what was marginal can become mainstream and vice versa. The peculiar demands and limitations of editing a volume make it impossible to include examples of all types of marginal religions in America, or even to definitely identify a particular religion as marginal. Listed below are the types of religious marginality represented in this volume:

1. Groups whose members separate willingly from the mainstream to preserve religious truth as they see it and tend to isolate themselves from what they consider to be a sinful world.

This first type describes the religious pattern that has been termed sectarian. In this volume, Shakerism is the best illustration of this pattern. The Pentecostals also can be seen as sectarians, although they do not isolate themselves so radically from mainstream culture.

2. Groups whose members may accept and conform to the social order, but reject the religious terms of the mainstream society. These groups tend to stress the importance of individual mystical experience.[14]

This second category refers to groups that sometimes have been labeled "cults" by the media. In this volume, the contributors do not find it necessary to use the word cult. It is assumed that these religions are worthy of study in their own right, and that there is no need to resort to pejorative labeling. Robert Ellwood points out that marginal religions of this sort appeal to people who feel marginal "behind the mask." People in this category are part of American mainstream culture, but have an inner sense of being different in their religiosity, and they reject the religious outlook of the American mainstream. This second category includes the specific organizations associated with Spiritualism, Theosophy, Christian Science, New Thought, and feminist spirituality.

3. Groups whose members feel excluded from the mainstream due to racism, so they are compelled (or choose) to form separate religious structures.

The third category is relevant to the chapter on the African American Spiritual churches in New Orleans by David Estes. African Americans have formed their own churches and denominations because of their experience of racism. Most persons outside the black community in New Orleans are unaware of the existence of the Spiritual churches. The next category of religious marginality is also relevant to the Spiritual churches.

4. Groups whose members feel excluded from the mainstream of society due to sexism, so they are compelled (or choose) to develop separate religious structures.

The fourth category describes the situation of black women in the Spiritual churches in New Orleans (Estes), as well as the feminist spirituality movement described by Cynthia Eller and the Women-Church movement described by Rosemary Radford Ruether. Women-Church is a fascinating example of women who remain in a mainstream religion (primarily Roman Catholicism), and yet feel forced by the patriarchy of that religion to seek separate women's spaces in order to develop women's liturgies and theology. Women in each of these cases develop autonomous spaces due to the sexism of their parent religion and/or culture. Interestingly, the women in each of these groups develop rituals to empower themselves and other women.

5. Groups which are foreign religions imported into the mainstream culture, and which have gained converts from the mainstream.

The fifth category refers to my study of American women who turn to imported religions in the Hindu and Buddhist traditions. This volume does not attempt to study these religions as immigrant religions.

Outside the Mainstream

The essays in this book have been grouped under three headings, each representing a family of religions. These are: "Women in the Spirit"; "Women in the Metaphysical Movement"; and "Contemporary Women as Creators of Religion." The reader will quickly notice that these "families" are not mutually exclusive and that the members of one family will demonstrate a close kinship to members of the other families.

The authors, as historians, folklorists, and theologians, have varied in their approach to the issues of the gender of deity, the Fall, the clergy, and the roles of women. To avoid repetition, these four points are not explicitly recited in every chapter, even though they are considered. In my following treatment of the material contained in the chapters, I attempt to summarize the general lessons that can be drawn relative to the four characteristics highlighted by Bednarowski. This section can be read as an introduction to the other essays. It can also serve as a summary review after reading the entire book.

The two religions in the section "Women in the Spirit," Shakerism and Pentecostalism, are Christian, and they are characterized by a concern to be in communion with the Holy Spirit. In the Christian tradition, this charismatic possession has been the most common way for women to exercise religious leadership and authority. In this way, Christianity is in continuity with animistic religions, in which shamanism provides a release of tensions, as well as an avenue to prestige and authority for the socially marginal.[15] One of these religions, Shakerism, has appeared to a number of scholars to be an early feminist religion, especially in its institutionalization of women's leadership, but closer investigation shows that this is not the case. The other, Pentecostalism, is highly patriarchal in its social structures and gender roles, but still allows scope for women to become preachers and ministers on the basis of their personal calling from God.

Shakerism, as one of the four groups examined by Bednarowski in 1980, possesses the features she considers to be positively correlated with women's leadership. Marjorie Procter-Smith pushes the analysis of Shakerism further to provide a corrective to the overly optimistic presentation of Shakerism as a early feminist utopia. Procter-Smith demonstrates that even when leadership may be shared equally by men and women in a religious institution, this does not mean that power is as well. On the basis of her study of the Shakers, Procter-Smith makes important suggestions for the development of a genuinely feminist religion. In so doing, Procter-Smith points to the problematic use of goddess imagery that is not sufficiently emancipated from patriarchal meanings. She suggests that "a female deity or image of the divine being is empowering to women only insofar as it remains independent of and critical of existing patriarchal social structures and experiences."

The chapter by Elaine Lawless on Pentecostal women ministers and preachers demonstrates that women can gain access to the pulpit in a context where the four features we are considering are not present, but probably because of the lack of these, their position as religious leaders is precarious. These women transcend the gender roles imposed by their patriarchal culture by the charismatic experience of God's calling to the ministry. This reinforces, once again, the observation that through charisma, exceptional women can successfully claim authorization to exercise religious leadership in patriarchal religions and cultures. However, this does nothing to question the patriarchal structures that subordinate and marginalize all other women.

The second section of the volume, "Women in the Metaphysical Movements," derives its title from J. Stillson Judah's discussion of *The History and Philosophy of the Metaphysical Movements in America.*[16] This religious stream has its roots in Transcendentalism, with strong influences from Swedenborgianism and European occultism. The religions considered here are Spiritualism, Christian Science, the Theosophical movement, and the New Thought movement, including the Unity denomination. Also included in this section is the chapter on American women who are attracted to various forms of Hinduism and Buddhism. Asian religions have much in common with the metaphysical point of view and have contributed to its development in America.

The metaphysical worldview is monistic, with God seen as an immanent, universal principle. The metaphysical movements differ on how the material world is regarded. Christian Scientists consider matter to be nonexistent. Spiritualists, members of New Thought groups, and Theosophists tend to see matter as devolving from, while remaining part of, spirit. Both points of view are found in the Hindu tradition. The metaphysical movements have optimistic views of human nature, rejecting the doctrine of inherited original sin. The human condition is not one of sinfulness, but of ignorance, and salvation comes through knowledge. The metaphysical movements tend to view the individual as always progressing, either in the afterlife, or through the process of reincarnation. Since what is needed is knowledge of one's true relationship with God, and not atonement in the orthodox Christian sense, Jesus is generally seen as "a wayshower and teacher of morals." The tendency is to distinguish between the Christ-principle and the man Jesus, who was one with it. The metaphysical movements stress the priority of spirit or thought and emphasize that personal thoughts have the power to affect material experience for good or ill. Well-being is predicated upon an understanding of the laws of the unseen reality, in order to work with these laws, rather than to be ignorantly at their effect.

The metaphysical movements, in offering monism as an alternative to western theism and scientific materialism, represent a resurgence of the animistic worldview, presented in terms understandable to people living in industrialized society. Within the metaphysical monism, there is scope for interaction with personal inhabitants of the unconditioned reality, for religious leadership exercised in the form of shamanism, as well as for the traditional concern with healing. Additionally, organizations within the metaphysical movements have developed leadership roles for women that are not legitimated primarily by charisma.

The chapters in this and the subsequent section suggest that contemporary feminist spirituality and theology have strong roots in the metaphysical movements. Spiritualism and Christian Science (Ann Braude), the Theosophical movement (Robert Ellwood and Catherine Wessinger), and the New Thought movement, which developed when Christian Science practitioners broke away from Mary Baker Eddy and which has been influenced by Theosophy, all tend to demonstrate the four characteristics we are considering. The same is true of certain Hindu and Buddhist groups in America. However, there is great diversity concerning the factor of ordination.

Spiritualism with its mediums, Christian Science with its readers and practitioners, and the parent Theosophical Society with writers, lecturers, and elected officers, offer ways of religious leadership that do not require ordination. While the passive role of public trance speaker in the 1850s reinforced patriarchal gender roles, it did provide a voice to women at a time when it was considered inappropriate for women to speak publicly. This type of shamanism, as well as the direct spiritual knowledge claimed by early women founders like Mary Baker Eddy (Christian Science), Helena Blavatsky (Theosophy), and Myrtle Fillmore (Unity), again point to the importance of charisma in the cases of exceptional women. Concerning ordinary, routine religious leadership in these groups, of particular interest is Ann Braude's description of the Christian Science practitioner as seeking to teach and empower her patient to heal herself. This suggests that the Christian Science practitioner can be said to be serving in a form of nonclerical ministry (see Ruether), in that dependency on the ministering agent is not encouraged.

The metaphysical movements developed at a time in American history when changes in economy, education, and understanding of gender were impelling middle- and upper-class white women to extend their activities beyond the domestic sphere. The United States was shifting from an agrarian society, in which men and women labored jointly on the homestead, to an industrialized culture in which men went off to work, and middle- and upper-class women were left at home to do the unpaid tasks of child rearing and housework. An ideology developed entailing the glorification of women, assigning to them the preservation of traditional values, while men engaged in the morally contaminating work of business and politics. This outlook, which has been termed the "cult of true womanhood,"[17] asserted that woman's place was in the domestic sphere, which she was to make into a peaceful sanctuary to which her husband could return at the end of a hard day. Since men were too busy to attend to religion, and probably lacked interest in it, religion became part of the women's sphere. Women were to exercise a subtle moral influence on their men, and raise their children in piety. Gradually, higher levels of education were made available to young women, so that they could be better wives and mothers.

The increasing education of women, along with the revivalist activity of the nineteenth century, began to break down the boundaries of the women's sphere. The ideology of true womanhood, which said that woman's place was in the home, began to be used to justify women's activity in society. Women began to pray, testify, and even preach before "promiscuous" gatherings of men and women, and women actively strove to convert friends, children, and husbands. Women took seriously their mission as their culture's guardians of morality and began to extend that mission into the outer world. For this purpose, women formed themselves into a variety of voluntary associations to work for temperance, prison reform, abolition of slavery, overseas missions, assistance to the poor, moral reform, and ultimately, women's rights. In these endeavors, women gained experience in management, writing, and speaking, and developed a sense of sisterhood with other women. Men began to be concerned that women Sunday School teachers and missionaries might next aspire to the ordained ministry. Methodist women in the holiness movement, which stressed the need for a direct experience of sanctification from God, were particularly active in preaching and reform activities. This is yet another example of women achieving a public voice via pentecostal/shamanistic phenomena.

J. Gordon Melton sees these factors as forming the social environment in which it was expected that women could and should exercise religious leadership in mainstream as well as marginal groups. Given the assumption that women were particularly competent in religious matters, and the nascent, but growing, acceptance of the equality of women, Emma Curtis Hopkins became the first woman to exercise the powers of a bishop in the 1889 ordination of twenty women and two men. Melton credits Hopkins with being the first to connect the concepts of female deity and women's equality and to create an institution that trained women for the ordained ministry and helped them to find employment.

Melton's essay, and my own essay on women in Hindu and Buddhist groups in America, suggest that whereas a nonmasculine divinity, an anthropology that does not scapegoat women, an absence of a traditional ordained clergy, and a broadened view of gender roles, support women moving into positions of religious leadership, the social expectation of the equality of women is crucial. For example, the Hindu and Buddhist traditions are not restricted to concepts of masculine divinity, yet they have been extremely sexist. When these religions were brought to the west, it became necessary to reevaluate their traditional views of women. Numerous American women have been attracted to Asian religions and in combination with American expectations of equality have found them liberating. However, it seems that a religion's view of God is not totally irrelevant for women's roles, since women's leadership has been most limited in the Hindu group that is strongly focused on a highly personal male deity, the International Society for Krishna Consciousness. The various world religions demonstrate that religions in patriarchal contexts remain patriarchal, even when they conceptualize the sacred in terms of goddesses and impersonal principles. But the case of the International Society for Krishna Consciousness, considered in conjunction with the historical situation in the Judaeo-Christian tradition, suggests that a male personal deity naturally reinforces a view of human nature in which men are perceived as the only real human beings.

The essays by me, Melton, Dell deChant on Unity, and, in the third section, David Estes on African American Spiritual churches in New Orleans, suggest that ordained leadership does open up to women given the other three factors and the social expectation of equality. The Unity denomination founded by Charles and Myrtle Fillmore in 1889, and the most successful of the New Thought groups, offers an interesting case. Unity is of significance in our study of women's religious leadership, since its ministry resembles that of mainstream denominations. DeChant shows that in this religion, which possesses the characteristics that would seem to ensure the equality of women in religious leadership, institutionalization works to exclude women from positions of authority. Whereas over half of the Unity ministers are women, men predominate in the highest positions of the Association of Unity Churches. Inevitably, men are found as ministers of the larger Unity churches, and it remains to be seen whether the recent (1992) majority of women on the Board of the Association of Unity Churches is a fluke or the start of a trend. DeChant observes that despite the egalitarian leanings of our culture, it is still male-dominated and "although theological assertions may support the religious leadership of women, they do not assure gender-balance in the political structure of a religious institution."

The essays in the section of the book entitled "Contemporary Women as Creators of Religion" are about twentieth-century women who are seeking to reconcile their religiosity with their desire to affirm their equality. The groups considered in this section are the Spiritual churches in New Orleans, feminist spirituality and wicca, the Women-Church movement consisting of Roman Catholic women, the Mormons, and the contemporary Theosophical movement. Women in these groups tend to be strongly influenced by metaphysical thought, even when they are not institutionally affiliated with a metaphysical organization.

David Estes describes the Spiritual religion in New Orleans as possessing three of the four characteristics we are considering, including the de-emphasis of male divinity by the reliance on John 4:24: "God is spirit, and they that worship him must worship him in spirit and truth." Spiritual women's authority is validated by ordination as evangelists, ministers, bishops, and occasionally, as archbishops. African American modes of worship are often pentecostal or shamanistic, but in other parts of the country, access to this charisma has not made the ordained ministry widely available to women in the black churches.[18] Estes suggests that, compared to the rest of the United States, the New Orleans environment is more hospitable to black women in ordained ministry, because of a history of black women's leadership in the voodoo religion practiced there in the nineteenth century. Additionally, the Spiritual religion in New Orleans is an heir of nineteenth-century Spiritualism, in which women commonly served as mediums. However, Spiritual women still find themselves to be in a cultural context that is suspicious of religious authority being exercised by women. Spiritual women ministers must be willing to face the hostility of their neighbors, relatives, and even male ministers in their denomination. In response they devise a variety of creative, self-empowering rituals.

Feminist spirituality is defined by Cynthia Eller as combining feminism with a non-Christian religious orientation. Feminist wicca (witchcraft) is the most focused segment of the feminist spirituality movement, in which a great deal of attention is paid to the creation of feminist rituals affirming the sacred as immanent Goddess. While there are strong continuities with the metaphysical movement, Eller points out that twentieth-century feminist spirituality's glorification of women's bodies and women's close rapport with nature differs from the nineteenth-century strategy of identifying the basis of women's personhood as spirit, and separate from their bodies. In the late twentieth century, greater economic independence and access to contraception frees women to affirm their bodily femaleness without having to give up the prerogative of an active worldly life. Eller's description of feminist spirituality's "sacred history," as providing a mythic explanation for the origin of patriarchy and sustaining the hope that patriarchy will come to an end, helps to supply a critical perspective that is lacking in numerous books on goddess spirituality.[19]

Roman Catholic women, while observing the growing incorporation of Protestant women into ordained ministry,[20] and while functioning in a variety of fulfilling nonordained ministries themselves, consistently have had the door slammed in their faces over the issue of ordination. Since ordination is the prerequisite for access to positions where church policy, ethics, and theology are defined, all of which affect the lives of women, it is the final test of whether women are regarded as partners in the mystery of redemption.[21] Under such circumstances, creative feminist theological and liturgical innovations are being produced by Roman Catholic women involved in the Women-Church movement. Currently, Women-Church is not separatist in intent, but seeks to transform the patriarchal church.

In her 1980 article, Bednarowski raised the chicken-and-the-egg question of whether women are attracted to certain marginal religions because of their characteristics favoring women's equal participation and leadership, or whether women deliberately shape these religions to have these characteristics. It is more difficult to discern which dynamic is primary in the nineteenth-century groups. The women who shaped these religions, and the women who were attracted to them, were acting on the natural impulse to either create or locate a religion supportive of women's autonomy and personhood, but most did not have an explicit feminist consciousness. Rosemary Radford Ruether points out that in the late twentieth century, the women of the Women-Church movement are *consciously* developing a feminist religion that possesses all of the characteristics profiled by Bednarowski. The same can be said of feminist spirituality and wicca. In Women-Church, the denial of the need for the traditional ordained clergy becomes a strong anticlericalism. The impact of feminist spirituality's recovery of goddess imagery on the Women-Church movement is obvious, and Ruether notes that an issue for future resolution is the extent to which Women-Church is post-Christian.

That we have to refer to both feminist spirituality/wicca and Women-Church as movements, rather than as institutions, indicates a feminist avoidance of authoritarianism and clericalism. In light of deChant's discussion of the detrimental effects of institutionalization on the position of women ministers in the Unity denomination, this looseness of structure is probably a strength. Yet the editor wonders if the current lack of institutionalization of Women-Church prevents it from having a stronger impact on the Roman Catholic Church. Braude's discussion of Spiritualism indicates that anticlericalism and individualism, resulting in lack of institutionalization, can be detrimental to the perpetuation of the group, and therefore to the women's leadership in that group. The issue of institutionalization is key for women struggling against marginalization. The chapters by Procter-Smith, Melton, and deChant all point to the fact that women are seldom found in positions that control the economic wealth of a large religious institution.

In the final essay, Mary Farrell Bednarowski reflects further on women as creators of religion by examining the recent thought of feminist women in the Mormon, Roman Catholic, and Theosophical traditions. In addition to the four points she highlighted in 1980, Bednarowski sees a number of additional themes in feminist women's theologies: a growing preference for either a Goddess or goddesses; affirmation of the body as well as spirit; and emphasis on immanence with its corresponding concerns with community, interconnectedness, and the spiritual journey as descent rather than ascent. When women have the opportunity to function as creative theologians, these views seem to predominate.

Immanence is a pervading theme in *Women's Leadership in Marginal Religions: Explorations Outside the Mainstream.* Most of the groups examined stress that one can find the divine within, whether it is done by "getting in the Spirit," liturgy or ritual, or individual meditation. Does this emphasis reflect the age-old reliance of women on direct inner experience for religious empowerment? Or does women's outlook tend naturally to a concern with interconnectedness? Even in moving beyond charismatic legitimation, women continue to be highly concerned with discovering the sacred within themselves, other persons, and nature. This perspective contrasts with definitions of the sacred as being transcendent, and "other."[22]

In addition to Bednarowski, several other scholars have seen certain marginal religions in America as having significance for feminist women. Robert Ellwood, writing in 1979 of the tradition of women-founded religions in America, stated that in these nineteenth-century and early twentieth-century religions that "a possible American feminine religion has already been indistinctly limned by certain common features of these movements, and that when its day comes it could break out of marginality with surprising speed."[23] An article by Thomas Robbins and David Bromley on "Social Experimentation and the Significance of American New Religions"[24] suggests that marginal or new religious movements (NRMs) serve as "laboratories of social experimentation."[25] Robbins and Bromley describe new religious movements as contributing to a "subterranean cultural tradition" in which the freedom is taken to experiment with alternative sexual arrangements, gender roles, theology, organizational structures, and manipulation of economic resources. After a period of experimentation on the margins of society, certain innovations may become part of the cultural "tool kit" that the mainstream groups may begin to utilize. At this point, specific innovations may begin to be adopted in ways more acceptable to people in mainstream religious groups.[26]

As American women are going beyond the reliance on extraordinary charisma to legitimate their religious leadership, they are also retaining the concern with the direct experience of the sacred. The direct experience of the immanent sacred is seen as being accessible to all, rather than the exclusive experience and source of authority of the founder or leader.

Common American cultural experience suggests that as the American ideal of equality is increasingly being claimed by women, cosmology and understandings of human nature, ministry, and gender roles developed in the metaphysical movement are being introduced into mainstream American religious institutions by feminist women.[27] However, on this point, the work of careful and extensive documentation remains to be done. Women's religious experience, roles, leadership, and theologies, outside and within the shifting boundaries of the mainstream, offer fascinating opportunities for the ongoing pursuit of understanding of human religiosity.

NOTES

1. By "highly patriarchal religion and culture," I am referring to what may be termed the "classic patriarchal pattern," which is patrilocal and patrilineal. Girls are married at a young age, often to older men, at which time they leave their natal homes to go live with the husband's extended family. The new bride has low status in her husband's family until she is older and the mother of sons. Descent and inheritance are reckoned through the male line. The wife should be sexually faithful to her husband, but the husband has sexual access to other women, including the possibility of other wives. Respectable women in the classic patriarchal pattern are always under the control of men—fathers, husbands, brothers, or grown sons. Women's work is restricted to the home, and they are dependent on men for economic support.

Women have greater status and autonomy in matrilineal and matrilocal cultures, in which their labor contributes materially to the family's maintenance, but men still control political power.

In industrialized societies, where changes in economy, education, and family structures set up conditions in which women can *begin* to be active outside the home, conditioning in gender roles and sexist attitudes restrict women's autonomy and self-development. A glance at the holders of religious, political, and economic power in industrialized countries reveals that women still have a long way to go to achieve equality.

2. Arvind Sharma, ed. *Women in World Religions* (Albany: State University of New York Press, 1987); Yvonne Yazbeck Haddad and Ellison Banks Findley, eds. *Women, Religion and Social Change* (Albany: State University of New York Press, 1985); Nancy Auer Falk and Rita M. Gross, eds. *Unspoken Worlds: Women's Religious Lives* (Belmont, Calif.: Wadsworth Publishing Company, 1989), particularly the chapter by Erika Friedl, "Islam and Tribal Women in a Village in Iran," 125–33.

3. For examples, see Clarke Garrett, *Spirit Possession and Popular Religion: From the Camisards to the Shakers* (Baltimore: Johns Hopkins University Press, 1987); and the following chapters in Falk and Gross, eds. *Unspoken Worlds:* Martha B. Binford, "Julia: An East African Diviner," 3–14; Youngsook Kim Harvey, "Possession Sickness and Women Shamans in Korea," 37–44; Kyoko

Motomochi Nakamura, "No Women's Liberation: The Heritage of a Woman Prophet in Modern Japan," 134–44; Karen McCarthy Brown, "Mama Lola and the Ezilis: Themes of Mothering and Loving in Haitian Vodou," 235–45. See also Janice Boddy, *Wombs and Alien Spirits: Women, Men, and the Zar Cult in Northern Sudan* (Madison: University of Wisconsin Press, 1989). This in-depth case study of women's *zar* possession in a Sudanese village demonstrates that the strategy of spirit possession is not consciously undertaken by women. Nevertheless, in a context in which the reality of spirits is taken for granted, possession can result in the negotiation of more life options for a woman in a culture with rigidly defined gender roles.

4. For an example, see Caroline Walker Bynum, "Women Mystics in the Thirteenth Century: The Case of the Nuns of Helfta" in *Jesus as Mother: Studies in the Spirituality of the High Middle Ages* (Berkeley: University of California Press, 1982).

5. Mary Farrell Bednarowski, "Outside the Mainstream: Women's Religion and Women Religious Leaders in Nineteenth-Century America," *Journal of the American Academy of Religion* 48 (June 1980): 207–31.

6. The standard works on religions in America to which Bednarowski refers are: Sydney Ahlstrom, *A Religious History of the American People* (New Haven, Conn.: Yale University Press, 1972), and Henry Warner Bowden, *Dictionary of American Religious Biography* (Westport, Conn.: Greenwood Press, 1977).

7. Rosemary Radford Ruether, "The Ecclesia of Patriarchy and Women Church" in *Miriam's Song II, Patriarchy: A Feminist Critique* (West Hyattsville, Md.: Priests for Equality, n.d.), 4–6.

8. Joseph Agonito, *Woman-Priest,* 1986. Film.

9. The Sacred Congregation for the Doctrine of the Faith, "Declaration on the Question of the Admission of Women to the Ministerial Priesthood," *Catholic Mind* 75 (May 1977): 52–64. Richard Beauchesne, Emmanuel College in Boston, has shown that this document's insistence on the necessity of a male priesthood rests upon a flawed application of the nuptial analogy representing the relationship of Christ to the Church. This analogy asserts that the priest = Christ/groom, and the congregation = Church/bride. The analogy is operable only on the congregational side of the altar, since the Church consists of both women and men. These priestly men insist, however, that the priest must be physically male in order to represent the Christ/groom. Beauchesne credits the failure of analogical reasoning to an underlying homophobia that views a female-female spousal relationship with discomfort. See Richard J. Beauchesne, "Women's Ordination, the Nuptial Analogy, and Homophobia" (Paper presented at the College Theology Society, New Orleans, May 1990).

10. Rosemary Radford Ruether conducts such a historical examination of the Christian tradition in her chapter "Christianity" in *Women in World Religions,* ed. Arvind Sharma. In this essay, Ruether notes that the Bible contains passages that support a "theology of equivalence" of women and men, and that other passages support the "theology of subordination" of women to men.

Passages of equivalence include Genesis 1:27, which states that woman and man are equally created in the image of God; Galatians 3:28, which states that "there is neither Jew nor Greek, there is neither slave nor free, there is neither male nor female; for you are all one in Christ Jesus"; and the interpretation of the Pentecost event recorded in Acts 2:17–18, which refers to the prophecy in Joel 2:28–29, that in the endtimes God's Spirit will be poured out on women and men alike.

The theology of subordination begins with the second story of the creation of humans found in Genesis 2–3. This is the story of Adam, Eve, and the serpent. In patriarchal Christianity, this myth has been interpreted as asserting that since Eve was secondary to Adam in the order of creation, and was primary in sin, all women should be subordinate to men. The theology of subordination is further buttressed by New Testament passages either written by Paul or attributed to Paul, which state that in the hierarchal order of creation, man is the head of woman, and that women should not speak, teach, or have authority over men in the church. See I Corinthians 11:2–12, I Corinthians 14:34–35; I Timothy 2:12–15, and other passages discussed by Ruether.

The theology of subordination was embraced by a number of church fathers, the most extreme example being Tertullian writing 196–212 C.E. in Carthage, who told women: "*You* are the devil's gateway; *you* are the unsealer of that (forbidden) tree; *you* are the first deserter of the divine law; *you* are she who persuaded him whom the devil was not valiant enough to attack. *You* destroyed so easily God's image, man. On account of *your* desert (i.e., punishment), that is death—even the Son of God had to die" (quoted in Ruth A. Tucker and Walter Liefeld, *Daughters of the Church: Women and Ministry from New Testament Times to the Present* [Grand Rapids: Zondervan Publishing House, 1987], 103).

For examples in Judaism of men blaming women for the Fall of Adam, thus making women responsible for bringing the punishment of mortality to humanity, see Judith Baskin, "The Separation of Women in Rabbinic Judaism," in Haddad and Findley, eds., *Women, Religion and Social Change,* 3–18.

11. John Paul II, "On the Dignity and Vocation of Women," *Origins* 18 (Oct. 6, 1988): 261, 263–83.

12. By "extraordinary charisma," I am referring to any sort of direct revelation defined as being available to the leader and not generally accessible to other members of the group. The leader with extraordinary charisma is, therefore, set apart from and over the followers. The terms "ordinary charisma" or "democratic charisma" can be used to refer to the direct experience of what is considered the sacred, which is accessible to any and all members of the group.

13. R. Laurence Moore, *Religious Outsiders and the Making of Americans* (New York: Oxford University Press, 1986), 48, 50–51, 93, 98.

14. These first two types of religious marginality draw on J. Robert Bumstead, "New Religions in America," in *The Religious World: Communities of Faith,* ed. Robert F. Weir, 1st ed. (New York: Macmillan, 1981).

15. Ernestine Friedl, *Women and Men: An Anthropologist's View* (Prospect Heights, Ill.: Waveland Press, 1975), 80, 139.

16. J. Stillson Judah, *The History and Philosophy of the Metaphysical Movements in America* (Philadelphia: Westminster Press, 1967).

17. This section on women in nineteenth-century America relies on Barbara J. MacHaffie, *Her Story: Women in Christian Tradition* (Philadelphia: Fortress Press, 1986). For the "cult of true womanhood," see Barbara Welter, "The Cult of True Womanhood: 1820–1860," *American Quarterly* 18 (1966): 151–74.

18. See the chapter entitled "The Pulpit and the Pew: The Black Church and Women" in C. Eric Lincoln and Lawrence H. Mamiya, *The Black Church in the African American Experience* (Durham: Duke University Press, 1990); James H. Cone, "New Roles in the Ministry: A Theological Appraisal"; Jacquelyn Grant, "Black Theology and the Black Woman," in *Black Theology: A Documentary History, 1966–1979,* ed. Gayraud S. Wilmore and James H. Cone (Maryknoll, N.Y.: Orbis Books, 1979).

19. See also Cynthia Eller's "Relativizing the Patriarchy: The Sacred History of the Feminist Spirituality Movement," *History of Religions* 30, no. 3 (Feb. 1991): 279–95. A helpful corrective to the popular theory of a perfect equalitarian, matrifocal, Goddess-worshipping Neolithic European culture that was destroyed by armed, nomadic and patriarchal invaders can be found in Margaret Ehrenberg, *Women in Prehistory* (Norman, Okla.: University of Oklahoma Press, 1989). Ehrenberg carefully demonstrates the difficulty of interpreting the archaeological record, as opposed to the overinterpretation supplied in the works of Marija Gimbutas.

20. J. Gordon Melton and Gary L. Ward, contributing editor, have collected the pertinent documents of the Roman Catholic church, the Protestant and Eastern Orthodox churches, Jewish groups, and the Mormons in *The Churches Speak On: Women's Ordination. Official Statements from Religious Bodies and Ecumenical Organizations* (Detroit: Gale Research, 1991).

21. "Partners in the Mystery of Redemption: A Pastoral Response to Women's Concerns for Church and Society," is the title of the first draft of the U.S. bishops' pastoral letter on women. It can be found in *Origins* 17, no. 45 (1988): 757ff. It seems noteworthy that the term "partners" was dropped in subsequent drafts of the pastoral letter. The second draft was titled "One in Christ Jesus," and the third draft was titled "Called to Be One in Christ Jesus." The fourth draft, entitled "One in Christ Jesus," was not adopted as an official pastoral letter by the National Conference of Catholic Bishops in November 1992. At that time, it was decided to suspend the attempt to write a pastoral letter on women in church and society. This last draft was criticized by Catholic feminists as representing the views of the Vatican more than the American Catholic women who were consulted. Due to restrictions from the Vatican, the American bishops were unable to follow out the logical implications of the affirmation that women and men are equal in dignity. Conservative Catholic women also disliked the fourth draft and saw it as an attempt to supplant John Paul II's pastoral letter on women, *Mulieris Dignitatum.* At the November 1992 meeting of the National Conference of Catholic Bishops, however, the American bishops discussed an issue that John Paul II has said is not open for discussion—the ordination of women. The fourth draft of the bishops' letter can be found in *Origins* 22, no. 13 (1992): 221 ff.

22. This sort of definition of the experience of the sacred often relies on Rudolf Otto, *The Idea of the Holy,* 2d ed. (London: Oxford University Press, 1950).

23. Robert S. Ellwood, Jr., "The Study of New Religious Movements in America," *The Council on the Study of Religion Bulletin* 10 (June 1979): 72, and quoted in Bednarowski.

24. Thomas Robbins and David Bromley, "Social Experimentation and the Significance of American New Religions: A Focused Review Essay," *Research in the Social Scientific Study of Religion* 4 (1992): 1–28.

25. Ibid., 1.

26. Ibid., 4.

27. One example is an article by R. Gustav Niebuhr entitled "The Lord's Name: Images of God as 'He' Loses Its Sovereignty in America's Churches," *Wall Street Journal,* Monday, Apr. 27, 1992, secs. 1A, 4A. The subheadings to the article read "More Worshipers Challenge Language That Describes Supreme Being as a Male" and "What Happens to the Trinity?" I am grateful to Loyola New Orleans student, Alisa Applegate, for bringing this article to my attention.

Part 1

Women in the Spirit

"In the Line of the Female": Shakerism and Feminism

Marjorie Procter-Smith

In 1774, the sailing ship *Mariah,* out of Liverpool, entered New York harbor. In addition to cargo, the ship carried nine passengers, taken on board at reduced fare because the ship was condemned. These nine people, a prophet from Manchester named Ann Lee and her eight followers, known in England as "Shaking Quakers," were looking for more hospitable missionary fields than England had proven to be. Although Lee died in 1784, the movement she had transplanted to America flourished and grew and survives still. The Shakers, both Ann Lee and those who came after her, understood themselves as being part of a tradition of Christian dissenters stretching from the Montanist prophets of the early church through the Quakers and other, more short-lived groups such as the Camisards. According to their self-definition, they were the remnant of the true church which had ever been marginalized and persecuted by the false anti-Christian church.

After Ann Lee's death the movement gradually took on the characteristics of an institution: the members built their own buildings, including houses of worship; they developed a complex social structure based on Lee's teaching of the necessity of celibacy and the requirements of communal life; and they developed a theological system. Because their social system demanded both male and female leaders (called Elders and Eldresses, Deacons and Deaconesses) and because their theology posited a dual incarnation (Ann Lee was the "Second Appearing of Christ in female form") and a dual Father-Mother God, many writers have argued that Shakerism is a feminist religion.

Edward Deming Andrews, in several of his many books on Shakerism, asserted that Shaker men and women enjoyed "perfect equality of rights," and cited as evidence the Shaker system of male and female leadership and their concept of a dual Father-Mother God.[1] French writer Henri Desroche and, more recently, feminist theorist Sally Kitch, build their arguments for Shaker feminism on the Shaker practice of celibacy.[2] Kitch in particular locates her assessment of Shaker celibate feminism in the context of current feminist critiques of marriage and sexuality.[3]

Contemporary feminist theologians, including Rosemary Radford Ruether, Barbara Brown Zikmund, Mary Farrell Bednarowski, and Linda Mercadante, approach the question of Shaker feminism from a different perspective.[4] In each case their analysis of Shaker feminism is influenced to some degree by the contemporary debates in the churches regarding women's religious leadership and the use of gender-inclusive language for God. Ruether, Zikmund, and Bednarowski are particularly motivated by the search for evidence of Christian movements or groups in the past that have empowered women. Mercadante focuses on the more recent question of the use of female language for God. However, all are driven by a commitment to the empowerment of women within Christianity, and not simply by a detached interest in the history of Shakerism.

While Bednarowski and Mercadante hold back from claiming that Shakerism is a feminist religion, like other feminist theologians they find much in Shaker doctrine and practice that anticipates contemporary feminist concerns. Is Shakerism feminist? All of the writers mentioned identify various characteristics that appear to foster women's religious leadership. Bednarowski identifies four of these characteristics that are found in several sectarian religions: (1) modification of an exclusively masculine interpretation of the divine; (2) tempering or denial of the doctrine of the Fall (according to which, in traditional Christian understanding, women bear the major responsibility for bringing sin into the world); (3) rejection of the need for conventional ordained clergy; and (4) a view of marriage that does not emphasize marriage and motherhood as the only means of fulfillment for women.[5] To some extent, Shakerism at certain times in its history reflected each of these characteristics. But Shakerism demonstrates other characteristics as well that parallel contemporary Christian feminist concerns, such as (1) a female founder and a tradition of strong female leadership; (2) equal numbers of women in leadership positions with men; and (3) modification of the traditional Christian understanding of a male Savior.

On the other hand, recent historical research into the role of women in communal or utopian sects in America has refined our understanding of Shaker history with regard to women. Such study has pointed to the ways in which Shaker theology and social structures reinforced gender stereotypes. Louis J. Kern and Lawrence Foster, for example, have noted the Shakers' retention of conventional nineteenth-century American division of labor along gender lines and their insistence that profound and inherent natural distinctions separate the sexes.[6]

The question "is Shakerism feminist" has been modified by these and other recent studies of women and Shakerism. Now the questions are "what was being a Shaker like for the women who joined the society?" "What can be learned from Shakerism about women and religion?" and "How did the Shakers succeeed at empowering women, and how did they fail?"

New Shaker studies, as well as the development of studies in the field of women and religion, enable answers to these questions. These studies have identified some of the complex relationships between women's social roles and women's religious roles, and between official statements about women and women's actual lived experiences. Such discoveries provide new and more refined ways of assessing the roles of women in Shakerism and of identifying the effects of gender ideology.

Restating the Question

One useful way of assessing the role of women within a religious group is to focus on the way in which a religion functions for women.[7] We can identify at least two functions, an emancipatory function in which religion enables women to transcend existing social restraints, and a sacralizing function in which religion interprets women's traditional roles as sacred. Both functions can be found in the history of Shakerism.

The purpose of the emancipatory function is to empower women to transcend existing social restraints and to behave in ways contrary to social expectations. This emancipatory function is well attested in early Shakerism and to some extent in later Shakerism as well. Certainly, the ecstatic movement that characterized early Shaker worship was considered by many to be antisocial behavior.[8] The ecstatic movement and speech (exercised by women as well as men) were a very public manifestation of the freedom from social constraints experienced by the converts. Since women generally were subject to more social restraints than men, it may be argued that women were accordingly more free. It was also useful for women that such operations were done "in the power of the Spirit," so that the individual was therefore not responsible for her outrageous behavior.[9] Outsiders may have been able to excuse such behavior as being "typically female," that is, hysterical or excessively emotional. There is no evidence, however, that they did so, and every reason to believe that it served a very different function for those within the ecstatic community, especially the women.

The ecstatic gifts of dancing, prophecy, and song were themselves tokens of a radical affirmation of the religious autonomy of each believer. Although all Shakers were not organized into communities until the late 1780s, from the beginning Shaker religion was strongly communal in identity. Nevertheless, the Believer's acceptance of Shakerism depended ultimately on internal and personal confirmation. Convert Elizabeth Johnson, on her first meeting with Ann Lee, experienced this internal authority thus: "[Mother Ann] came singing into the room where I was sitting, and I felt an inward evidence that her singing was in the gift and power of God."[10]

Moreover, this powerful internal authority was interpreted to be "of God," and could not be denied. A non-Shaker observer once asked a woman believer if she could be stopped in her exercise of the gifts of shaking and whirling by the use of brute strength. She informed him that "it would be a blasphemy against God to attempt such a thing."[11] Implicitly, then, if not explicitly, women's religious autonomy was a basic emancipatory element of Shakerism from the beginning of the movement.

The social counterpart to religious autonomy for Shaker women was the rejection of the existing family structures through the advocacy of celibacy and the substitution of the Shaker family for the biological family. Celibacy was preached by Ann Lee as the surest way to salvation, and so its primary acknowledged function was freedom from sin. However, the subversive consequences of the Shaker rejection of marriage and family ties did not go unnoticed by contemporary critics. Daniel Rathbun, a Shaker apostate, reported in 1785 that among the Shakers "the greatest abominations are committed: children abusing their parents in the most shocking manner that was ever heard of, . . . and ruling over their parents; and wives ruling over their husbands, all of which is against the laws of God and nature."[12]

Shakerism's effects on the lives of women were not overlooked by Ann Lee or by early Shakers. Celibacy was, in effect, a reliable method of birth control. It freed women from the dangers of childbearing and gave them a measure of control over their own bodies that existing patriarchal family structures, in which women had little or no control over sexuality or pregnancy, did not allow. To Lee, women did not need to be "saved through childbearing," as the author of Timothy advises (I Tim. 2:15); rather, they needed to be saved *from* childbearing. Her pragmatic concern for women and children is revealed in the following conversation with a poor woman named Beulah Rude: "The family being very poor, Mother asked Beulah how many children she had. She answered, 'five.' 'Five! (said Mother,) When you had one, why did you not wait, and see if you was able to bring up that as you ought, before you had another? And when you had two, why did you not stop then? But now you have five!' "[13]

Celibacy was not unambiguously emancipatory for Shaker women, although it was potentially so, and probably was in reality for many Shaker women. During the early years of Shakerism, however, Shaker women married to unbelieving husbands found little support from Shaker leaders. Ann Lee herself apparently discouraged women from leaving their husbands. She reportedly returned Daniel Bacon's wife and child to him and advised even Lucy Markham, whose husband was a Shaker, to be obedient to him.[14] By the early 1800s a policy was apparently in place that regulated relationships between a Shaker spouse and a non-Shaker spouse. "If the wife believes, and not the husband, according to the order of the church she must still abide with her husband, and take up her cross according to the faith ... If the husband will voluntarily give her up, the church will then receive her to live among believers. But if the husband believes, he is counselled to forsake her, and have no union with her; and if he pleases, he can take his children from her."[15]

Celibacy was only part of the Shaker reconstruction of the patriarchal family, albeit a symbolically powerful element.[16] For women who were able to get free of their marriages, acceptance of the Gospel was given a higher priority than previously existing familial obligations, and critics of the Shaker movement frequently accused the Shakers of breaking up families. Replacing the traditional family was the Shaker community, which, during the lifetime of Ann Lee, was a family of "Sisters" and "Brothers" with a spiritual "Mother." Thus women converts to Shakerism in the early period were freed from the restraints of patriarchal marriage, particularly the dangers of childbirth, and were empowered to express that freedom in ecstatic speech and movement. Ann Lee, as "Mother" of the community, was its center. The familial context from which they derived their new identity was thus firmly gynocentric, woman-centered, at least to the extent that it centered on Ann Lee and her charismatic leadership. A radical sense of equality pervaded the community, expressed in the use of familial language of "Sisters" and "Brothers." Although some of the first members of the movement were called "Father" and "Mother" by some Believers, Mother Ann Lee was clearly the mother of them all, and she called no one "Father" or "Mother."

Shakerism offered women an alternative to conventional marriage and family, and the movement placed commitment to the Shaker family above ties to the biological family. At the same time, early Shaker leaders failed to support women who were converted to Shakerism independently of their husbands, instead accepting the cultural norms that asserted men's control over their wives and children, and thereby limiting the emancipatory possibilities of Shaker celibacy and alternative family.

After Ann Lee's death, the gynocentric structure of the community rather quickly gave way to a patriarchal structure under the pressure of increased competition with other religious movements and a concern for the movement's public image.

During Ann Lee's lifetime, from 1774 until her death in 1784, Shaker leadership and community organization were somewhat fluid. There seems to have been an inner circle of leaders, predominantly but not exclusively male, who functioned variously as public speakers, community organizers, and spiritual advisors to Believers and inquirers.[17] At the center of this circle, however, was Ann Lee, whose charismatic presence was the primary focus of the community's energy and identity. After her death, male members of the inner circle moved into leadership. Lee was immediately succeeded by "Father" James Whittaker. His successor, "Father" Joseph Meacham instituted the principle of joint headship of the order with the elevation of Lucy Wright as "Mother" before his death in 1796.[18] Beginning with Whittaker and continuing through Meacham's leadership, the communities were gradually organized into highly structured "families" with a clearly identified hierarchy. Although Wright's long period of primary leadership (1796–1821) was formative, the hierarchical structure remained unchanged.

Together with this evolution came a move to the other possible use of religion for women, that is, the sacralization of women's traditional experiences and roles, both biological and social. At its best, a sacralizing religion reveals the dignity and holiness of women's work, which is usually ignored or demeaned. At its worst, however, such a religion may provide justification for maintaining traditional roles that limit women's power and freedom. While most of the examples of this use of religion are to be found in later Shakerism, the seeds are present in the earliest days of the movement in two forms: the use of "Mother" as a formative image for the community's identity, and the use of traditionally female housekeeping tasks as models for the divine life.[19] Although both images have complex histories, it is not too much of an oversimplification to say that their initial function was to redefine and transform traditional reality but that as they evolved, they came instead to represent a justification of traditional reality.

The Shaker use of the image of "Mother" is an example of this process. As it evolved from the lifetime of "Mother" Ann Lee through the leadership of "Mother" Lucy and the appearance of "Holy Mother Wisdom," it is the image most constant and most uniquely characteristic of Shaker life and thought. But it is also an image that is ambiguous as well as somewhat ambivalent.

Adrienne Rich, in *Of Woman Born,* makes an important distinction between motherhood as experience and motherhood as institution. When Rich refers to the first meaning of motherhood as experience, she is referring to "the *potential relationship* of any woman to her powers of reproduction and to her children." The second meaning, which she notes has been "superimposed" on the first, is the institution of motherhood, "which aims at insuring that that potential—and all women—shall remain under male control." The overlaying of the patriarchal institution of motherhood, Rich concludes, "has alienated women from our bodies by incarcerating us in them. . . . Most women in history have become mothers without choice, and an even greater number have lost their lives bringing life into the world."[20]

Ann Lee's own experience of motherhood, if the accounts of it are reliable, was an example of this. Married against her will, she reportedly bore four children, all of whom died in infancy.[21] This experience of alienation from and bondage to her own body, in particular its sexuality and the terror of giving birth, apparently precipitated the profound religious experience that led her to found her own religious movement and to value celibacy. Lee frequently used language drawn from her own experiences of sexuality and childbirth to speak of her own and Believers' religious experiences and lives. Lee describes her spiritual conversion experience in terms of labor and childbirth: "Thus I labored, in strong cries and groans to God, day and night, . . . until my soul broke forth to God; which I felt as sensibly as ever a woman did a child, when she was delivered of it."[22] Similarly, she describes her work with new converts as "labor in the Gospel," by which she brings forth the members of a new community.[23] And her ongoing relationship with Christ is described in boldly erotic language, describing him as her "Husband" and her "Lover," in whose arms she lies down, and with whom she walks "hand in hand."[24] Once again, however, the patriarchal institutions of marital love and childbirth, which are imposed on women without their consent, are radically recontextualized by Lee into ecstatic, autonomous experiences of spiritual liberation.

Within early Shakerism, during the lifetime of Ann Lee, Lee's motherhood was experiential. Ann Lee was "Mother Ann" because her followers experienced her as a mother. Men and women alike described the affectionate relationship they enjoyed with Lee in terms of the mother-child relation-ship. A convert who joined the Shakers at the age of 19 remarked, "Indeed I felt myself as a child blessed with the best of mothers," and another one called Lee his "Mother in Christ," because "she has verily brought me forth into the family of Christ."[25] These early Believers' perceptions of Lee as mother depended not on romantic ideals of "True Motherhood," but on their pragmatic experience that it was through the labor of Ann Lee that they had been born into the new life that they now enjoyed, and it was by her ongoing care, instruction, and reproof that they continued to survive.[26] More importantly, Lee accepted the title "Mother" in a radically new way, distanced as much as possible from the institution of the patriarchal family. The requirement of celibacy and separation from one's biological family placed the term "Mother" in a wholly new context.

After Ann Lee's death, however, motherhood became institutionalized within the office of eldress, which was part of a pyramidal leadership structure. Although the early Shaker community was gynocentric in structure, the balanced male-female leadership system that evolved in Shakerism promoted some women into positions of power and authority, at the cost of the religious autonomy of all Shaker women. The "Mother" of a Shaker family was not the center of a gynocentric community, but one of two authority figures in a rigid hierarchy.[27] The memory of Ann Lee was reified into a semidivine mother who not only gives birth to and nurtures the life of Believers, but also reflects the nature of the Heavenly Mother at the side of the Heavenly Father.[28] This figure of the Heavenly Mother, shadowy at first, or perhaps simply wearing Ann Lee's face, was further developed during the period of internal revival in the 1830s. As Holy Mother Wisdom, this divine female figure became a kind of "Goddess of Domesticity," advising young women on proper deportment, and expressing a highly romanticized picture of womanhood. Although the image of Holy Mother Wisdom may have originated in the authentic response of Shaker women to Ann Lee's reinterpretation of motherhood, and although the prophetic gifts given to women by Holy Mother Wisdom legitimized women's religious autonomy, the hierarchical leadership soon assumed control of the image, using it to reinforce loyalty to the leadership and control of women.[29]

Complicating the question of the meaning of "motherhood" in Shakerism is, of course, the Shaker doctrine of celibacy. For Ann Lee, celibacy was a necessary means of freeing herself and other women from the bondage of patriarchal motherhood. However, celibacy is also open to another interpretation and another use, quite at odds with Lee's apparent purposes. In a patriarchal society, celibacy can become an intensified expression of the alienation from our bodies that begins in the institution of patriarchal marriage. When required of women especially, celibacy can be used to control women's lives and choices by controlling their bodies. Thus, in celibate Shakerism, women were not bound to bear children against their will, but neither could they bear children if they chose to. They could earn the title "Mother" only by being chosen to join the ministry, an office to which they could be appointed only by their superiors in the hierarchy.[30]

To return to our categories of emancipatory or sacralizing functions of religion, then, it appears that the religious movement Ann Lee began served an emancipatory function for her and for other women. Motherhood and sexuality, activities associated with women in patriarchal society, were radically reinterpreted and recontextualized to enable women's freedom and autonomy. But through the replacement of hierarchical structure for gynocentric leadership and the substitution of order for religious ecstasy, celibacy and motherhood became institutionalized in ways that restricted rather than emancipated women, although some restrictions were already present in limitations on married women's ability to join the Shakers.

It was after the institutionalization of Shakerism in the nineteenth century that sacralizing functions appear, particularly in the development of theories of specialized spiritual roles for women and the elevation of women's traditional work, especially cleaning, to religious significance. Theories of specialized spiritual roles for women were developed as part of the Shaker theological system. The authoritative statement of Shaker theology, Benjamin Seth Youngs' *The Testimony of Christ's Second Appearing,* first published in 1808, articulates these roles clearly: "It was also necessary, that Christ should make his second appearing in the line of the female, and that in one who was conceived in sin, and lost in the fullness of man's fall; because in the woman the root of sin was first planted, and its final destruction must begin where its foundation was first laid."[31]

The development in the 1840s of rituals such as "the cleansing gift" and "Mother Ann's Sweeping Gift," which combined actual and metaphorical cleaning, and "The Midnight Cry," which involved solely metaphorical cleaning, claimed women's daily work as a revelatory sign of God's purifying power and activity. The negative consequences of Shaker gender dualism were acceptance of gender hierarchy and the association of women with the origins of sin. The positive consequences were an elevation of traditional gender work, especially women's work, to sacred status.

Rethinking the Shakers

We have already looked at some of the ways in which Shakerism either challenged or sacralized women's conventional roles, and we have examined in particular the way in which the image of Mother has functioned. If we now examine the three major periods of Shaker history—with an eye to the consequences for women of changes in community structure, worship practice, and general theological beliefs—we can perhaps offer a fresh look at Shakerism's complex impact on women.

The earliest period of Shakerism, the time of charismatic community during Ann Lee's lifetime, from 1774–84, challenged the existing patriarchal family structures of the society by demanding celibacy of all converts and by providing as an alternative a community that was marked by gynocentric leadership and structure. Ecstatic, unmediated worship expressed believers' experience of freedom in the gospel as proclaimed by Mother Ann. The religion of this period reflects Lee's own personal struggles as a woman and her development of a religion that took seriously her anxiety over sexuality and her fears and griefs over childbirth and family life. Lee's personal spirituality never denied her femaleness, in spite of the centrality of celibacy in her teaching. The language and imagery in which she described her religious experiences were explicitly drawn from her experiences of childbirth and sexual love. Her relationship with Jesus was described in terms which are openly erotic, and this language was consistent with the ecstatic spirituality of the movement during this period.

After Lee's death, between 1784 and 1857, the community was organized into communal families with communalistic finances and resources. Leadership was dual, and division of labor along gender lines was strictly maintained and strictly conventional. Each Shaker "family" was governed by the ministry, which consisted of two elders and two eldresses, who exercised spiritual authority, and two deacons and two deaconesses, who exercised temporal authority. The ministry of each family was appointed by the head ministry, an elder and eldress, in New Lebanon, the first among the communities. Although apparently symmetrical in shape, the responsibilities of the family leaders were quite uneven. The responsibility for handling money and property, an increasingly important task as Shaker communities grew in size and wealth, was entirely in the hands of the male deacons and trustees. Deaconesses, by contrast, were responsible for overseeing the execution of household tasks and the production of goods for sale to "the world." Even though this work brought in no little income to the community, women did not have control over their finances, apart from providing the supplies needed to produce the items for sale.[32]

An official theology (produced by male Shakers) argued that male-female differences were both divinely ordained and also reflective of the nature of the divine sphere.[33] The culturally defined roles of men as leaders and women as followers were seen to reflect the relationship between God the Father and God the Mother (or the Holy Ghost) who is the Father's "helper." This orderly, dualistic theological system was reflected in the orderly, dualistic dances used in worship in place of the earlier ecstatic movement. Individually inspired, autonomous religious exercises, normative in the early days of the movement, during the lifetime of Ann Lee, were increasingly brought under the control of the "Elders."[34] It was under the leadership of Joseph Meacham, who became Elder of the whole society in 1787, that the use of structured communal dancing was established as the normative form of worship, with emphasis on order and uniformity.

It was perhaps inevitable that institutionalization of Shakerism should follow the death of a strong, charismatic leader such as Lee. But in this case the shift to structured community resulted in the loss of the gynocentric system. Strong female leadership thenceforward had to be exercised within a hierarchical system that limited the number of those who could exercise power within the community. Power and authority thus came through the hierarchy rather than through the Spirit. Lucy Wright, who became "Mother" Lucy when Joseph Meacham established the dual ministry, exercised powerful and determinative influence on Shakerism until her death in 1821. For twenty-five years, from Joseph Meacham's death in 1796 until her own death, Mother Lucy exercised supreme authority in the community, in spite of apparent internal resistance to her leadership. Nevertheless, she did not modify the hierarchical theological system that could only have undermined her own religious authority. The period of established Shakerism meant a net loss of women's autonomous exercise of power rather than a gain.

Thus the outbreak of "spiritual gifts," initially at least uncontrolled by the leadership, was in some sense inevitable. Between roughly 1837 and 1847 the communities underwent a period of internal revival known at the time as "Mother Ann's work." During this period women again began to exercise some of the spiritual power that had been known in the first period of the movement's history. Women were again prominent as prophets, "instruments," and artists who received these spiritual gifts quite independently of the hierarchy or the ministry.[35] Mother Ann and Holy Mother Wisdom, the female face of God, appeared to the communities by means of female "instruments," and ecstatic gifts were once again exercised. But the Shakers had been conventional too long, and the presence of prophetic gifts was too threatening to an established hierarchy. Holy Mother Wisdom became a spokeswoman for all of the conventional nineteenth-century feminine virtues, and urged women to not talk too much or too loudly, to be meek and agreeable, and thus to find their place in the divine plan. Whatever potential for power there may have been in the image of Holy Mother Wisdom, it was an image very swiftly domesticated.

Moreover, although the instruments, both male and female, normally received their spiritual gifts directly from God or benign spirits, the exercise of those gifts was controlled by the ministry as much as possible. While some women instruments may have been able to exercise considerable artistic and religious autonomy, others, such as Paulina Bates, felt compelled to submit themselves and their spiritual gifts to male Shaker authority, and even to emphasize their lowliness and inadequacy as females in order to find legitimacy.[36]

Rethinking Women and Religion

What then can we learn about the emancipatory functions of religion from the Shakers? Let us return to the characteristics identified earlier: women's leadership, alternatives to patriarchal marriage and family structure; modification of a male image of God; alternative interpretation of the Fall; rejection of clergy; and modification of a male savior.

According to Rosemary Radford Ruether, "continuing female leadership of a group was more likely if the founder was a woman. But even then it was not assured unless there was a definite theory of female empowerment in the ideology and structure of the community."[37]

Lee's theory of female empowerment, so far as she may be said to have had one, was that empowerment came through embracing the Gospel, which then freed women from enslavement to sin. It was the same process for men. So Shakerism was entirely egalitarian. It also recognized that women were under more severe restraints than men, and took women's lives and struggles with seriousness, especially with regard to sexuality, childbirth and family life. On the other hand, in spite of Ann Lee's own struggles with her husband over sex, she seems to have made no provisions to assist other women who wished to live as Shakers, but whose husbands were unconverted.

Yet in spite of the evident power of Lee's personal spiritual vision and its apparent attractiveness to her contemporaries, perhaps because of her apparent failure to assert that females had an equal right to and responsibility for spiritual leadership, Lee's power as leader of the community did not pass from her to another woman leader, but to "Father" James Whittaker.

At the same time, we must acknowledge that it was probably because of the memory of Ann Lee's personal power as a woman that the idea of dual leadership was even possible after her death. The structure of dual leadership, however, was held in place during the establishment of Shaker communities not so much out of a commitment to female empowerment or leadership but by the demands of order within a mixed celibate community.

The same might be said about the likelihood of equal numbers of women in leadership positions insuring equal sharing of power. It was primarily the practical need for women leaders to deal with the women in a celibate community that insured equal numbers of women leaders, but power was not, apparently, so evenly divided. Division of labor tended to follow traditional practices, which meant that men usually dealt with money, property, and business dealings with "the world." Women bore internal responsibilities for care of food, clothing, and young children.

Men were most often the theologians and writers and theoreticians. Therefore, although leadership was shared equally by men and women, power was not. Male leaders retained control over property, money, and ideas on behalf of the community, at least until the male membership declined to such an extent that control necessarily passed to women.

The Shaker community structure also had its advantages and disadvantages for women. On the one hand, Shaker women were free from the dangers in childbirth, threat of loss of male support, and the isolation and loneliness suffered by many of their non-Shaker sisters. The Shaker family did indeed provide women a secure and supportive community in which to live, and for some, it also provided the opportunity to travel and to exercise leadership skills that probably would have been impossible for them to display in the world. On the other hand, the strict division of labor demanded by the celibate community channeled women into narrow and largely uncreative work that could and, at times did, become burdensome.[38]

It was not until after Ann Lee's death and the growing understanding of her as the Messiah in female form that the Shaker image of God began to be modified to speak of anything but a male God. Once again, it is undoubtedly an indication of the power of Lee's personality that her memory should be so influential. But the theology of this middle period, expressed in theological writings and in hymns, demonstrates the same duality that is reflected in the community structures and worship of the time, with similar advantages and disadvantages for women.

This duality was, at best, egalitarian in portraying Lee as equal to Jesus, and God the Mother as equal to God the Father. From this "separate but equal" theology, however to "separate and different" was a rather short step. The relationship between Mother Wisdom and the Heavenly Father mirrored an archetypal patriarchal family, with a governing, leading Father and a nurturing, tender Mother. In other words, the use of parental images, growing in part out of the early community's transforming relationship with Lee as Mother, led to an uncritical acceptance of prevailing cultural definitions of gender identity and stereotypical parental models and application of those definitions and models to the divine.

Shakers cannot rightly be said to have modified the doctrine of the Fall as regards women's role. Shaker theologians generally accepted the notion that women bear responsibility for the introduction of sin into the world, and they defined sin primarily as lust. Nor, as we have seen, did they ultimately eliminate a clergy class, although they avoided the tendency of non-Shaker Christian groups to associate ministerial leadership with male prerogative.

It was in articulating the meaning of Ann Lee as Christ's second appearing that Shaker theology departed most dramatically from conventional Christianity. In claiming that it was necessary for Christ to come a second time as a woman, Shaker theologians opened up the possibility of a systematic restructuring of the maleness of Christianity's central symbol. Ironically, however, the theory that made that second, female appearance necessary, according to male Shaker theologians, was the belief in women's need for salvation because of their greater sin. The emancipatory possibilities of a female Christ figure are thus lost.

Constructing a Women's Religion

Feminist theology has concerned itself in general with identifying the religious sources of women's oppression and proposing changes in order to bring about women's emancipation. As feminist theologians have discovered, such a process is complex because women's place in religion has been and continues to be complex. We have examined some of these complexities in relation to Shakerism. Now we are in a position to examine more closely some of the implications of women's complex experience in Shakerism for the construction of a religious tradition that is truly emancipatory for women.

1. Ann Lee was a leader whose religion was shaped by her own personal struggles as a woman, yet her religion attracted men as well as women. This suggests that it is possible to universalize from women's experience as readily as from men's.
2. Failure to prepare a female succession can result in the loss not only of female leadership, but also of a matriarchal or gynocentric structure as well.
3. An equal number of women in leadership positions does not necessarily result in equal sharing of power. Attention to the function of those leaders and the nature of their office is also necessary to overcome cultural assumptions about male and female roles.
4. A powerful female founder or leader can affect a community's experience of God.
5. However, a female deity or image of the divine being is empowering to women only insofar as it remains independent of and critical of existing patriarchal social structures and experiences.
6. Parental images of God, because they tend toward dualism, can be used to justify dualistic theories about human and divine nature. A parental image, as of Ann Lee as mother, can avoid

this only when it is primarily experiential rather than institutional. It is a demonstration of the power of ideology that the Shaker's strongly patriarchal definition of male and female characteristics and roles should be developed within a community which practiced sexual celibacy and eschewed traditional family structures. Ideological parenthood, in other words, is independent of biological parenthood.

7. Romanticization of female experience, whether motherhood or any other aspect of women's lives, lends itself to use as justification for perpetuation of denial of power and freedom to women. On the other hand, when firmly grounded in the realistic assessment of women's lives, a genuinely woman-centered religion is possible.

The final phrase is indicative: woman-centered religion is possible. From early Shaker history we learn that it is possible to create a religion that is gynocentric and therefore takes women's lives and experiences and needs seriously, that encourages women's religious leadership, and that is grounded in female images that are both historical and divine. What seems to be far more difficult is to sustain such a religion. The challenge for our time is to construct such a religion in a way that it can endure.

NOTES

A slightly different version of this essay is published as a monograph under the title, *Shakerism and Feminism: Reflections on Women's Religion and the Early Shakers* (*Shaker* Monograph Series #1), by the Shaker Museum and Library, Old Chatham, N.Y., 1991. Jean Humez, Stephen Stein, Diane Sasson, and Catherine Wessinger provided valuable comments and suggestions on earlier drafts.

1. Edward Deming Andrews, *The People Called Shakers: A Search for the Perfect Society* (1953; reprint, New York: Dover Publications, 1963), 56, 60; see also Andrews, *The Community Industries of the Shakers* (Albany: The University of the State of New York, 1932), 179–80; Andrews, *The Gift to Be Simple* (New York: Dover Publications, 1940), 5–6.

2. Henri Desroche, *The American Shakers,* trans. John Savacool (Amherst: University of Massachusetts Press, 1971; originally published in French in 1955); Sally L. Kitch, *Chaste Liberation: Celibacy and Female Cultural Status* (Urbana: University of Illinois Press, 1989).

3. See especially Kitch, *Chaste Liberation,* 186–214. Kitch confines her study to the years 1870–1910; thus her analysis cannot be extended to other periods of Shakerism without great care. Although Shaker insistence on celibacy was a constant, their interpretation of it was not.

4. Barbara Brown Zikmund, "The Feminist Thrust of Sectarian Christianity,"

in *Women of Spirit,* ed. Rosemary Reuther and Eleanor McLaughlin (New York: Simon and Schuster, 1979), 206–24; Rosemary Radford Reuther, "Women in Utopian Movements," in *Women and Religion in America, the Nineteenth Century,* ed. Rosemary Radford Reuther and Rosemary Keller (New York: Harper and Row, 1981), 46–100; Mary Farrell Bednarowski, "Outside the Mainstream: Women's Religion and Women Religious Leaders in Nineteenth-Century America," *American Academy of Religion Journal* 48 (1980): 207–31; Linda A. Mercadante, *Gender, Doctrine, and God: The Shakers and Contemporary Theology* (Nashville: Abingdon Press, 1990).

5. Bednarowski, "Outside the Mainstream," 209.

6. Louis J. Kern, *An Ordered Love* (Chapel Hill: University of North Carolina Press, 1981); Lawrence Foster, *Religion and Sexuality* (New York: Oxford University Press, 1981).

7. See especially Nancy Auer Falk and Rita M. Gross, eds., *Unspoken Worlds: Women's Religious Lives in Non-Western Cultures* (New York: Harper and Row, 1980).

8. Some sense of the outrage generated by the sight of Shakers dancing in worship may be gleaned from eyewitness descriptions of their exercises by outsiders, who until the mid–1800s often attended Shaker Sunday meetings to see what was going on: Valentine Rathburn, *An Account of the Matter, Form and Manner of a New and Strange Religion* (Providence, R.I., 1781); Amos Taylor, *A Narrative of the Strange Principles, Conduct, and Character of the People Known By the Name of Shakers* (Worcester, Mass., 1782); William Plumer, "The Original Shaker Communities in New England," F. B. Sanborn, ed., *New England Magazine* 22 (May 1900): 303–9.

9. Marjorie Procter-Smith, *Women and Shaker Community and Worship* (Lewiston, N.Y.: Edwin Mellen Press, 1985), 88–89. For the significance of ecstatic religion, for women as a marginalized group, see I. M. Lewis, *Ecstatic Religion* (Baltimore, Md.: Penguin Books, 1971), 31–33, 66–126.

10. [Seth Y. Wells and Calvin Green, eds.] *Testimonies Concerning the Character and Ministry of Mother Ann Lee,* (Albany, N.Y., 1827), 90.

11. Plumer, "The Original Shaker Communities in New England," 306.

12. Daniel Rathbun, *Letter from Daniel Rathbun, of Richmond, . . . to James Whittacor, Chief Elder of the Church Called Shakers* (Springfield, Mass., 1785), 83.

13. [Rufus Bishop and Seth Y. Wells, eds.] *Testimonies of the Life . . . of our Ever Blessed Mother Ann Lee . . .* (Hancock, Mass.: J. Talcott and J. Deming, 1816), 313.

14. [Bishop and Wells] *Testimonies* (1816), 138–39; 321–22; 313.

15. Thomas Brown, *An Account of the People Called Shakers,* (Troy, N.Y.: Parker and Bliss, 1812), 287. It is interesting to speculate on whether these restrictions on married women's admission into Shaker communities might have motivated them to such vigorous missionary activity within their family that they were often responsible for the well-documented and frequent conversion of whole families to Shakerism.

16. On the symbolic importance of celibacy for women see Kitch, *Chaste Liberation,* 23–43.

17. On the structure of early Shaker community, see Clarke Garrett, *Spirit Possession and Popular Religion* (Baltimore: Johns Hopkins University Press, 1987); Stephen A. Marini, *Radical Sects of Revolutionary New England* (Cambridge, Mass.: Harvard University Press, 1982).

18. Standard histories on this period of Shakerism commonly assume that Lucy Wright was chosen by James Meacham, and they cite prophecies of Mother Ann before her death promising future leadership for Meacham. See Andrews, *The People Called Shakers,* 55–56, 60; Calvin Green, "Biographical Account of the Life, Character and Ministry of Father Joseph Meacham" (*Shaker Quarterly* 10 [1970]: 59). However, Anna White and Leila Taylor, *Shakerism: Its Meaning and Message* (1904; reprint, Columbus, Ohio: AMS, 1971), argue that Ann Lee selected her before her death. See further Procter-Smith, *Women and Shaker Community and Worship,* 39–44.

19. See Virginia Weis, "With Hands to Work and Hearts to God," *Shaker Quarterly* 9 (1969): 35–46.

20. Adrienne Rich, *Of Woman Born: Motherhood as Experience and Institution* (New York: W. W. Norton, 1976), 13.

21. Stephen A. Marini, "A New View of Mother Ann Lee and the Rise of American Shakerism," *Shaker Quarterly* 18 (Summer 1990): 52, says that Lee's marriage to Abraham Stanley was "arranged." Shaker histories usually report Lee's early aversion to sex and (presumably) marriage, but it is difficult to know how much historical credence to place in these accounts. See *Testimonies* (1816), 3.

22. *Testimonies* (1816), 47.

23. Procter-Smith, *Women and Shaker Community and Worship,* 10–13, 106–10.

24. *Testimonies* (1816), 206–7, 211, 325. See further Procter-Smith, *Women and Shaker Community and Worship,* 100–102.

25. *Testimonies* (1827), 47–48, 129, respectively.

26. Lee was also experienced as stern and judgmental by her followers; but testimonies collected from Believers in 1827 on Lee's motherhood tend to emphasize her love and tenderness. Jean Humez characterizes Lee's motherhood, as expressed in the 1816 *Testimonies,* as "the stern mother," in "Images of Ann Lee in the 1816 *Testimonies:* A Study in Orally-Based Sacred Biography" and in " 'Ye Are My Epistles': The Construction of Ann Lee Imagery in Early Shaker Sacred Literature," *Journal of Feminist Studies in Religion* 8 (Spring 1992): 83–103.

27. White and Taylor, *Shakerism,* 79–112.

28. "The Father [in heaven] is first in the Order of the new Creation, and the Mother is second, the glory, wisdom, and perfection of the Father. And in and by the Son and Daughter, . . . the Father and Mother are both revealed and made known." Benjamin Seth Youngs, *The Testimony of Christ's Second Appearing,* 2d ed. (Albany, N.Y.: The United Society, 1810), 542. Ann Lee is here understood as the Daughter, who reveals the Mother as Jesus reveals the Father.

29. In Paulina Bates, *The Divine Book of Holy Wisdom,* (Canterbury, N.H.: n.p., 1849). Holy Mother Wisdom describes herself as "endless love, truth,

meekness, . . . purity, peace, sincerity, virtue, and chastity" and advises young married woman to yield to their husbands and to be "the crown of his enjoyment, and the bright morning star of his existence," 661, 516–17. See also Barbara Welter, "The Cult of True Womanhood," *American Quarterly* 18 (1966): 151–74, and Procter-Smith, *Women and Shaker Community and Worship,* 174–208.

30. The complexity of the use of the symbol "Mother" for God within the Shaker celibate system is analyzed by Mercadante, *Gender, Doctrine, and God,* 152–54.

31. Youngs, *Testimony of Christ's Second Appearing,* 438.

32. Procter-Smith, *Women and Shaker Community and Worship,* 64, 66–67. Priscilla Brewer, in *Shaker Communities, Shaker Lives* (Hanover: University of New England Press, 1986), 188–89, notes that during the 1870s a Hancock elder proposed permitting women trustees to hold money in their own name, the reason being the decline in male membership in the community.

33. Benjamin Seth Youngs, John Meacham, and David Darrow wrote their first edition of the *Testimony of Christ's Second Appearing* in 1808. But it was reportedly edited and revised by the ministry for another forty-eight years, so it is much more of a communal reflection. Of course, it reflects primarily, probably exclusively, the work of the male members of the ministry. See Mercadante, *Gender, Doctrine, and God,* 76–89.

34. The *Testimonies,* originally collected and published in 1812, as many of the last of the original members began to die, was edited and republished in 1888. Much material was removed which was regarded as indelicate or offensive.

35. The original revival activity originated among the "marginalized" members of the communities: the young, the "out-families," and the women. For a summary of interpretations of this period and its significance for women, see Procter-Smith, *Women and Shaker Community and Worship,* 174–208, and Mercadante, 100–113, 116–46.

36. Jane Crosthwaite analyzes the ways in which one instrument, Eleanor Potter, exercised considerable religious and political authority by means of her spiritual messages in "Eleanor Potter's Spiritual Spectacles: Reading, Writing, and Drawing in the Era of Manifestations" (Paper). For analysis of Paulina Bates's work and her strategy as an instrument, see Mercadante, 100–113.

37. Reuther, "Women in Utopian Movements," 51.

38. See Procter-Smith, *Women and Shaker Community and Worship,* 56–69; Kern, *An Ordered Love,* 129–34; Foster, *Religion and Sexuality,* 59, 231–232; D'Ann Campbell, "Women's Life in Utopia: The Shaker Experiment in Sexual Equality Reappraised," *The New England Quarterly* 51 (1978): 23–38.

Not So Different a Story After All: Pentecostal Women in the Pulpit

Elaine J. Lawless

Pentecostalism is a twentieth-century, American-born, conservative, Bible-based and Bible-inspired, patriarchal religion[1] that affords women the opportunity for direct religious experience and sometimes to exercise pastoral leadership.

Founded on the premise that "baptism" needs to be experienced both in water and in the Holy Spirit via speaking in tongues, the Pentecostal movement has received much publicity. In recent years, the inclination toward a more experiential, spirit-filled religious encounter has invaded the most stalwart of the traditional, "mainline" churches, including the Roman Catholic church. Yet, because Pentecostals have insisted on the charismatic, enthusiastic, public tongue-speaking experience as necessary for salvation, their animated religious services, their proselytizing, and their conservative, fundamentalist outlook have earned for them the epitaph "marginal" by all those religions that hold these religious attributes to be outside the mainstream. In terms of *numbers,* however, the Pentecostal movement, which includes the Assemblies of God, claims to be the fastest growing denomination in the world, and the recent advent of television evangelism, even with its blatant corruption, leads this nation in visibility and following.[2]

Males founded Pentecostalism, and males dominate the leadership roles in Pentecostalism, although a few charismatic women leaders, such as the healer Kathryn Kuhlman (1907–76) and Four-Square founder Aimee Semple McPherson (1890–1944) come to mind immediately because theirs were very public ministries. Although men generally dominate the public and political aspects of Pentecostalism, they do not dominate the energetic religious church services; women do. Men do not testify the longest and the loudest; women do. As I have argued elsewhere,[3] the Pentecostal religious service, while officiated by male leaders, affords an astoundingly receptive forum for female virtuosity, both in spiritual/physical encounters and in the art of spontaneous testifying. Women can actually dominate a religious service simply through their spirit-filled encounters with the Holy Ghost, their tongue-speaking and "falling out" experiences, and their long, elaborated testimonies, which might continue long into the night, preventing the pastor from ever having the chance to deliver his sermon.

While it certainly is not the norm, one will, on occasion, encounter a female preacher in a revival service or a female pastor of a Pentecostal congregation. At first it is difficult to ascertain why women can hold prime leadership roles in this religion that takes the Bible very literally and which openly supports a male-dominated hierarchy—from God, to Jesus, to Men, to Women, to Children, to Animals—and which subscribes to the traditional view that in the home the man is "king" and the woman is to be submissive to her husband and father (and to the general public of men) in all things. In fact, literal interpreters of Pauline's writings have kept Pentecostal dress codes a prevalent feature of the Pentecostal group identity. Paul says of women "your hair is your glory," and many Pentecostals take this to mean that women should *not* for any reason cut their hair.[4] In Paul, too, Pentecostals find scriptural support for their dress codes which insist that women wear high necklines, long sleeves, long dresses, and wear no make-up or jewelry. Pentecostals quote Paul on many occasions and are clearly aware of his admonition for women to keep silent in the churches (1 Cor. 14:34–35 and 1 Tim. 2:11–14). In light of this adherence to the scriptures, it seems unlikely that one would ever encounter Pentecostal clergywomen. Yet, in fact, one does.

Field research done primarily in central Missouri, in the heart of conservative American Christianity, yielded a sizable number of Pentecostal clergywomen, most of them in small rural towns. Given that rural Missouri is not the most likely spot to find avowed feminists or proponents of gender equality, it is puzzling how women in these small farming communities could acquire access to the pulpit and maintain it. In response to such questions as "How *is it* that you are a Pentecostal preacher?" or "How have you been able to maintain your position as the pastor of this church for more than seventeen years, in this small rural town, in central Missouri?" generally one receives first a quick denial that the woman is a "feminist," or a "bra-burner," or "you know, one of those ERA women." Rather, what is often offered are call-to-preach narratives. The carefully articulated, almost formulaic style, content, and structure of the call-to-preach narratives are, in fact, a part of the answer to the questions but are answers not readily discernible to the listener and possibly not totally conscious on the part of the narrators.

The stories are very similar, even from women who might never have met. Narrators most often begin with their own dismay, chagrin, and disbelief when they felt the call to preach from God. Some of the women heard a voice in the night; some were "slain" in the spirit in religious meetings; some heard voices in the woods; others heard God speak to them while they did the family laundry. *All* resisted the call. Their narratives clearly articulate their own misgivings about such a call; their first response was to deny the call or resist it. Most told elaborate stories about how, after ignoring the call at first, God returned to them in subsequent encounters, and sometimes he made the message clear in dramatic ways. For example, one woman fell on the ice and permanently crippled her hand during this time. She is convinced that it was God's way of making her pay attention to the call for her to preach.

Almost all the women then narrated how they tested God's calling. Each developed an elaborate "test," whereby, for example, if a particular person called them by six o'clock on a given evening and asked them to take the Sunday evening service, and that incident occurred exactly as outlined, then the woman conceded that indeed the call was from God and was not to be avoided. The narratives went on to explain how the woman made her calling from God public, and may have encountered opposition from fathers, mothers, pastors, and congregations. All spoke of the hardship of those times and the determination they had to acquire to "do God's will." Most of these women become itinerant preachers, traveling from church to church by invitation, from revival to revival, all across the state and region. Most never attain the status of pastor of a church, but a few do.

Many times, after serving as an interim pastor for several months or years, a woman will be "called" by a church to be their pastor. This was the case of one woman I came to know well. Sister Anna, as I have referred to her, has been pastor of one congregation for seventeen (now twenty) years in a small farming community in south-central Missouri. When this congregation got to know her and appreciate her stamina and devotion to her work, they finally agreed to make her their pastor. It is important to note that most Pentecostal churches are autonomous and are not part of elaborate, hierarchical, central organizations that determine policy for individual churches. Each church makes its own rules and regulations. So, while Pentecostalism can openly discourage the notion of a woman in the pulpit, in actual practice, women do often stand in the pulpit and can, in fact, gain the pastorship. Certainly, most of the female pastors I was able to locate were situated in churches in very small rural towns; the larger town and city congregations almost always have male pastors.

In time, the message of the call-to-preach narratives becomes more evident: the oft-repeated stories of how these women got a call from God serves to validate their calling. Pentecostalism is a religion that claims that all persons, male and female, young and old, are equally subject to the benefits of salvation. Pentecostals are generally not in the habit of questioning other believers' testimonies of a personal spiritual encounter with God. The religion is soundly based on the premise that Spirit-filled encounters can and do happen to everyone who seeks them. They believe that all who convert and are baptized in both the water and the Spirit have achieved a place next to God and Jesus in the hereafter. Therefore, the call-to-preach narratives are sacred stories, honored by the group as believable encounters with God Almighty.

While Pentecostals rely on an interpretation of Paul that keeps governance in the hands of males, women find argument for their own voice in the "end-time" language of the Bible as well. The most oft-quoted verse justifying women's active roles in religion comes from Joel: "It shall come to pass afterward, that I will pour out my spirit upon all flesh; and your sons and your daughters shall prophesy" (Joel 2: 28–29). Pentecostals believe these are "the last days" and that "the rapture" is apt to come at any moment, in the "twinkling of an eye." Therefore, given the women's call as perceived as coming directly from God and the directives for the need to convert the world before the final days, Pentecostals will—if all these criteria are successfully met—endorse the ministry of a woman. Any Pentecostal layperson has only to publicly attest to a spiritual call to preach from God to be considered "ordained" in many Pentecostal groups. Some sects of the religion have developed a mail-order "license" to preach, and certainly the more mainstream Assemblies of God have their own Bible colleges and ordination procedures. But the most critical aspect of the aspiration toward the ministry is the call from God.

The women's call-to-preach narratives, then, serve the function of verifying their personal call from God. The narratives further attest to the woman's unwillingness to take on a role she openly, at first, discounts as a possibility for a woman. Her ritual disclaimers all serve to illustrate that she has not sought this role *on her own;* this is God's doing and not hers. Sister Anna says that she asked: "God, do you know what you are doing? I am a wife and a mother. I am happy doing what I am doing. I don't *want* to preach. Do you really know what you are doing?" These women test God, they say, as their narratives move toward convincing their audience that should they, too, question, it shall all be in vain. This is, indeed, the will of God, and there is really nothing anyone can do about it. Part of the answer to the question "How did you ever get to be a Pentecostal woman preacher?" then, becomes "because *God* called me, and there was really nothing I, nor anyone else, could do about it." While Pentecostal female preachers decry the feminist movement and deny that they have chosen a strong, feminist stance against the dictums of their world, they have nevertheless clearly chosen for themselves an alternative life-style, often against the wishes of husbands, family, and friends.

Feminist scholarship that deals with narrative strategies in literature can aid us in understanding how these midwestern women have chosen to "re-script" their lives to fit an acceptable model. In her discussion of twentieth-century women writers, Rachel Blau DuPlessis suggests that, unlike nineteenth-century women writers whose characters basically could choose only between marriage and/or death, many contemporary women writers are "writing beyond" those restrictive endings for women's stories.[5] We can better understand both the lives of female preachers and their narrated "life stories," by relying on DuPlessis's understanding of narrative strategies that stretch women's possibilities, and Jeff Titon's notion of these as created "fictions."[6] It is constructive, then, for us to view the lives of women preachers as alternative living strategies, and the reconstructions of those lives—in the form of life stories—as narrative strategies that reinforce and validate the identity sought in the living "script." The ability of the women to create elaborations of "reality" may stem from what Patricia Spacks has termed the "female imagination," or the "power that penetrates the inner meaning of reality but also a power that creates *substitutes* for reality."[7] Our task is not to determine where "truth" leaves off in these narratives and where "imagination" begins; rather, it is most productive for us to view the narratives as stories with identifiable characteristics, structure, and content—stories that embody a shared understanding of the world. The life accounts may or may not actually reflect historical fact, but for the women who develop and recount them, they become very real indeed. As real, in fact, as the alternative life-style they have chosen. Both the women's lives and their fictive reconstructions of their lives serve as alternative strategies for women.

In our examination of the roles of women in this particular cultural milieu, we might ask several other pertinent questions concerning the leadership roles of women in Pentecostalism: How do women preach? What do they preach about? How do they become pastors of churches and maintain that role of authority? A brief discussion will following that will address these issues and point to where I think further research will lead us in our attempt to understand how and why women continue to be limited in their attempts to achieve equal footing with men in the world of religious ministry.

There is no single answer to the question—"How do women preach?" Different women have different preaching styles, just as different women have different walking and talking styles. Of course, the question often emerges whether women preach differently from men or if they preach about different things than men do. These are, on one level, legitimate questions, and certainly in gender-based studies appropriate ones. Field research suggests that female pastors of white congregations are less likely to be as forceful, exuberant, and physically dramatic as their male counterparts. This is not true across the board, but in general female pastors are more quietly subdued in their pulpit presentations than male pastors in similar churches on similar religious service occasions. However, the preaching styles of itinerant female preachers, who travel from church to church and from revival to revival, are vastly different from the preaching styles of female pastors who largely preach only to their home congregations. Female revivalists are likely to stomp back and forth on the platform, beat the pulpit with their fists, throw down the microphone, dance in the aisles, sing, chant, and speak in tongues in a manner rarely observed by women pastors. Possibly, the women who travel from church to church and town to town are not faced with the same restrictions on style and delivery in terms of proper decorum as those encountered by female pastors. Traveling preachers are expected to "revive" languid congregations, to stir them up, to incite the spirit to come amid them and cause them to swoon and speak in tongues. Some of the traveling female preachers are particularly good at this; their style matches the expectations of the audience. However, the female pastors of churches must maintain the image they seek to portray in the community and in the congregation. They have worked extraordinarily hard to achieve the power and authority they hold; it would not be acceptable for a female pastor to scream at her congregation, to admonish them for their indecorous behavior, to make herself a spectacle on display. One begins to understand that power and authority have a price tag, that gender is still very much at issue, and that style of presentation is often aligned with success. The traveling revival preachers have not attained power and authority; they have not achieved leadership positions and equal status with men. They have gained only temporary access to the pulpit—their liminality provides them license in performance style not available to the female pastor.

Folklorists are interested in the narratives people tell (i.e., the call-to-preach narratives discussed above). We study performance styles and verbal art and are tuned to the content of stories and other verbal genres. Several studies have appeared that are concerned with the performance styles and the content of "folk preaching."[8] Most of these works have focused on the African American tradition of spontaneous, chanted preaching styles. As examples of oral tradition, the sermons have been examined in terms of their delivery style, punctuated structure, use of formulas and clichés, imagery, and content. Similarly, in the spontaneously rendered oral sermons of women, examined as representations of verbal art and oral tradition in a modern context, we can point out the formulas, the repeated patterns, the clichés and the repeated images that serve the women in their sermon weaving.[9]

As with white male preachers, white female preachers are greatly varied in their use of patterned formulaic phrases, Bible verses and clichés, lines from songs and hymns, and their use of the staccato-like, chanted delivery style. Some move easily into a chant during their preaching of a sermon, and some never reach that sing-song, heavily punctuated style at all. Ethnopoetic renderings of orally performed sermons enable us to transcribe sermons verbatim and attempt to illuminate style in performance.[10]

The folklorist is interested as well in the themes of women's sermons. Is it possible that women's concerns are different? Are their approaches to issues different? Do they utilize storytelling in unique and gender-based ways? Are they more this-world oriented or inclined toward the next world? Without question, women have a style of preaching that is unique to their gender. They are less likely to criticize their congregational members or admonish them for misbehaving; they are more likely to cajole and urge them into good behavior, "nurture" them if you will.[11] A "woman's way of knowing" certainly appears to be in operation in the way women pastors relate to their congregations: "Women resolve conflicts not by invoking a logical hierarchy of abstract principles but through trying to understand the conflict in the context of each person's perspective, needs, and goals—and doing the best possible for everyone that is involved."[12] Female pastors rarely dwell on rules and restrictions, dress codes and moral conduct; they are more inclined to speak about the importance of cooperation, of interaction, of concern and brotherly/sisterly love. An interesting project will be to compare the sermons of clergywomen from other denominations with those preached by Pentecostal women.

Female pastors often utilize certain images as strategies to guard their tenuous positions in the pulpit. They often use images of children and family, of reproduction and mothering, of household duties and wifely concerns, images utilized to authenticate both their religious power and their church authority. The maternal and reproductive images they employ as religious strategies serve to strip their presence behind the pulpit of its most threatening aspects.[13]

Most of the sermons delivered by these Pentecostal clergywomen include two main themes. The first of these is the examination of what "total sacrifice" really means. In one guise or another, a great many of the sermons pose questions about how one can make a total sacrifice to God and to God's work. Many stress the importance of unquestioned, total sacrifice to God of one's body, soul, and mind. The final questions at the conclusion of these sermons are: What are *you* doing for God? Are you giving your all? What more could you do for the Lord? Another theme that dominates the women's sermons is a concern about making it into heaven. Sermon after sermon is woven around the image of making it to St. Peter's door only to be turned away. One woman spoke on several occasions of fearing she might meet St. Peter and be "found wanting, found wanting; only to make it to the pearly gates and be found wanting." Another woman often turned to an old hymn about being "left standing outside" as the structural and thematic basis for her sermons. She recalled many times how, as a young girl, so young her feet didn't touch the floor, she would be singing that old song and weeping for fear that she, too, would get to heaven and be "left standing outside." The message here, by the end of the sermon, was always "come to Jesus, now, before it is too late and you are left standing outside."

In some ways, both of these dominant themes in women's sermons are problematic. Both seem to point to the possibility of fears evident in the women themselves about their religious roles and how, in fact, these roles may be received by those around them and, ultimately, by God.[14] Their sermon messages deal primarily with life on this earth in terms of complete obedience to God's will, total self-sacrifice while on this earth, and a rejection of their own intrinsic worth and capabilities—all with a view of the possibility of rejection by God in the end.

The religious worldview of Pentecostals includes an omnipotent, vengeful, male God who will become angry at disobedience and who can "cast you out" if provoked. This God must be approached on his terms and at the appropriate moments; he is quite capable of rejecting late pleas for help. These women sometimes preach what they recognize as an "old-fashioned" message complete with hell-fire and brimstone. They preach the devil as a "real being" who lurks around every corner, ready to tempt them and tell them they need not be so careful. But they also share a belief about the Judgment Day that will come at heaven's gates, where some will be left "standing outside."

Women raised in conservative, patriarchal American religions such as Pentecostalism are acutely aware of the equation of "man's fall" with Eve's transgression in the Garden of Eden. They are fully aware that most believers in these religions, male and female, have accepted Eve's guilt and blame her for the banishment from the Garden. They equate their own life's tribulations, in fact, to punishment for Eve's sin. Perhaps they become preachers to save their own souls. Perhaps that seems to be the very closest they can walk with God; on the other hand, they recognize the criticism that often comes from their community.

Finally, it seems important to ask why women in the very smallest rural towns are able to achieve leadership roles as pastors more often than in the larger towns and cities. The irony is that in the most conservative regions of the Midwest, where God, home, and family are sacred, private, and preserved by the Father in heaven, a woman has a better chance of gaining access to the pastorship if and because she is more likely to assert the God-given rightness of this worldview, than the male pastor who, in a less conservative cultural context, may wish to take the congregation into a more public and political arena. These female pastors are able to employ the system to their advantage by basing their roles as preachers and pastors on the traditional spiritual religiosity, which is still closely aligned with nineteenth-century notions of religion as part of the woman's sphere, maintained close to hearth and home.[15] A woman brought up in this culture, who remains submissive even as she acquires religious power and authority, can assert that, with God's blessing, she is protecting the sanctity of hearth, home, and church. It may not be a feminist's dream, but that is because these women are not feminists. They are strong-willed, determined, hard-working religious women doing remarkable things in a constricted atmosphere. Their mere presence in the pulpit offers hope to those who would follow them, but it would be a mistake to assume that Pentecostalism is a liberal-minded religion that has taken great strides toward the equality of the sexes. Only a few women make it into the pulpit in this religious movement, and we must be cautious in how we read their experience.

If the clergywoman can assure her conservative congregation that she will keep the religion closely connected to the spiritual realm and the family-based community, and as far away from the secular as is possible, then she has a better chance of gaining the pastorship. Her disregard for the public arena and her inclination toward the hearth, the home, and the family, represent everything the congregation holds dear. By making a clear commitment to these central configurations and pronouncing her intention and ability to keep the church within the domestic/spiritual sphere, she can win their confidence. And, further, if she "mothers" the congregation, cares for them, nurtures them, empathizes with them, counsels them, and can pray their souls into heaven, then they are all that much more likely to allow her to fill the job of pastor. It is her ability as a religious woman to confer with God's Spirit that makes her a legitimate spiritual being; therefore, she can utilize this perception of her natural powers in order to assume a position of authority within the church.

In general, women are not granted equality in authority in the Pentecostal religion; in fact, it is not at all unusual to find that in many of the churches with a woman pastor, the ruling board of deacons is made up entirely of men or that the business meetings of the church are held with only men present (with the woman pastor), or with men only (and the pastor) allowed to speak and to vote. But the weight of the call from God to preach is profound, and combined with the belief in the urgency of these as the "final days," women have found a way into the pulpit.

For many, Pentecostalism remains a "marginal" religion, set apart from mainstream religions in this country by both doctrine and practice. Although some women have gained access to the pulpit in Pentecostalism, their position there is a precarious one. The situation of Pentecostal women preachers and pastors certainly does not suggest what Janet Wilson James has termed a flood of women in the religious scene searching out the "liberating promises of scripture to revise theologies,"[16] nor is it, as Mary Farrell Bednarowski suggests, "a different story."[17]

Bednarowski's article certainly provides exciting "liberating promises" that include revising images of the divine, denying the traditional doctrine of the Fall as the transgression of Eve, offering new possibilities for ordination, power and authority, and creative possibilities for the life scripts for women. We should not be surprised that these characteristics are right at the forefront of the religious expectations and goals of religions founded by women. However, the four points highlighted by Bednarowski are not found to be relevant to white Pentecostal women's religious leadership. The comparison, though, is critical and useful. By illustrating that none of these criteria fit contemporary Pentecostalism, we are forced to probe even deeper to understand how it is that women in this restrictive denomination do enter into leadership roles and how they maintain and preserve them.

It is worth noting that in my current research with clergywomen from a variety of different "mainstream" denominations, I am finding a consistent effort on the part of the female clergy to approach each of Bednarowski's four points with energy and determination. Unlike most Pentecostal clergywomen who have never attended seminary, the life experiences and the seminary experiences of clergywomen in mainline denominations have motivated them to face each of these critical issues head-on. Clergywomen from a variety of denominations—Episcopalians, Methodists, Disciples, Baptists, Unitarians, Unity ministers, and a host of others—are dealing with the issues of inclusive language, with reimagining the traditional scriptural stories and acquitting Eve, of stressing the importance of decentralizing church hierarchies and democratizing the religious service, and insisting on the rights of all people to choose alternative life-styles. While it is important for us to study marginal religions, noting how women have gained leadership positions there, we must take note of what clergywomen in mainline religions are attempting to accomplish as well. Here, Bednarowski's question, "Why is it that women were [are] able to achieve positions of leadership in some religious movements, contrary both to established tradition and to cultural assumptions about the proper role of women as well?" remains pertinent and critical. Furthermore, it is within mainstream American religion that both the "established tradition and the cultural assumptions about the proper role of women" are also being questioned and revised.

NOTES

1. See Vinson Synan, *The Holiness-Pentecostal Movement in the United States* (Grand Rapids, Mich.: Eerdmans, 1971).

2. See Carol Flake, *Redemptorama* (New York: Penguin, 1984).

3. See Elaine J. Lawless, "Shouting for the Lord: The Power of Women's Speech in the Pentecostal Service," *Journal of American Folklore* 96 (1983): 433–57.

4. See Lawless, "Brothers and Sisters: Pentecostals as a Folk Group," *Western Folklore* 43 (1983): 85–104; Lawless, " 'Your Hair is Your Glory': Public and Private Symbology for Pentecostal Women," *New York Folklore* 12 (1986): 33–49.

5. Rachel Blau DuPlessis, *Writing Beyond the Ending: Narrative Strategies of Twentieth-Century Women Writers* (Bloomington: Indiana University Press, 1985).

6. Jeff Todd Titon, "The Life Story," *Journal of American Folklore* 93 (1980): 276–92.

7. Patricia Meyer Spacks, *The Female Imagination* (New York: Alfred A. Knopf, 1972), 4.

8. See Gerald Davis, *I Got the Word in Me and I Can Sing It, You Know* (Philadelphia: University of Pennsylvania Press, 1985); Catherine Peck, "Your Daughters Shall Prophesy: Women in the Afro-American Preaching Tradition" (Master's thesis, University of North Carolina, 1983); Bruce A. Rosenberg, *The Art of the American Folk Preacher* (New York: Oxford University Press, 1970), reissued as *Can These Bones Live? The Art of the American Folk Preacher,* rev. ed. (Urbana: University of Illinois Press, 1988); Jeff Todd Titon, *Powerhouse for God* (Austin: University of Texas Press, 1988).

9. Cf. Christine M. Smith, *Weaving the Sermon: Preaching in a Feminist Perspective* (Louisville, K.Y.: Westminster Press, 1989); Elaine J. Lawless, *Handmaidens of the Lord: Pentecostal Women Preachers and Traditional Religion* (Philadelphia: University of Pennsylvania Press and the American Folklore Society, 1988).

10. For discussions of ethnopoetics, see Jerome Rothenberg and Diane Rothenberg, eds., *Symposium of the Whole: A Range of Discourse toward an Ethnopoetics* (Berkeley: University of California Press, 1983); Dennis Tedlock, *The Spoken Word and the Work of Interpretation* (Philadelphia: University of Pennsylvania Press, 1983).

11. For a discussion of these as female characteristics, see Carol Gilligan, *In a Different Voice* (Cambridge: Harvard University Press, 1982).

12. Mary Field Belenky et al. *Women's Ways of Knowing: The Development of Self, Voice, and Mind* (New York: Basic Books, 1986).

13. These images are discussed in detail in Elaine J. Lawless, "Piety and Motherhood: Reproductive Images and Maternal Strategies of the Woman Preacher," *Journal of American Folklore* 100 (1987): 469–79.

14. It must be noted that in conversations with Sister Anna, she has strongly denied any fears about making it into heaven. I have discussed this problematic in detail in " 'I Was Afraid Someone Like You . . . an Outsider . . . Would Misunderstand': Negotiating Interpretive Differences between Ethnographers and Subjects," *Journal of American Folklore* 105 (Summer 1992): 302–15, and "Women's Life Stories and Reciprocal Ethnography as Feminist and Emergent," *Journal of Folklore Research* 28, no. 1 (Fall 1991): 35–61.

15. See Barbara Welter, *Dimity Convictions: The American Woman in the 19th Century* (Athens: Ohio University Press, 1976).

16. Janet Wilson James, ed. *Women in American Religion* (Philadelphia: University of Pennsylvania Press, 1976).

17. Mary Farrell Bednarowski, "Outside the Mainstream: Women's Religion and Women Religious Leaders in Nineteenth-Century America," *Journal of the American Academy of Religion* 48 (June 1980): 207–31.

Part 2

Women in the Metaphysical Movement

The Perils of Passivity:
Women's Leadership in
Spiritualism and Christian Science

Ann Braude

Is religion oppressive to women, or is it liberating? During the last ten years much of the discussion of women's religious history has focused on the question of whether religion has functioned to reinforce societal limitations on women's roles and to limit opportunities, or, in contrast, whether it has empowered women to exceed normative social roles, and to reject previously accepted limitations on their activities. Feminist historians have looked to religious movements founded by women in search of models for female empowerment. Yet, despite early enthusiasm, attempts to find an unequivocal feminist in Anne Hutchinson, Ann Lee, or Mary Baker Eddy have proved unsatisfactory. As research continues, what one scholar cautiously called "The Ambiguous Feminism of Mary Baker Eddy" seems to be as much as can be claimed for most female founder figures.[1] If the gender of the founder does not determine whether a religion will be empowering to women, what does? Should we look to the content of doctrine or the structure of polity? Should we examine images of the divine or political platforms? Or should we expect all of these to reflect and reinforce a single feminine ideal?[2]

Spiritualism and Christian Science provide tempting examples for exploration of these questions because each presents so many features apparently conducive to female leadership. Both portray the divine in a way that allows men and women equally to identify with the image of God, who is referred to as both Mother and Father and as principle. In Spiritualism, communication with an abstract divine principle takes place through individual spirits, both male and female, while the Christian Science concept of God is summarized in seven "synonyms"—Mind, Spirit, Soul, Principle, Life, Truth, and Love—all devoid of gender specificity. Both groups reacted against the doctrine of the Fall and viewed human beings as naturally good and whole from birth, thus rejecting the idea that woman caused sin to enter the world. Both saw important roles for women beyond home and family, and did not view marriage or motherhood as the only normative roles for women. And, finally, both rejected the idea of an ordained clergy, thus undercutting the traditional source of legitimation for the exclusivity of male religious leadership.[3]

It is clear that these two new religious movements did indeed generate unprecedented examples of women's leadership. Spiritualism emboldened hundreds of women to exceed the boundaries of acceptable behavior and made feminine characteristics normative for religious leadership. Christian Science assaulted traditional gender roles by elevating a powerful female founder to a position of immense authority. But the types of leadership generated by the two movements formed parts of utterly incongruous organizational structures, and had very different implications for their female members. In addition, Spiritualism's support for women's leadership resulted in active advocacy of women's rights throughout the movement, while in Christian Science advocacy of women's rights remained a low priority. This essay will compare women's leadership in Spiritualism and Christian Science in order to suggest some of the difficulties of predicting what sort of religion will be empowering to women. In the process, it will explore the perils of applauding feminine passivity as a basis for women's religious leadership, as well as the perils of rejecting passivity as a spiritual path in a culture that assumed that this was an inherent attribute of women's nature.

Spiritualism

In Spiritualism, women's leadership rested on the centrality of the role of medium.[4] Spiritualism began as a popular movement in 1848 in upstate New York when two adolescent girls, Kate and Margaret Fox, heard raps on the walls and furniture of their family home, which their neighbors attributed to the spirit of a dead peddler buried in the basement. Based on the premise that communication with the spirits of the dead provided empirical proof of the immortality of the soul, Spiritualism spread "like a prairie fire" throughout the Northeast and the old Northwest. Americans hungry for communication with the dead gathered around séance tables in hope of discovering human mediums in their midst who could serve as vehicles for messages from beloved friends and family members who had passed beyond the veil. They found such messages most convincing when they came through figures like the Fox sisters: untrained, unlettered teenage girls. These figures epitomized the ideal feminine characteristics of the Victorian period: purity, piety, passivity, and domesticity.[5] Untainted by the corrupting influence of the world beyond the home—or even by the sexual contact implied in marriage—teenaged girls were believed to make good mediums because their own characters were not powerful enough to interfere with an external intelligence's use of their bodies. Because the goal of mediumship was to serve as a passive vehicle for spirits, the characteristics that usually qualified men for leadership—education, experience, will—all became disadvantages. Spiritualists concurred with their contemporaries in believing that an inclination toward religion was an inherent aspect of the female character. But, instead of viewing the qualities that inclined women toward piety as disqualifications for public roles, Spiritualism made the delicate constitution and nervous excitability commonly attributed to femininity a qualification for religious leadership.[6]

Most mediums limited themselves to private séances, at which they conveyed personal messages from departed friends or family members to those seated with them around a table. But many became trance speakers who delivered spirit messages at public lectures. Trance speakers emerged during the 1850s as the first sizable group of American women to speak in public.[7] In the figure of the medium, Spiritualism manipulated nineteenth-century gender ideals so that both religious leadership and public speaking became natural extensions of woman's role. By providing divine sanction for the reinterpretation of gender roles, Spiritualists overcame women's internalized gendered self-image more effectively than those who attempted to alter woman's role without a religious justification.

But the manner in which Spiritualism encouraged women's leadership had a cultural significance of its own. At public events the Spiritualist platform juxtaposed unconscious women voicing poetic visions inspired by external intelligences with conscious men expressing their own opinions on spiritual, social, and political subjects. This sexual division of labor presented the passivity of women in bold relief. In view of this, some may question the applicability of the term "leader" to spirit mediums. Can one speak of the "leadership" of an unconscious adolescent? Most mediums were not leaders in the sense of exercising power or authority. Would it be more accurate to find the leaders of Spiritualism in the male figures who organized Spiritualist conventions and societies, or served as managers for female mediums? In my view, these men were leaders, but so were mediums. Very simply, where mediums went, Spiritualists followed, and there was no Spiritualism without them. Believers and investigators alike traveled long distances to sit at the séance table of a renowned medium. Trance speakers were the missionaries of the movement, drawing converts to the faith from the large crowds they attracted as they spoke in town after town. In some cases there was a man at the door who had rented the room and who collected an admission fee, but it hardly makes sense to call him a religious leader. Many trance speakers traveled alone, making their own arrangements and handling their own finances. Where they were accompanied by husbands, fathers, or managers, these were often met with skepticism. After a visit from the tremendously popular medium, Cora Hatch, a Spiritualist in Troy, New York, wrote to a coreligionist, "You ask how we like Mrs. Hatch? Very much and *Mr.* Hatch very little." The following year the eighteen-year-old trance speaker won a divorce from her husband and manager because of his exploitative treatment. He responded with a damning pamphlet attacking Spiritualism for its immoral tendencies and for the inevitability of mediumship leading to the destruction of marriages. Three subsequent husbands left little mark on Spiritualist history while Cora, under a variety of married names, remained a revered speaker with a large following for half a century.[8]

Although the passive nature of mediumship had intrinsic problems for female leaders, it could be equally problematic for male Spiritualists whose presumed rationality, worldliness, and 'organized' mental capacities were believed to make them poor vehicles for spirit communication. Men could become mediums, but only if they showed the feminine characteristics that would disqualify them for more traditional forms of leadership. Mediumship was closely associated with femininity, and Spiritualism defined no comparable public role for men. While men did become Spiritualist leaders, each had to find his own role, whether as manager for a female medium, as conference organizer, or as newspaper editor. While hundreds of women gained respect, admiration—and sometimes a living—as spirit mediums, publishing a newspaper was about the closest thing to ministry that the new faith offered to male advocates.[9]

Because the new religion relied on direct spiritual communication it rejected not only ordained clergy, but all forms of religious authority. Individuals were advised to seek unique encounters with religious truth through their own investigations at séances and through attention to their own inner promptings. Spiritualists denied the validity of anyone exercising authority—spiritual or otherwise—over anyone else. Advocates regarded the clergy, the Bible, and the hierarchy of the churches as so many obstacles on the path to spiritual truth. Their rejection of authority caused them to question the political order as well as the religious order, and formed the basis of their critique of slavery and of marriage, because each interposed the authority of another human being between the individual and his or her divine nature. Because they recognized no source of religious authority, Spiritualists had no basis for enforcing uniformity either in doctrine or in religious practice. Without authority there could be no orthodoxy. Without orthodoxy, there could be no heterodoxy. Thus Spiritualism accommodated a broad spectrum of opinions and

practices. Spiritualists insistence on radical individualism made their movement an amorphous one, that ultimately proved impervious to organization.
Spiritualists' absolute rejection of authority provides an extreme case of
the anticlericalism that many scholars have identified as encouraging
women's leadership.

Christian Science

Christian Science arose in a population in which Spiritualism and its
individualist premise were familiar and widely accepted. Considering how
much it shared with Spiritualism in basic cosmological outlook, Christian
Science could not have been more different in its group structure or in its
attitude toward authority. Founded in 1875, Christian Science quickly
became a tightly organized movement, with a firm structure designed to
insure the authority of its founder, Mary Baker Eddy, as the sole basis of
the church. Scholars looking for models of women's leadership have often
turned to Christian Science because they see in Eddy one of the most
effective female leaders in American history. Her towering presence over-
shadows the role of women in general in Christian Science both in the
institutional forms that evolved after her death, and in historical treatments of the movement. The closest thing to an official history the church
has produced is a three volume biography of its founder.[10] But the focus
on Eddy is not limited to in-house scholarship. In *Notable American
Women,* the standard biographical reference work in American women's
history in which the length of each entry reflects the editors' estimate of
the figure's historical import, Eddy's entry is second in length only to that
of Harriet Beecher Stowe, who Abraham Lincoln called "the little lady
who caused this big war." It is nearly twice as long as those on Susan B.
Anthony and Frances Willard, three times as long as the one on Ellen
Gould White, founder of a much larger denomination, the Seventh-Day
Adventists, and, perhaps justly, five times as long as the combined entry
covering Kate and Margaret Fox as well as their older sister Leah.[11]
    What did Eddy do that placed her second in significance only to the
nineteenth century's best selling novelist, credited, if only in jest, with
causing the Civil War? Her unique accomplishment was to exercise a
degree of authority unprecedented for an American woman. She created a
long-lasting movement thoroughly identified with her own religious ideals
and insights, for which she wrote the authoritative text and provided an
organizational structure that guaranteed the authority of her teachings
after her death. According to her own account, Eddy discovered that,
following a fall on the ice in 1866, she could heal herself through the
application of mental principles based on the New Testament. She began

teaching her new system of healing and published the first edition of *Science and Health* in 1875. Eddy asserted the absolute power of Spirit over matter, of Mind over body. Christian Science recognized no objective physical reality, but only the reality of Spirit, an infinite, all encompassing principle of goodness, also called God. The physical world and all evidences of evil were seen as resulting from the workings of Mortal Mind, the opposite of Spirit, which had no ultimate reality, but resulted only from human thoughts. Christian Scientists agreed with Spiritualists that there is no change at death, but while Spiritualists found proof of immortality in the ability of spirits to make their physical presence felt after death—to tip tables, hold pens, or ring bells—Christian Scientists asserted that the body never existed in the first place, so that physical evidence of spirit presence proved nothing.

But the most important difference between Christian Science and Spiritualism lay in the enduring role of its founder. While Spiritualism had no founder, no scripture, and no orthodoxy, Eddy's role as founder and author of *Science and Health* meant that her movement could not countenance the extreme individualism so central to Spiritualism. In Christian Science worship selections from *Science and Health* replaced sermons, and those who presided were called "readers" rather than "ministers," because their function was to read the words of Mary Baker Eddy, not to interpret scripture on their own. In order to justify her solitary role as leader Eddy needed to explain her rejection of the egalitarian model of leadership implied in mediumship. In a chapter of *Science and Health* devoted to distinguishing Christian Science from Spiritualism, Eddy explained that Spiritualism did indeed empower female mediums, but that it empowered them to use their own minds to generate the appearance of false manifestations, not to gain true spiritual knowledge.[12]

While the Spiritualist understanding of mediumship implied that women as a group had natural qualities of spiritual leadership, Christian Science asserted that one woman had unique leadership attributes. Although the new movement produced an extraordinary female leader in its founder, it discouraged other women from following her example. Christian Science did empower women within certain well-defined limits; it asked them to lead worship services, to become healers, and to assume a variety of public roles within their church. However, Eddy censured any who emulated her by aspiring to religious authority in any way comparable to hers. She prohibited the use of writings on Christian Science other than her own, and limited the terms of readers to three years, so that no local leader could ever attract a personal following. The authoritative role of Eddy's teachings left no outlet for the creativity of other believers and forced Eddy to expel some of her most effective spokespersons. Christian

Science did produce a number of powerful female leaders, most notably Emma Curtis Hopkins, Ursula Gestefeld, and Augusta Stetson—all of whom became religious leaders in their own right after being severed from the Christian Science church. Christian Science promoted the exclusive authority of one woman rather than promoting women's leadership as a principle.[13]

Eddy's commitment to the exclusivity of her own teachings created a tension between Christian Science doctrine and the organizational structure she established to promote that doctrine. Although the structure ascribed a unique role to Eddy, the doctrine suggested that all human beings have the potential to achieve the perfection of thought that allowed her to discover the principles of Christian Science. On one hand Christian Science paralleled Eddy's role to that of the Virgin Mary, which, in a singular interpretation of the incarnation, it elevated almost above the role of Jesus. The Virgin Birth was an important tenet in Christian Science because it showed that biological functions could be controlled by Spirit. Just as the Virgin Mary gave birth to Christianity through the conception that resulted from her perfect communion with God, so Mary Baker Eddy gave birth to Christian Science through her conception of *Science and Health,* which resulted from the same cause.[14] Christian Science urged all believers to strive for such communion, and assured them it was possible. Yet, if they felt they had achieved it to the point that they could express the truth of Christian Science in original writing or teaching, they were expelled from the church. Eddy prohibited an ordained clergy, *not* to diminish authority within her movement, but rather to increase her own authority and that of her text, *Science and Health.* Where Spiritualists emphasized personal spiritual knowledge, Christian Scientists emphasized doctrinal uniformity.

While Christian Science did not offer women the opportunity to emulate its powerful founder, it did offer them smaller roles that nevertheless exceeded the degree of power and autonomy accessible to women in mainstream religious groups or in society at large. The by-laws of the Mother Church mandated the appointment of one male and one female reader.[15] This was an extraordinary move when the by-laws were written in 1891, when only a few small churches allowed the ordination of women. Ironically, Christian Science offered the same appealing leadership opportunities to men. Eddy's attempt to maintain sexual parity in the reader's stand placed a premium on male members, who constituted no more than 25 percent of church membership. Because Eddy kept the most capable men in Boston to run the Mother Church and the publishing concern, regional churches were generally started by women. The requirement of a male reader forced these women,

many of whom showed great personal ambition, to seek male cooperation and converts.

Perhaps the aspect of Christian Science that had the most significant
implications for women's autonomy was its concept of healing. Here, the
egalitarian implications of Christian Science doctrine were embodied in
religious practice. Because Eddy believed that God is good and God is all,
she viewed all disease and misfortune as resulting from errors in human
thought devoid of ultimate reality. In Christian Science the nature of Spirit
and of its opposite, Mortal Mind, were revealed to individuals through
experiences of illness and healing. Eddy's teaching rested on a reciprocal
relation between healing and revelation in which "to be healed is to
understand the true nature of God, and to understand the true nature of
God is to be healed."[16] Thus healing lay at the core of Christian Science,
and, unlike the structure she proposed for her church, Eddy offered an
egalitarian model for the process through which healing could be obtained.[17]

Early Christian Science was organized on the model of the medical
profession. Potential Scientists enrolled in classes at Christian Science
Institutes, where they studied mental healing. Upon completing the course
students became "practitioners" who were entitled to accept fees for
treating sick patients according to the principles of Christian Science. The
relationship between patient and practitioner was one of relative equals.
Both were likely to be women, often of the same age and marital status.
The treatment initiated the patient into the system of knowledge of which
the practitioner was a specialist. Ideally, each patient would become a
church member, and, ultimately, a practitioner.

The egalitarian approach of Christian Science becomes clear in contrast to another system of healing that arose at the same time to address
the ills of the same urban, educated women from whom Christian Scientists were recruited: gynecology. The new medical specialty of gynecology based treatment on the belief that woman's general health and well-being
depended on her reproductive health, and especially on the state of her
ovaries and her uterus. Gynecologists treated a broad range of physical
and nervous disorders according to this theory, including of course,
hysteria—"womb-disease." The relationship between doctor and patient
in gynecology mirrored the ideal relationship between men and women in
Victorian society. Many doctors claimed that the success of their cures
rested on their ability to achieve the submission of the patient's will to the
superior authority of the doctor. The physician was the active party in the
cure, whether he performed one of the new radical surgical techniques on
an etherized patient or merely prescribed the details of her daily regimen:
what she ate, what she read, with whom she spoke, and what her hours of
rising and retiring would be. The patient's role was to accept unquestioningly

the authority of her doctor, just as she was supposed to accept that of her father or husband. After the treatment, she remained as ignorant of the workings of medicine as before.[18]

Not only did Christian Scientists propose a more egalitarian model of healing than gynecology, but the diseases with which they were most concerned suggest that an active role for women was essential to their understanding of health. Christian Science healing did not differentiate between diseases. Teachers and practitioners insisted that they did not perform diagnosis because illness was not real, therefore its symptoms told nothing about its nature or cause. All illnesses received the same treatment: mental healing. But they did report cures in the *Christian Science Journal,* where they list the full range of complaints treated by medical practitioners of the day, including many specious diagnoses and psychosomatic ailments.[19] No particular class of disease predominates. However, two complaints were especially expressive of Christian Science concerns and appeared more frequently in general discussions of healing than they did in reports of cases—these were poisoning and paralysis.

Although Christian Scientists denied the reality of evil, they were preoccupied with fighting the dangerous temporal impact of false belief in evil. From her conviction that mind could control matter Eddy concluded that if thoughts could heal, they could also harm. Especially in the early years, Christian Scientists attributed much disease to the force of malicious animal magnetism or mesmerism—that is, to the power of one person's belief in evil on the well-being of another. Eddy taught that disease could be caused by the malicious intent of one's enemies. She attributed her husband's death to arsenic placed in his body by the thoughts of those who wished her ill.[20] Poisoning imaged the essential feature of malicious animal magnetism—the involuntary subjugation of the victim's will to that of the mesmerist. Like poison, a foreign element invaded the victim and took control of her system. Paralysis represented the most dread result of animal magnetism—the inability to act. The state of being mesmerized—or subject to animal magnetism—was characterized by loss of power and volition. It was often compared to drunkenness. Descriptions of victims of animal magnetism used the terms "inactivity," "indifference," "procrastination," and "impotence." One article explained that "Christian Scientists will find the effect of the approach and attack of mesmerism to be a sort of paralysis, or inaction of mind which will be revealed upon the recovery of the right condition of thought, by the vitality and Life that has destroyed the numbness and fear."[21] Illness inevitably accompanied animal magnetism. Eddy wrote in the monthly column on animal magnetism: "Even if the mental operator is not intent on making his victims sick, but only determined to make him believe a lie, this error will also produce physical sufferings, and these sufferings show the fundamental principle of Christian Science—that error and sickness are one, and truth is their only remedy."[22] The mesmerist deprived the victim of self-control. Physical illness literally expressed the victim's inability to act.

Mesmerism rendered its victims passive through physical and spiritual incapacitation. But Eddy viewed passivity as unacceptable even in the absence of animal magnetism. Passivity was openness to error—truth and health required constant vigilance. Eddy extolled incessant activity in the struggle against animal magnetism. If one did not actively oppose mesmeric forces, one opened oneself to their influence. The *Journal* explained,

> God, the source of all being . . . is Radiation, continual action. . . . That constant Radiation of Light is the armor of righteousness, which always protects man from his enemy, the devil (mortal mind). All mortal mind is the counterfeit, or opposite of this life principle, and is absorption, blackness and stagnation which strives . . . to render its victim absorbent of all that is evil and erroneous, causing stagnation and death . . . man cannot at the same time radiate and absorb.[23]

The ideals of activity and personal power espoused by Christian Science clearly differed substantially from the norms for feminine behavior of the period. The ideology of Christian Science asserted that women, like men, could and should be active outside the home. In the doctrine of animal magnetism it recognized that many felt forceful inhibitions to such activity. Christian Science asserted that passivity was not part of woman's nature, but was imposed on her by mesmerism, an external force that placed destructive limitations on her ability to act. Where Spiritualism applauded feminine passivity as a qualification for religious leadership, Christian Science waged war on passivity in women as an invitation to spiritual error.

Conclusion

What can this comparison tell us about the role of religion in encouraging or discouraging women's leadership? It confirms what much social theory in other areas would lead us to suspect that the content of religious doctrine can influence whether a group will take an active role in promoting women's rights, as well as what its position will be on women's issues. For Spiritualists the empirical demonstration that reveals the true nature of reality is spirit communication, for Christian Science, healing. The one heals a rift in the social fabric, the other a rift in the individual's harmony with divine order. Spiritualism's social orientation encouraged concern with the reform of society, including the emancipation of women. The Christian Science concept of healing, in contrast, suggested that individuals, whether male or female, could solve their own problems through the power of their minds, so that little attention need focus on changing the status of groups of people within society.

Second, and more importantly, the comparison of Christian Science and Spiritualism complicates interpretations that focus on the benefits offered to women by anticlericalism. While religious beliefs and practices clearly effect women's roles, there is not a simple correlation between specific doctrines and female empowerment. Many studies observe that women's leadership occurs most often in religious contexts that recognize the authority of direct spiritual knowledge or experience rather than the authority of office represented by ordination or education. The present comparison suggests that while such anticlericalism supports women's leadership, it also presents problems. Recognition of direct spiritual contact as a legitimation for leadership is most likely to exist early in the development of a religious movement. If the movement is able to perpetuate itself into a second and third generation, it is likely to partake of some form of institutionalization. Generally, institutionalization is accompanied by the legitimization of authority through hierarchical structures, thus leading to a decline in the conditions that fostered women's leadership. Thus, while new movements may be more likely to have female leaders than old ones, even those founded by women show a tendency to move away from those conducive conditions if they survive.

In Christian Science and Spiritualism we have two examples of anticlericalism in a new religious movement, one in a group that succeeded in institutionalization, one in a group that did not. Christian Science was enabled to forge an effective structure for its own perpetuation by accepting the authority of its founder to an extent that limited leadership opportunities for other women. In contrast, Spiritualists remained loyal to individualist principles, generating a movement with a broad base of female leadership and strong support for women's rights, but lacking an effective organizational structure for its own perpetuation. The example of Spiritualism suggests that the rejection of authority has dangers for the perpetuation of any group, and, therefore, ultimately, for women's leadership in that group. There may be costs as well as benefits to conditions that foster women's leadership.

NOTES

1. Susan Hill Lindley, "The Ambiguous Feminism of Mary Baker Eddy," *Journal of Religion* 64 (1984): 318–31. On Ann Lee, see the article by Marjorie

Procter-Smith in this volume. For a somewhat problematic attempt to interpret Anne Hutchinson as a "feminist" see Selma R. Williams, *Divine Rebel: The Life of Anne Marbury Hutchinson* (New York: Holt, Rinehart and Winston, 1981).

2. Although so much important twentieth-century social theory describes a dialectical relationship between religious doctrine and social structure, some scholars still resist the idea that the symbolic and theological content of a religion are inextricably bound to the gender norms it promotes. On the dialectic between religion and culture see, for example, Emile Durkheim, *The Elementary Forms of the Religious Life,* trans. Joseph Ward Swain (New York: Free Press, 1965); Peter L. Berger, *The Sacred Canopy: Elements of a Sociological Theory of Religion* (New York: Doubleday, 1969).

3. Mary Farrell Bednarowski, "Outside the Mainstream: Women's Religion and Women's Religious Leadership in Nineteenth-Century America," *Journal of the American Academy of Religion* 48 (1980): 207–31. Spiritualism and Christian Science were two of the four groups that provided the data from which Bednarowski formed her profile, so they fit it very well.

4. I have discussed mediumship, and Spiritualism in general, at greater length in Braude, *Radical Spirits: Spiritualism and Women's Rights in Nineteenth-Century America* (Boston: Beacon, 1989).

5. Barbara Welter, "The Cult of True Womanhood: 1829–1860," in *Dimity Convictions* (Athens: Ohio University Press, 1976), 217.

6. Some recent scholarship has challenged Welter's description of the "Cult of True Womanhood" as the single normative paradigm of femininity during this period. The Spiritualist sources support the view that it was not the only normative model available to women, but suggest that it was an important one, especially in discussions of women as religious leaders. For an opposing view see Frances B. Cogan, *All-American Girl: The Ideal of Real Womanhood in Mid-Nineteenth-Century America* (Athens: University of Georgia Press, 1989).

7. Braude, *Radical Spirits,* 90–92.

8. Benjamin Starbuck to Achsa Sprague, 1 June 1857, Achsa W. Sprague Papers, Vermont Historical Society, Montpelier, Vermont. B[enjamin] F. Hatch, *Spiritualist Iniquities Unmasked, and, the Hatch Divorce Case* (New York: B. F. Hatch, 1859). On Cora Hatch see Harrison D. Barrett, *Life Work of Mrs. Cora L. V. Richmond* (Chicago: Hack & Anderson, 1895).

9. Ann Braude, "News from the Spirit World: A Checklist of American Spiritualist Periodicals, 1847–1900," *Proceedings of the American Antiquarian Society* 99 (1989): 409.

10. Robert Peel, *Mary Baker Eddy,* 3 vols. (New York: Holt, Rinehart and Winston, 1966–77).

11. Edward T. James, Janet Wilson James, and Paul Boyer, *Notable American Women,* 3 vols. (Cambridge: Harvard University Press, 1975).

12. Mary Baker Eddy, *Science and Health* (Boston: Christian Science Publishing Co., 1875), 78.

13. Peel, *Mary Baker Eddy: The Years of Trial,* 177–80. Peel, *Mary Baker Eddy: The Years of Authority,* 231–35, 329–43. "Gestefeld, Ursula Newell," *NAW,* 2:

27–28; "Hopkins, Emma Curtis," *NAW,* 2: 219–20; "Stetson, Augusta Emma Simmons," *NAW,* 3: 364–66. Charles S. Braden, *Spirits in Rebellion: the Rise and Development of New Thought* (Dallas: Southern Methodist University Press, 1963), 138–49.

14. Peel, *Mary Baker Eddy: Years of Trial,* 69; Eddy, *Science and Health* (1934), 517.

15. Mary Baker Eddy, *Church Manual of the First Church of Christ, Scientist, in Boston, Massachusetts* (Boston, 1896), 24.

16. Mary Farrell Bednarowski, *New Religions and the Theological Imagination in America* (Bloomington: Indiana University Press, 1989), 30.

17. This interpretation owes a great deal to Peter Brown's *The Cult of the Saints: Its Rise and Function in Latin Christianity* (Chicago: University of Chicago Press, 1981), which argues that the relationship between the source of healing (the saint) and the sick person (devotee or pilgrim) was paradigmatic of the ideal human relationships in feudal Europe.

18. John S. Haller, Jr., and Robin M. Haller, *The Physician and Sexuality in Victorian America* (Urbana: University of Illinois Press, 1974); B. J. Barker Benfield, *The Horrors of the Half-Known Life: Male Attitudes Toward Women and Sexuality in the Nineteenth-Century America* (New York: Harper and Row, 1976); Carroll Smith-Rosenberg, "The Female Animal: Medical and Biological Views of Women in Nineteenth-Century America," *Journal of American History* 60 (1973): 332–56; "The Hysterical Woman: Sex Roles and Role Conflict in Nineteenth-Century America," *Social Research* 39 (1972): 652–78.

19. *The Christian Science Journal,* published in Boston, served as the main organ of the church during the 1880s and 1890s.

20. Peel, *Mary Baker Eddy: Years of Trial,* 38–40, 50–57, 113–15; 129.

21. *Christian Science Journal* 5 (1887): 46.

22. Ibid., 6 (1888): 250.

23. Ibid., 5 (1887): 45.

The Feminism
of "Universal Brotherhood": Women in
the Theosophical Movement

Robert Ellwood and Catherine Wessinger

The modern Theosophical movement, formally inaugurated with the founding of the Theosophical Society in New York in 1875, has had significant female leadership and possesses characteristics that are supportive of the religious leadership of women, both in its fundamental worldview and its institutional expression. Theosophical women leaders have been a diverse lot, so this treatment will focus on three of Theosophy's most prominent women. Helena P. Blavatsky, the spiritual founder, was an enigmatic Russian noblewoman known as much for her sharp tongue and ample girth as for her mysterious initiations, psychic "phenomena," and voluminous literary output. Annie Besant, celebrated president of the Society for approximately the first three decades of the twentieth century, was an estranged Anglican clergyman's wife and sometime freethinker of liberal social views. Katherine Tingley, known as the "Purple Mother," was a social reformer, founder of the utopian Theosophical community on Point Loma, California, and head of a Theosophical Society associated with it. All three—and numerous other Theosophical women as well—had in common strong intelligence and powerful gifts for spiritual leadership. They additionally shared difficult marriage experiences and an antipathy, based in no small part on personal frustrations, toward "orthodox," male-dominated religion, science, and education. All three struggled to assert their autonomy and innate creativity in the context of the limitations and opportunities presented women in Victorian/Edwardian society. For them the answer came in a small though worldwide and, at the same time, widely publicized and controversial spiritual organization, which embraced numerous tenets likely to antagonize that "orthodox" establishment. This organization, which was not quite a church and not quite a feminist conventicle, aroused unsparing ridicule and fervent opposition disproportionate to its small numbers and at the same time allowed its women and men leaders alike to travel the world lecturing and organizing. In it, women no less than men rose to the highest positions of responsibility. Today, the Theosophical movement continues to provide ample scope for women's leadership, and it, perhaps inadvertently, has made important contributions to contemporary feminist spirituality.

Helena Blavatsky and
the Origins of the Theosophical Movement

Theosophy initially was founded as something new, which intended to meet the intellectual and spiritual crises of the modern day by an appeal to something old. Its immediate roots were in the mid-nineteenth-century vogue for Spiritualism. Helena Blavatsky, the movement's principal figure, had first tried to focus and comprehend her disturbingly energetic inner powers and guides by means of that movement. Of her migration in 1873 to the United States, the homeland of modern Spiritualism, she remarked that she was drawn to it as "a Mohammedan approaching the birthplace of his prophet." "For the sake of Spiritualism," she added, "I have left my home, an easy life amongst a civilized society, and have become a wanderer upon the face of this earth."[1] She wrote for major Spiritualist publications of the day, such as the *Banner of Light* and the *Spiritual Scientist,* and she first met her long-time Theosophical collaborator, Henry Steel Olcott, at the spirit-manifestations being mounted in Vermont by the dour Eddy brothers. But the ascerbic and exotic lady's relations with American Spiritualists were never smooth, and she plainly yearned for something more. She began speaking to Olcott, her "Theosophical Twin," of "Brahma Vidya" or "Eastern Spiritualism," ultimately to replace "the cruder Western mediumism," and the manifesting masters she presented him began to wear turbans.[2]

After meeting in Vermont, Blavatsky and Olcott, both maritally estranged, proceeded to live and work in close proximity in New York City. Their residences quickly became magnets for New York's coterie of seekers and bohemians. Along with unforgettable parties, they were sites of lectures and discussions on the mysteries of the ages, mysteries of which Spiritualism was said to be only a token. Olcott and Blavatsky believed that if the nonsubstantial realities of which Spiritualism hinted could be penetrated and joined with the science and the progressive spirit of the day, then the unity of life might again be grasped. Like so many Victorians, the first Theosophists sensed the challenge of science to scriptural and religious authority to be the most agonizing issue of the hour. Blavatsky and Olcott believed that the apparent conflict between science and religion could be resolved only through a radical redefinition of both contenders, and that the march forward could be made only after a giant step backward, to the days of the "Ancient Wisdom."

Thus, in his inaugural address as president of the Theosophical Society in the fall of 1875, Olcott said,

> If I rightly apprehend our work, it is to aid in freeing the public mind of theological superstition and a tame subservience to the arrogance of science. Our Society is, I may say, without precedent. From the days when the Neoplatonists and the last theurgists of Alexandria were scattered by the murderous hand of Christianity, until now, the study of Theosophy has not been attempted.
>
> To the Protestant and Catholic sectaries we have to show the origin of many of their most sacred idols and most cherished dogmas; to the liberal minds in science, the profound scientific attainments of the ancient magi. Society has reached a point where *something* must be done; it is for us to indicate where that something may be found.[3]

The initial program of the Theosophical movement is thus evident: to get behind the orthodox religion and doctrinaire science of the day, to show up their limitations and false assumptions about their origins and the uniqueness of their present achievements, and to build again on older and deeper foundations. In her first major book, *Isis Unveiled* (1877), Blavatsky labored at those tasks at considerable length, constructing a remarkable farrago of polemics, unorthodox sermons, and stories of marvels performed by lamas and shamans in out-of-the-way places. The philosophy in *Isis Unveiled* draws on Neoplatonism, the Cabala, and certain Indian texts. *Isis* was an argument for Platonic or Hermetic philosophy as "the only possible key to the Absolute in science and theology."[4] In *Isis,* Blavatsky indicated how humans and the cosmos could be seen as a subtle mix of matter and a different—but also natural—spiritual substance. The Theosophical cosmology of a spirit-matter universe, emanated from an impersonal Unknown Root, offered an alternative to Western theism and scientific materialism. Within this universe, entities of spirit-matter-derived individual consciousness precipitated into being.

In Blavatsky's second magnum opus, *The Secret Doctrine* (1888), drawing more heavily on Indian thought, the individual centers of consciousness were described as "Pilgrims" whose long journey away from the Source and back again would take them through seven worlds, the fourth and most material of which was ours. Through the process of reincarnation governed by *karma,* the Pilgrim underwent a full course of evolution on each world (buddhic, mental, astral, material, and on the return higher versions of the first three). In our earthly system, the Pilgrim moved through the kingdoms of nature, and as human through seven "root races" with their various cultures and religions. Men known as the "masters" were simply those Pilgrims who were well in advance of the norm in collective evolution. The masters were ranked in an "Occult Hierarchy," and they directed the divine plan of collective evolution back to the Source.

Fundamental features of Theosophical teaching have included *karma,* reincarnation, cosmic evolution, a hierarchy of masters, and a general affirmation of the reality of psychospiritual forces from which humans could draw power. Sometimes this worldview has been expressed in highly mythological-seeming language, sometimes with near-scientific abstraction, and its importance has waxed and waned in various periods of Theosophical history. A number of Theosophists are content with the broadly-delineated original mission of the Society, especially as encapsulated in its often reprinted three objectives:

> To provide a nucleus of the Universal Brotherhood of Humanity, without distinction of race, creed, sex, caste, or color.
> To encourage the study of Comparative Religion, Philosophy, and Science.
> To investigate unexplained laws of Nature and the powers latent in man.

But what has all this to do with women? And with marginality? Certainly some Theosophical women, like some Theosophical men, were marginal in the sense known to sociological jargon as "status inconsistency"[5]—that is, the situation of people who sense within themselves a capacity, or a reality, inconsistent with the position forced upon them by their social environment. In reference to religion, this might be a person with innate gifts of spiritual leadership or theological articulation who is denied the opportunity to develop them in a respected mainline theological school and to practice them as a priest or minister in an established denomination, for reasons of race, economic deprivation, lack of social standing—or gender. Not a few unconventional religious movements, needless to say, have stemmed from the handiwork of such gifted but thwarted individuals. In nineteenth-century America, Spiritualism, in particular, provided venues for such persons among women and the economic underclass.[6] Olcott wrote of such autodidacts as a housepainter learned in Greek philosophy among New York Theosophists, but he and Blavatsky, like many others, were relatively privileged in some ways.

Henry Steel Olcott (1832–1907) was a denizen of the sturdy American middle class whose career was a model of Yankee get-ahead spirit. During the Civil War, Olcott had earned the title of Colonel by investigating fraudulent suppliers to the Union forces. In postwar New York, Olcott was noted as a busy lawyer, journalist, writer, and man-about-town. When his collaboration with Helena Blavatsky began, Olcott had behind him a failed marriage to a piously Christian woman, and apparently unmet yearnings for adventure on both this-worldly and otherworldly planes, which his interest in Spiritualism had only begun to channel. Olcott is an example of an outwardly successful person of socially acceptable status, who nevertheless possesses a spiritual identity that differs from that offered by the normative mainstream religions. Olcott illustrates that a mainstream individual can possess an identity of marginality, in rejecting the religious terms of the mainstream culture behind an outer conventional appearance. This is not the same phenomenon as status inconsistency. The concept of status inconsistency is more directly relevant to the life experiences of Helena Blavatsky, as it is to numerous other nineteenth-century women Theosophists.

Helena Blavatsky (1831–91) was born Helena von Hahn, the daughter of an artillery officer (of German descent) in the Czar's army, and a princess-novelist of an ancient Russian house. Helena's mother hated cantonment life with its frequent moves and stifling society, and found little response to her sensitivities in her unimaginative husband, apparently no more than a typical military man of his time and place. Into this unhappy scene came Helena, a wild, precocious, temperamental, and virtually undisciplinable child, who was given to hiding for hours to the despair of the household, and to telling fantastic stories about the lives and past lives of the stuffed animals in her grandfather's private museum. Interestingly, Helena seemed to have been closer to her father than her mother. The latter was highstrung and sickly, and relations with her strong-willed, energetic daughter were difficult. On the other side, the tomboyish Helena was the darling of her father's batallion, and she loved riding with the soldiers on maneuvers or answering smartly to their racy talk.

Yet all was not what it seemed. Though outwardly privileged, Helena Blavatsky's upbringing offered little to a girl of her precocious intellect and fiery independence. Her governesses afforded her the grounding in French and English that would enable her to carry her mission internationally, but nothing of the scholarly rigor that might have helped her avoid later embarrassing critiques, and certainly nothing that would help her comprehend her burgeoning psychic powers. Moreover, she was aware of the precariousness of women in a society like hers. Her mother, a popular novelist whose stories inevitably turned on the sufferings of women at the hands of callous men, died when Helena was only twelve.

After her mother's death, Helena lived much of the time on the vast estates of her maternal grandfather, a provincial governor. There, the unusual child grew into an ungainly and still-independent teenager, who with her undoubtedly brilliant intellect read deeply of the esoterica in the grandfather's library and fiercely rejected "normal" interests in society and romantic love. She once scalded her leg with boiling water so she would not have to go to a viceroy's ball, and later said of those days that "If a young man had dared to speak to me of love, I would have shot him like a dog."[7] Nonetheless, at the age of only seventeen she married a man more than twice her age, Nikifor Blavatsky, a civil servant who had risen to the post of vice-governor of Erivan, Russian Armenia.[8] This impulsive step was probably in response to her father's recent remarriage, to taunts that such a mean-tempered young woman could not find a husband, and to a passionate desire within herself to enter a new stage of her life and be on her own. Though she disappointed her husband—as she had warned him she would—by denying him all conjugal rights during the honeymoon at a mountain resort, she came into her own by abandoning him before the intended two-month sojourn was over and commencing her long traveling career. She first landed in Constantinople, where she found employment as a companion to an elderly, wealthy Russian lady who traveled widely and shared Helena's interest in the occult.

Next came more than twenty hidden years—though, as Marion Meade and other biographers have shown, it is possible to uncover numerous clues regarding a visit to London at the time of the Great Exhibition, relationships with a Serbian opera singer and a Russian psychic investigator, a child and the child's death a few years later, tutelage under the famous medium Daniel D. Home, and a long stay back in Russia among relatives whom she amazed with psychic performances.[9] According to her own later recitations, Helena Blavatsky spent those years in a search for esoteric wisdom under the guidance of masters in Tibet, with whom she finally attained high initiations. There may be levels of inner or outer verity to both narratives, and, in both, some use of the "blinds" she later acknowledged had their place in her discourse.

Blavatsky surfaced in Cairo in 1871, where she was briefly connected with a Spiritualist society, returned to Russia, went on to Paris, and finally booked steerage passage to the United States in 1873, landing worn and impoverished in New York like so many millions of other immigrants from the Old World in those years. She was at loose ends for a time, but ended up a Spiritualist writer. She and Olcott met in 1874, and established the relationship that would produce the Theosophical Society the following year. Intended to be the next step beyond Spiritualism, Theosophy sought to recover the Ancient Wisdom from Eastern as well as Western sources. Helena Blavatsky became a U.S. citizen in 1878, but partly in pursuit of the Ancient Wisdom, she and Olcott went to India in 1879. There, Theosophy was controversial but remarkably successful among persons, both British and indigenous, sympathetic to the Indian cultural renaissance and the nascent independence movement, in no small part because of its affirmation of the value of the Indian spiritual heritage long smothered by imperialism. In 1882 the international headquarters of Theosophy was established at an estate they purchased at Adyar, near Madras. Adyar was, however, to be the scene of a devastating event a few years later.

Controversy was generated by the delivery of letters from the masters through a box in the "Shrine Room," and other psychic phenomena associated with Blavatsky. A report issued in 1885, following an investigation by a representative of the Society for Psychical Research, charged Blavatsky with fraud. In the uproar that followed, she returned permanently to Europe. Although the Theosophical Society was damaged by this scandal, it was not destroyed, and while staying at the home of Countess Wachtmeister in Germany, Blavatsky wrote her major work, *The Secret Doctrine*. She then moved to London, where she founded the Blavatsky Lodge, and continued to write and instruct her disciples until her death in 1891.

All this appears to be par for Theosophy as a marginal spiritual movement. It can, in its early decades, be characterized as a marginal movement for people who do not look marginal, but who in some inner dimension of their being, experience themselves as precisely that. It is for people who have a sense of being marginal behind the mask. This may be due to pressures relating to status inconsistency, or it may be due to an inner sense of difference, rooted in personal autobiography, that is more difficult to identify. In its first two or three decades, Theosophy attracted not only its treasury of millionaires and countesses, and its gallery of artists and composers, but also such diverse personalities as the creator of *The Wizard of Oz*,[10] a prime minister of New Zealand, and several founding fathers of the Indian Congress party. Yet if one looks closely at the lives of each of these persons, one will find an important respect in which that person was in tension with her or his milieu and its expectations regarding not only the role one plays but also the subjectivity that is supposed to go with it. This is an especially common phenomenon, needless to say, for bright and potentially very creative women. Here, we will find the key to understanding what Theosophy has meant to its generally well-bred women spiritual leaders.[11]

Helena Blavatsky possessed a sense of her own spiritual power, a power that women could wield as well or better than men. The exact nature of this power is not easy to define. Undoubtedly, it involved a combination of real psychic gifts (unquestionably Blavatsky had her share of them), the hypnotic force of her penetrating blue eyes, her ability to weave wonderful stories in which her listeners found themselves enmeshed, and her rich store of occult wisdom. Regrettably, she sometimes exercised this power to baffle or manipulate people, including supportive males such as the ever eager and loyal Olcott. In this odd but rewarding relationship, each profoundly needed what the other had to offer: she, the credibility and lawyerly *savoir faire* that made him first president of the Theosophical Society and he, the realms of wonder and adventure she opened for him. In a social order in which institutional power in both church and state was heavily weighted in favor of men, the kind of personal spiritual power exercised by Blavatsky was almost the only kind accessible to a brilliant and spirited woman of her class. The gender role set out for women prohibited her from becoming a priest, professor, prime minister (like her cousin, Count Sergei Witte), or a lawyer and administrator, like Col. Henry Steel Olcott. Outside marriage or genteel spinsterhood at home, the primary options were to become someone's governess, someone's lady-companion, or someone's mistress. None of these was likely to appeal permanently to a woman as much her own person as Helena Blavatsky. The doctrine Blavatsky communicated with her spiritual power was one holding attraction to other women finding their way toward autonomous spirituality, and men willing to accompany them—or serve them—in that quest. Blavatsky possessed a charismatic source of religious authority in claiming that her teachings came from masters who, though all male, spoke to her via inner or covert means, rather than through any institution controlled by earthly men.

The Theosophical picture presents features that help one to understand its attraction for middle- to upper-class, well-educated, and intellectually-oriented women of the late nineteenth and early twentieth centuries. First, its evolutionary monism clearly fits the "harmonial," nurturing style of spirituality that has characterized most woman-dominated religious movements of that era, whether Spiritualism, New Thought, or Christian Science. Ahlstrom has defined harmonial religion as encompassing "those forms of piety and belief in which spiritual composure, physical health, and even economic well-being are understood to flow from a person's rapport with the cosmos."[12] Theosophical monism is based on a concern with immanence of divinity, and a sense of interconnectedness follows from that immanence. Second, the doctrine of *karma* enabled the understanding of the conditions of one's life, including gender, in a "scientific" kind of way as circumstances for which there is a reason. Third, the heavily verbal—books and lectures—quality of typical Theosophical communication fitted the finishing-school, liberal Protestant milieu of upper-class Boston, New York, or San Francisco, from which American Theosophical women were most likely to be recruited. Fourth, Helena Blavatsky, in tracing the Ancient Wisdom through the world's cultures and faiths, pointed out that in many venues it has given much more generous place to female forms and symbols than in the Protestant Christian: in the Mother Goddesses of antiquity, the Sophias and Aeons of Gnosticism, the Shaktis and Prajnas of the East, and more. Fifth, because it was said that Theosophy was not inconsistent with the underlying truth of any religion, it was also possible for women sympathetic with it to participate in a respectable church of the dominant faith, as many had to for family or social reasons. Sixth, the ascetic side of Theosophy, which taught that one's lower nature motivated by base desires should come under the control of one's higher spiritual nature, had its appeal for women caught in situations contaminated by sexual or alcoholic excess.

Finally, and no doubt most important of all, the example of prominent Theosophical women, from Helena Blavatsky on down, suggested a) that women could take full control of their lives, b) that such self-controlled female lives could be eminently productive and useful to the world, and c) that women in such cases could have direct, unmediated access to spiritual truth and power, outside the male-written scriptures or man-powered churches.

When Blavatsky was asked if women in the Theosophical Society enjoyed equal rights with men, she answered that in the esoteric part of the Society as well as in the ranks of the adepts, one's sex had no bearing on one's standing. The important thing was one's desire to serve others and the willingness to labor for that goal.[13] The subsequent history of women in the Theosophical movement demonstrated that in the doctrines presented, as well as in the institutional forms of the Theosophical Society, Blavatsky and Olcott started something of significance to feminist spirituality.

Women Leaders after Blavatsky

The points cited above were not lost on the two energetic women, Annie Besant (1847–1933) and Katherine Tingley (1847–1929), who constitute the foremost of the second generation of Theosophical leadership. The lives of Besant and Tingley parallel each other in many ways, but primarily in their deep commitment to the alleviation of hurtful social conditions and the establishment of "universal brotherhood" in the world. Both began their religious quest by questioning the meaning of suffering, and were ultimately drawn to Theosophy's answer in the doctrines of *karma* and reincarnation. Before becoming Theosophists, Besant and Tingley were social activists, and they had despaired of whether social work alone could make a lasting change in the human condition. They both concluded that a change in human nature was needed before social problems could be eliminated. In Theosophy, they found not only an answer to the question of evil, but the concept of a divine plan that would bring about the transformation of humanity. Besant and Tingley were drawn naturally to Blavatsky's stress that the monism of Theosophy should result in a life of "pure altruism."[14] However, these two unusually talented women with a shared vision of universal brotherhood did not work together, but regarded each other as rivals, each claiming to head the "real" Theosophical Society. Both Besant and Tingley combined within themselves the charisma and religious authority of Blavatsky, and the administrative ability of Olcott.

Annie Besant

The Englishwoman, Annie Besant, had a great impact on the spread of Theosophy internationally, and in the United States, which she toured on five occasions. Before her conversion to Theosophy in 1889, Besant had gained notoriety in England as an atheist, materialist, and freethinker, who was closely associated with Charles Bradlaugh and his National Secular Society. In 1877, Besant and Bradlaugh were prosecuted for their publication of a pamphlet on contraception. During this period, Besant gained a reputation as one of the foremost woman orators of the day. In 1885, she joined the Fabian Society, hoping that socialism would provide the means to alleviate the social problems caused by industrialization. She helped organize the famous strike of the Bryant and May match girls in 1888, and she became a member of the London School Board, where she worked for free meals for poor children.

Besant began to question the basing of her efforts for social reform on a materialistic cosmology, and increasingly began to investigate the unseen aspects of reality. For a brief time in the late 1880s, she explored the mysteries of mesmerism and the sèance table. In 1889, after reading the newly published *The Secret Doctrine* and meeting Blavatsky, she became a Theosophist and immediately put her great oratorical and organizational skills to use for the Theosophical cause. In 1893, Besant was one of the speakers at the Theosophical Congress at the World's Parliament of Religions held in conjunction with the Columbian Exposition in Chicago. In the 1890s, Besant cultivated her psychic senses, because she believed these experiences offered scientific proof of the divine reality underlying matter. Besant's occult investigations were always in partnership with another Theosophist, Charles W. Leadbeater. One product of their research was a book entitled *Thought-Forms* (1901),[15] a forerunner of contemporary ideas concerning "positive thinking" or "creative visualization."

After the death of Olcott in 1907, Besant was elected international president of the Theosophical Society. Besant came to regard India as her homeland by virtue of past incarnations and her love for Indian philosophy and religion. She founded the Central Hindu College, which would become the Benares Hindu University, as well as numerous other schools for Indian youth. Besant worked for Indian Home Rule, and she was elected president of the Indian National Congress in 1917. She lost her popularity to Mohandas Gandhi, because of her opposition to his radical new tactics and her disagreement with his eventual demand for complete independence from the British Commonwealth.

The primary motivation for Besant's work as a Theosophist was her concern to bring the world into a millennial condition, and she believed that her work was guided by the masters. Her work in India would benefit the entire world, because India would become the spiritual leader of the nations and bring them into the "New Civilization." In 1908, Besant began lecturing on the imminent appearance of a master known as the World-Teacher (or the Christ or the Lord Maitreya), who would present a teaching that would lead to the establishment of the New Civilization. The New Civilization would develop as a new human type was evolved, which possessed a faculty by which universal unity would be perceived. Besant promoted an Indian boy, J. Krishnamurti, as the physical vehicle of the World-Teacher, and an international organization of 30,000 members, the Order of the Star, was built up around him. After 1925, Krishnamurti began speaking and teaching as the World-Teacher, but found that, because he was regarded as a savior, his followers were not able to hear his message of personal responsibility for one's transformation. Therefore, he dissolved the Order of the Star in 1929 and went on to present his message independent of the Theosophical Society. Besant died in India on September 30, 1933, still convinced that Krishnamurti's message would bring the world into the New Civilization.[16]

Katherine Tingley

The American Katherine Tingley likewise hoped that her Theosophical work would bring about the Kingdom of God on earth. Tingley was born in Newbury, Massachusetts, into a family of Puritan heritage. In her youth, she experienced two unsuccessful marriages, and in undocumented years, she possibly worked in a traveling theatrical company. By the late 1880s, she was married to the unobtrusive Philo B. Tingley and was organizing efforts for social reform. Tingley had been attracted to Spiritualism, and sometimes raised funds for her social work by giving spiritualistic readings. During the winter of 1892/93, while feeding poor women and children at her Do-Good Mission on the East Side of New York City, Tingley met William Q. Judge, a founding member of the Theosophical Society. At that time, Judge was general secretary of the American Section of the Theosophical Society and international vice-president. In the aftermath of Blavatsky's death, Judge became involved in a power struggle with Olcott and Besant, during which he was accused of forging letters from the masters. An official inquiry did not resolve the matter, and in 1895 the greater portion of the American Section seceded from the Theosophical Society under Judge's leadership.[17]

Judge believed that Tingley was in mediumistic contact with Helena Blavatsky, and after his death in 1896, Tingley emerged as the Leader and Official Head by convincing key persons that she was channeling messages from Judge and that she was in contact with the masters. She renamed the organization The Universal Brotherhood and Theosophical Society, and focused her efforts on the building of a Theosophical community, a "white city," at Point Loma, near San Diego.[18] (This organization is now known as The Theosophical Society with headquarters at Pasadena. From this point on, the larger organization will be referred to as the Theosophical Society [Adyar].)

Tingley's work as a Theosophical leader, like Annie Besant's, was intended to benefit humanity. She organized relief work for wounded soldiers returning from the Spanish-American War, and in 1899, she carried her relief work to Cuba. When Tingley turned her attention to building her white city, she succeeded in creating a community that was noted for its unusual architecture, and the horticultural and artistic accomplishments of its residents. Point Loma attracted the most public attention by its elaborate productions of Greek and Shakespearean dramas, which Tingley felt illustrated the principles of the Ancient Wisdom. Tingley's efforts to transform human nature relied primarily on a system of education, aimed at educating the whole person in its physical, emotional-aesthetic, mental, and spiritual aspects, which she called Raja Yoga. She was unable to set up an international chain of Raja Yoga schools, but at Point Loma more than twenty-five hundred children were educated, including over a thousand Cuban children.[19] Thirteen years after Tingley's death in 1929, the Point Loma community had to be closed due to financial problems and the onset of World War II.

Continuation of Female Leadership

The Theosophical movement in America has continued to provide ample opportunity for women to exercise leadership in a variety of ways, although there was a period in which women were not found in the highest positions. Joy Mills's book, *100 Years of Theosophy,* recounts the activities of the numerous women (and men) in the Theosophical Society in America (Adyar) who have served in administrative and executive positions, as traveling lecturers and teachers, experts, and writers. It must be noted, however, that the Theosophical Society in America (Adyar) did not have a woman president until 1965, when Joy Mills became president. From 1965 until 1993, the presidency of the Theosophical Society in America (Adyar) was filled by women. In addition to Mills, Ann Wylie and Dora Kunz have served.[20] In 1990, Dorothy Abbenhouse was elected to her second term as president of the Theosophical Society in America (Adyar). On the international level, there was no woman president of the Theosophical Society (Adyar) after Annie Besant until Radha Burnier was elected president in 1980. In the Tingley organization, now the Theosophical Society (Pasadena), Tingley was succeeded in Leadership[21] by men, until Grace F. Knoche became Leader in 1971.[22] The temporary lapse of women's presence in the highest offices seems to indicate that despite the aspects of Theosophy supportive of women's leadership, there still must be present a social expectation that women can function in important positions of leadership. It is probably not accidental that the increase of women in leadership positions has coincided with the contemporary women's movement, whereas the leadership of the early Theosophical women roughly corresponded with the "first wave" of the women's movement. Space limitations preclude extended discussion of other important women in the Theosophical movement, but Alice Bailey (1880–1949), Margaret Cousins, and Elizabeth Clare Prophet should be mentioned.

Alice Bailey, an Englishwoman living in America, was the founder of the Arcane School, and claimed to be the amanuensis for the master called D. K. the Tibetan, with whom she communicated via mental telepathy. The books produced in this manner express a millennial view similar to that of Besant, including the expectation of the World-Teacher or Christ. The Bailey works and their focus on the "New Age" or "Age of Aquarius" are an important source of the contemporary New Age movement.[23]

The Irishwoman Margaret Cousins is a noteworthy example of a woman whose Theosophy informed her feminism. Cousins, who can be regarded as the mother of the women's movement in India, helped to found the Women's Indian Association in 1917 and the All India Women's Conference in 1927. Annie Besant was the first president of the Women's

Indian Association, however, the rights of women were not the primary focus of Besant's work in India. When she began speaking in favor of later marriage and education for Indian girls, Besant, backpedaling from the feminism of her early years, argued that Indian women should be educated to make them "lights of the home" and "true helpmates of their husbands." Nevertheless, Margaret Cousins saw Besant as an example for future women, writing that "she is the Forerunner of the New Age of which already the prominent feature is the emergence of Woman to power in all aspects of public service."[24]

The American Elizabeth Clare Prophet, the current leader of the Church Universal and Triumphant, is the most recent of the controversial women in the Theosophical movement, and claims authority based on her contact with the masters.[25] Called "Mother" by her followers, she has founded a community on thirty-three thousand acres in Paradise Valley, Montana, adjacent to Yellowstone National Park. Prophet differs from her foremothers in the Theosophical movement in her emphasis on the possibility of catastrophic change, which she combines with survivalism. She and her followers have built fall-out shelters in anticipation of a nuclear attack by the former Soviet Union. Prophet has been misrepresented as setting dates for the end. In response to government aggression in 1993 against the Branch Davidians near Waco, Texas, church staff reportedly removed privately owned firearms from church property. Much more study needs to be done on this international church.[26]

In relation to women's continued leadership in the Theosophical movement, it finally must be noted that there are numerous small groups in America with a Theosophical orientation, but no official Theosophical affiliation, that usually meet in private homes. These groups more often than not consist of women and are led by women. A concern for alternative forms of healing and the channeling of information from unseen entities is not unusual for these groups.[27]

Conclusions

The Theosophical movement has offered a variety of leadership opportunities to women. It has not always been easy for the Theosophical women leaders in their struggle against socially restricted gender roles. Yet the Theosophical movement has offered a number of features that facilitate the leadership of women, such as the absence of an ordained ministry. Whenever there has been the social expectation that women can serve in important leadership roles, there has been no institutional bar to women doing so. Likewise, in Theosophy there is no theological barrier to equality. The Christian myth of the Fall is rejected, and there is no reason to blame the imperfections of the human condition on women. Katherine Tingley, for example, in reaction to her Calvinistic heritage was most firm in rejecting human depravity.[28] Tingley stressed that "true progress" must begin with persons realizing "the essential divinity of their own nature."[29] In Theosophy, sex distinctions have no ultimate validity due to its monism and the doctrine of reincarnation, that teaches that all individuals will experience male and female rebirths. Additionally, in Theosophy, the concept of male divinity is de-emphasized. In the complex cosmology presented in *The Secret Doctrine,* the divine is described in male and female terms, but at its root, the ultimate is impersonal. In response to a student's query, "Is the first differentiation from the absolute IT always feminine?" Blavatsky replied, "Only as a figure of speech; in strict philosophy it is sexless."[30] Despite the view that the divine is impersonal and monistic, Theosophists do not hesitate to draw on female and male God-imagery drawn from the various religions of the world. Since 1925 when Annie Besant proposed the imminent appearance of the World-Mother to complement the coming of the World-Teacher, the concept of the World-Mother has continued to be meaningful for some Theosophists. Often the World-Mother is regarded simultaneously as a female member of the Occult Hierarchy, and the "mother aspect of Deity."[31]

Theosophy has consistently affirmed and practiced gender equality, and has provided a spiritual home for many actively feminist women. It must be remembered, however, that beyond this, the movement as a whole has not promoted any particular feminist program, though individual members and occasionally large units have. On this issue, as on many others, Theosophy has harbored a wide range of points of view. Some Theosophists have addressed themselves to the "man-woman question," and have seriously questioned gender roles, or have ended up reaffirming them.[32] Many Theosophists seem completely unaware of feminist issues. For instance, Theosophists are just beginning to be aware of the need for the use of inclusive language.[33]

In the late twentieth century, a close relationship can be discerned between Theosophy and feminist spirituality. The volume compiled by Shirley Nicholson, *The Goddess Re-Awakening* (1989), marks the awakening of some Theosophists to feminism and feminist spirituality. The introduction to this book written by feminist author, Merlin Stone,[34] demonstrates the natural conjunction of Theosophy's concern for the Ancient Wisdom with the concern of feminist spirituality to recover the ancient goddess religions. Theosophy and feminist goddess spirituality share the strategy of looking to the ancient past for wisdom that can be employed in creating a better world for the future.[35] In so doing, the Theosophical and feminist spirituality movements share an eclectic approach to the world religions. Further, a great deal of the cosmology and view of human nature of feminist spirituality is drawn from Theosophy, sometimes explicitly, often not. Long-time feminist Diane Stein's *The Women's Book of Healing*[36] explicitly cites Theosophical authors in asserting that the human being consists of various subtle bodies (as manifested in the aura), as well as the gross-physical body. Her use of concepts such as the *chakras,* the *kundalini,* and *prana* are drawn from Theosophy's presentation of these Indian ideas to the West. Stein even devotes a chapter to the healing technique developed by Theosophists Dora Kunz and Delores Krieger that they have termed "Therapeutic Touch." In another example, the discussion of "Thought-Forms" by eminent feminist thealogian and witch, Starhawk, does not explicitly acknowledge Besant and Leadbeater's book by that name, but her statement that it is "an underlying principle of magic that consciousness itself has structure, and that structure manifests in the forms of the material world," and her definition of magic as "the art of changing consciousness at will"[37] owe a great deal to the Theosophical worldview. Finally, reincarnation, a doctrine that was popularized by the Theosophical movement, is a widely held belief in the feminist spirituality movement.

Whereas much of Theosophy has not been consciously feminist, the Theosophical worldview and institutional expressions have been very supportive of the equal leadership of women. Currently, Theosophical ideas inform much of feminist spirituality, which may also be considered part of the story of women in the Theosophical movement.

NOTES

1. Letter by Helena Blavatsky in the *Spiritual Scientist* 1 (3 Dec. 1874): 148–49. Excerpted in *H. P. Blavatsky: Collected Writings, 1874–78,* vol. 1 (Adyar, Madras: Theosophical Publishing House, 1966), 47.

2. Henry Steel Olcott, *Old Diary Leaves: America 1874–1878,* 1st ser. (Adyar, Madras: Theosophical Publishing House, 1895), 15.

3. Henry Steel Olcott, "Inaugural Address of the President of the Theosophical Society," facsimile centenary ed. (Wheaton, Ill.: Theosophical Society of America, 1975).

4. H. P. Blavatsky, *Isis Unveiled,* H. P. Blavatsky Collected Writings 1877 (Wheaton, Ill.: Theosophical Publishing House, 1972), 1: vii.

5. Kenneth L. Wilson and Louis A. Zurcher, "Status Inconsistency and Participation in Social Movements: An Application of Goodman's Hierarchical Modeling," *Sociological Quarterly* 17 (Autumn 1976): 520–33. The bibliography of this article cites the sociological literature that validates as well as questions the effects of status inconsistency. The status factors usually considered in these studies are education, occupation, income and ethnicity. This study of Wilson and Zurcher

supports the commonsense observation that overrewarded inconsistents, combining, for example, high-status income with low-status occupation and/or education, tend to participate in social movements resisting change; and that underrewarded inconsistents, combining, for example, low-status income with high-status occupation and/or education, tend to participate in social movements agitating for change. The concept of status inconsistency illuminates the attraction of marginal religions to women of high or relatively high social class, possessing leisure, intelligence, and an amount of education, but who find their opportunities for self-fulfillment are circumscribed by the traditional feminine gender role. Our thanks to Dr. Thomas Robbins for providing us with this reference and his comments on leisured, high-class women in new religions in the nineteenth century and first half of the twentieth century.

6. Ann Braude, *Radical Spirits: Spiritualism and Women's Rights in Nineteenth-Century America* (Boston: Beacon Press, 1989); Alex Owen, *The Darkened Room: Women, Power and Spiritualism in Late Victorian England* (Philadelphia: University of Pennsylvania Press, 1990).

7. Mary K. Neff, comp., *Personal Memoirs of H. P. Blavatsky* (1937; reprint, Wheaton, Ill.: Theosophical Publishing House, 1967).

8. Despite Helena's later attempts to portray her husband as a doddering senior, he was only thirty-nine at the time of the wedding.

9. Marion Meade, *Madam Blavatsky: The Woman behind the Myth* (New York: G. P. Putnam's, 1980). Though containing some speculation presented as virtual fact, this work is sympathetic to Blavatsky as a woman and at the same time critical toward some of the legends that have surrounded her. See also Sylvia Cranston, *H. P. B.: The Extraordinary Life of Helena Blavatsky* (New York: G. P. Putnam's, 1993), a sympathetic new biography that emphasizes her influence on the modern world. Readers should also turn to Neff, comp., *Personal Memoirs of H. P. Blavatsky,* a treasury of her own scattered autobiographical writings; Jean Overton Fuller, *Blavatsky and Her Teachers* (London: East-West Publications, 1988), a fresh scholarly discussion of major biographical issues that generally ends up supporting the traditional Theosophical view; and Michael Gomes, *The Dawning of the Theosophical Movement* (Wheaton, Ill.: Theosophical Publishing House, 1987), a vigorous reexamination of the 1874–79 period, which among other things casts serious doubt on the often repeated but seldom rechecked assertion that substantial parts of *Isis Unveiled* are plagiarisms.

10. Frank L. Baum's classic new-world fairy tale has been read as a populist political allegory, a feminist allegory, and an allegory of the mystical quest; but through the influence of an aunt, Baum was a serious student of Theosophy, and perhaps meaning should be looked for there as well.

11. The novel by Edith Wharton, *The House of Mirth* (first published in 1905), dramatizes the ennui and anguish of a young high-class woman, Lily Bart, who has been socially conditioned to display her beauty as an ornament to the wealth and status of men, but who ultimately cannot bring herself to sell her body and soul for material support from a rich husband. Although her inner being rebels at

this conventional woman's fate, Lily's slavery to her gender conditioning and the limited economic opportunities for women of her day, prevent her from finding a way to put her intelligence and creativity to good use. Lily is unable to become an active subject rather than a beautiful object. Edith Wharton, *The House of Mirth* (New York: Bantam Books, 1984).

12. Sydney E. Ahlstrom, *A Religious History of the American People,* vol. 2 (Garden City, N.Y.: Image Books, 1975), 528. While Ahlstrom's definition of harmonial religion is descriptive of the religions in the metaphysical movement, it is not unique to these. From the perspective of the study of the world's religions, the concern to be in harmony with the unconditioned reality underlying the manifested universe is commonly found in animistic religions, as well as in those religious traditions that have developed out of animistic contexts. As suggested earlier in this chapter, Theosophy can be seen as offering an alternative to Western theism and scientific materialism. Theosophy, as well as the other metaphysical movements, represents a resurgence of the ancient animistic worldview among people living in industrialized society.

13. F. Henrietta Muller, "Theosophy and Woman," in *The Theosophical Congress Held by the Theosophical Society at the Parliament of Religions, World's Fair of 1893, at Chicago, Ill., September 15, 16, 17. Report of Proceedings and Documents* (New York: American Section Headquarters T.S., 1893), 169. Our thanks to Dr. Nancy Anderson for bringing this and other materials to our attention.

14. W. Emmet Small, ed. and comp., *The Wisdom of the Heart: Katherine Tingley Speaks* (San Diego: Point Loma Publications, 1978), 16–17, 30, 33, 76, 93; Catherine Lowman Wessinger, *Annie Besant and Progressive Messianism* (Lewiston, N.Y.: The Edwin Mellen Press, 1988), particularly 178–81; Emmett A. Greenwalt, *The Point Loma Community in California 1897–1942: A Theosophical Experiment* (Berkeley: University of California Press, 1955), 77.

15. Annie Besant and C. W. Leadbeater, *Thought-Forms* (Wheaton, Ill.: Theosophical Publishing House, 1969). The paintings in this book have had an impact on abstract art. See Edward Weisberger, ed., *The Spiritual in Art: Abstract Painting 1890–1895* (New York: Los Angeles County Museum of Art and Abbeville Press, 1986).

16. Wessinger, *Annie Besant and Progressive Messianism;* Arthur H. Nethercot, *The First Five Lives of Annie Besant* (Chicago: University of Chicago Press, 1960); Arthur H. Nethercot, *The Last Four Lives of Annie Besant* (Chicago: University of Chicago Press, 1963); Wessinger, "Service to India as Service to the World: Annie Besant's Work in India for Human Rights," *Theosophical History* 3 (Jan. 1990): 19–32; Part II in 3 (Apr. 1990): 51–60.

17. Greenwalt, *The Point Loma Community in California,* 12–15; Katherine Tingley, "Recollections," in *The Wisdom of the Heart,* 25–33; Wessinger, "Democracy vs. Hierarchy: The Evolution of Authority in the Theosophical Society," in *When Prophets Die: The Postcharismatic Fate of New Religious Movements,* ed. Timothy Miller (Albany: The State University of New York Press, 1991); Nethercot, *The Last Four Lives,* 24–32.

18. Greenwalt, *The Point Loma Community in California,* especially 16, 18,

22, 32, 38–39; Bruce F. Campbell, *Ancient Wisdom Revived: A History of the Theosophical Movement* (Berkeley: University of California Press, 1980), 131–42.

19. Greenwalt, *The Point Loma Community in California*; Katherine Tingley, "The Reconstruction of the Race and Higher Education. From a Theosophical Standpoint," *The Theosophical Path* 23 (Oct. 1922): 315–25.

20. Joy Mills, *100 Years of Theosophy: A History of the Theosophical Society in America* (Wheaton, Ill.: Theosophical Publishing House, 1987), 160, 194, 209. In 1993, John Algeo was elected president of the Theosophical Society in America (Adyar).

21. In the Theosophical Society (Pasadena), the Leader holds that office for life or until she or he resigns. See "Constitution" (As Amended Aug. 27, 1971), published by International Headquarters, Pasadena, California. Our thanks to W. T. S. Thackara and Kirby Van Mater for providing us with this and other materials from The Theosophical Society, Pasadena.

A presidential election is held in the Theosophical Society (Adyar) every seven years. All presidents since Olcott have been continuously reelected until death. The only exception is C. Jinarajadasa, who in 1953, decided not to run for reelection. (Mills, 141) The term of office for the president of the Theosophical Society in America (Adyar) is three years.

22. Campbell, *Ancient Wisdom Revived*, 142.

23. See "Epilogue" in Wessinger, *Annie Besant and Progressive Messianism*.

24. See Wessinger, "Service to India as Service to the World." A considerable amount of research is currently being done on the relation of Theosophy to feminism. Nancy Fix Anderson, Loyola University, New Orleans, is doing research on Annie Besant and the difficulties of cross-cultural feminism. Joy Dixon, Rutgers University, is preparing a dissertation on the relationship between gender and Theosophy in Great Britain. See her unpublished paper, "Feminism and the Occult in England, 1880–1930." Catherine Candy, Loyola University Chicago, is researching the life of Margaret Cousins for her dissertation.

25. Campbell, *Ancient Wisdom Revived*, 150–53, 163.

26. Bill Shaw and Maria Wilhelm, "The Cloud Over Paradise Valley," *People* 33 (4 June 1990): 48–53; "Church prepares for Armageddon," *The Register-Guard*, Mar. 15, 1990; "Tensions heighten as cult creates trouble in Paradise," *Register-Guard*, Apr. 24, 1990; and field trip to C.U.T. headquarters by Catherine Wessinger in 1993.

27. Campbell, *Ancient Wisdom Revived*, 153–54. The groups reported by Meredith McGuire with the assistance of Debra Kantor in *Ritual Healing in Suburban America* (New Brunswick: Rutger University Press, 1988), probably draw heavily on the cosmology and view of human nature disseminated by the Theosophical movement.

28. Katherine Tingley, "Why I Am a Theosophist," in *The Wisdom of the Heart*, 75; Tingley, "The Reconstruction of the Race," 318.

29. Katherine Tingley, "Foreshadowings," in *The Wisdom of the Heart*, 105.

30. H. P. Balavatsky, *Transactions of the Blavatsky Lodge of the Theosophical Society* (Covina, Calif.: Theosophical University Press, 1946), 4.

31. Nethercot, *The Last Four Lives*, 402–6; Geoffrey Hodson, "The World Mother" in *The Goddess Re-Awakening: The Feminine Principle Today*, comp. Shirley Nicholson (Wheaton, Ill.: Theosophical Publishing House, 1989), 108–12; Corine McLaughlin, "The Mystery of the Veiled Mother of the World," *The Quest: A Quarterly Journal of Philosophy, Science, Religion & the Arts* 3 (Summer 1990): 56–65.

32. Theosophists who have considered the issue of gender roles have tended to speak of the need for a balance of feminine and masculine cosmic principles. Therefore, Theosophists have tended to be very attracted to the thought of C. Jung. Some recent articles in *The Goddess Re-Awakening* express a sense of ambiguity over the specific characteristics of a masculine principle and a feminine principle. See Mary Farrell Bednarowski, "Women in Occult America," in *The Occult in America: New Historical Perspectives*, ed. Howard Kerr and Charles L. Crow (Urbana: University of Illinois Press, 1983), 183–87; Roberto Assagioli and Claude Servan-Schreiber, "A Higher View of the Man-Woman Problem," and Mary Ann Mattoon and Jennette Jones, "Is the Animus Obsolete?" in *The Goddess Re-Awakening*.

33. The Theosophical Society in America (Adyar) has recently proposed a By-Law Amendment stating "That without changing the intent of our by-laws, all sexist language will be removed." See "Proposed By-Law Amendments," *American Theosophist* 78 (May/June 1990): 9.

34. *The Goddess Re-Awakening* is referenced above. Merlin Stone is the author of two books that have greatly influenced feminist goddess spirituality: *When God Was a Woman* (New York: Harcourt Brace Jovanovich, 1976), and *Ancient Mirrors of Womanhood* (New York: Sibylline Books, 1979).

35. For a history and analysis of the "utopian poetics" of goddess feminism, see Mary Jo Weaver, "Who Is the Goddess and Where Does She Get Us?" *Journal of Feminist Studies in Religion* 5/1 (Spring 1989): 49–64.

36. Diane Stein, *The Women's Book of Healing* (St. Paul: Llewellyn Publications, 1987).

37. Starhawk, *Dreaming the Dark: Magic, Sex and Politics*, new ed. (Boston: Beacon Press, 1988), 13, 18.

Emma Curtis Hopkins:
A Feminist of the 1880s and Mother
of New Thought

J. Gordon Melton

On January 10, 1889, on Chicago's South Side, people gathered for the graduation of twenty-two students from the Christian Science Theological Seminary. Those who assembled, either as participants in the service, as well-wishers, or as seminary students viewing what they soon would pass through, did so with a sense that they were involved in a momentous happening. One speaker, Louisa Southworth, dubbed it the "ceremony of the New Era."[1] Elizabeth Boynton Harbert, the featured speaker, said she had once thought it impossible that such an event could ever occur.[2] Southworth's and Harbert's exuberance was occasioned by the fact that twenty of the twenty-two graduates of the seminary were women. Moreover, the person who had trained these graduates was a woman. But most important, after their graduation, the same woman who trained them was to exercise the office of bishop and ordain these women and men to the Christian ministry. In this ceremony, Emma Curtis Hopkins (1849–1925)[3] became the first woman to assume such powers in modern times.[4]

The history of Hopkins's audacious action, certainly as significant for women in the larger Christian and religious communities as the 1974 ordination of women to the Episcopal priesthood, is only beginning to be recovered by the scholarship.[5] Given the perspective of a century, the 1889 ordination can now be seen as the culmination of several trends of the nineteenth-century women's movement, and the originating point of other trends in feminist theology and ministry, which would be important in the twentieth century.

Hopkins in Context

In the voluntary society that developed in America in the nineteenth century, a stage was set for the organization and mobilization of women, and women began to agitate for their equal status. In numerous and various ways, women developed groups in which they could carry on their work, both for their own pleasure and the betterment of the world. By the 1830s, there were hundreds of women's organizations scattered across the country, not a few of which were dedicated to the abolition of slavery. The first women's schools had appeared in the 1820s, and in the 1830s, college education became obtainable for some women. Women writers called for a new society.

In the nineteenth century, religion provided a context in which women could organize and from which feminist impulses could be generated. Before there were women's clubs, women's schools, and women's rights groups, women's mobilization began in the churches. In addition to the longstanding existence of women's orders within the Roman Catholic church, as early as 1800, Baptist women in Massachusetts organized the Boston Female Society for Missionary Purposes. Within two decades similar societies had spread among the Congregationalists, Reformed, Lutherans, and Methodists. Although the churches continued to give voice to traditional sanctions to keep women confined and limited, the church also provided a rationale for women seeking equality in a realized kingdom of God.[6] The women's Protestant missionary societies provided places for women to socialize, exercise power, and contribute financially and otherwise to the ministry of the churches. These missionary societies promoted female education, offered employment to women executives, teachers, and writers, opened avenues for social services, and gave women limited access to the highest echelons of church power.

An additional avenue for women's activities was provided by the deaconess movement among Lutheran, Methodist, Episcopalian, and Presbyterian women.[7] Akin to Roman Catholic women's religious orders, deaconesses engaged in the full range of ministries supported by the missionary societies. For instance, Lucy Rider Meyer, the founder of the Methodist deaconess movement, was one of the first female physicians in the country. Beginning in Chicago in the 1880s, she developed and managed a hospital, a training school, a baby fold, an orphanage, two old folks' homes, and several boarding schools. Organizations such as the one created by Meyer also forced open positions of power in the larger denominational structures. Meyer, for example, became the first lay woman seated at the Methodist Episcopal church general conference (legislative body) as a duly elected representativie.[8]

Revivalism, and particularly the holiness movement among Methodists, opened even more ways for women to participate in American religious life.[9] Central to the holiness movement was a belief that the life of perfection could and should be attained in an experience of sanctification by the

Holy Spirit. In holiness revivals, women increasingly began to speak and pray before mixed audiences. At the beginning of the nineteenth century, the revivalistic Primitive Methodists in England began to recruit and license female preachers, and by 1881 twenty percent of their ministers were women. The first female licensed preacher in America was Ruth Watkins of the Primitive Methodists, who arrived in New York in 1829.[10] The connection between the holiness movement and women's religious leadership was apparent when in 1853, holiness minister and founder of the Wesleyan Methodists, Luther Lee, preached at the Congregationalist ordination in South Butler, New York, of the first woman minister, Antoinette Brown (1825–1921).[11]

Throughout the last third of the nineteenth century, no religious movement or church in America was so open to female leadership as was the holiness movement. Beginning with the example of Phoebe Palmer (1807–74), who moved from conducting informal prayer meetings in New York City in the 1830s, to preaching at large revivals with her husband,[12] other female evangelists, such as Amanda Smith (1837–1915),[13] found that within the holiness movement women could preach and do almost everything a male minister could do, except administer the sacraments. The movement also produced a theological rationale for the ordination of women to the ministry. In 1859, Phoebe Palmer published a 421-page defense of women preaching, *The Promise of the Father.*[14] The promise, found in Acts 2:17, was that in the latter days women would prophesy. Building on Palmer, women such as Fannie McDowell Hunter[15] and Catherine Booth[16] would further develop the case for female ministers. One by one, the new holiness denominations would find room to accept them, beginning in 1902 with Alma White's founding of the Pillar of Fire.[17] The holiness movement also became the breeding ground of Pentecostalism, which from its beginning at the turn of the century, became open to women leaders.

One organization which many of the holiness women in America joined was the Women's Christian Temperance Union (WCTU). No organization so naturally embodied the sanctification ideal of the movement, and through it women were able to reach out and attempt to alter society in ways not open to them elsewhere. Under the capable leadership of its second president, Frances Willard (1839–1898), the WCTU became active in every area of women's rights.[18]

The holiness movement was among the important forces working for the general elevation of women in the social structures of nineteenth-century America, and the single most important force within the larger religious community opening space for women to exercise power and hold positions previously reserved for men alone. The holiness movement pioneered the ordination of women, and over the decades of the nineteenth century, through associated movements such as the WCTU, it empowered hundreds of thousands of women and provided them with new arenas for action. The emergence and importance of Emma Curtis Hopkins (as well as other nineteenth-century female religious leaders such as Helena P. Blavatsky, Ellen G. White, and Mary Baker Eddy) cannot be understood apart from the appreciation of the tremendous opening of new space for women in the religious community created by the holiness movement, and the atmosphere of longing and expectation it generated among women in other religious groupings.[19]

The Development of
the Christian Science Theological Seminary

Emma Curtis was born in 1849 and grew up in the Congregational milieu of Connecticut. She attained an education and in 1874 married a school teacher, George Hopkins. In 1881, she had a healing encounter with Christian Science, the details of which are unknown. The founder of the Church of Christ, Scientist, Mary Baker Eddy, was in the process of establishing her center in Boston, and in December 1883, Hopkins traveled to Boston to take Eddy's standard introductory class. Hopkins became Mary Baker Eddy's devoted pupil. She moved to Boston, and by February 1884, Hopkins was listed as a Christian Science practitioner. That same month, Hopkins's first article for the *Christian Science Journal* appeared. In April, when Eddy left for an extended trip, she turned the *Journal* over to Hopkins's able editorial control. Hopkins was made the permanent editor the following September. After a year of dedicated service, Hopkins broke with Eddy on ideological and financial grounds. She left her post as editor, and resigned from the Christian Science Association, the organization of Eddy's students. Hopkins and her husband moved to Chicago, and she opened her own office as an independent Christian Science practitioner.

Hopkins found in Chicago a vital women's movement. An active women's network had functioned in Chicago since the days of the Sanitary Commission, which was formed to supply bandages and food to Union soldiers during the Civil War. The Chicago Women's Club had been formed in 1876, and the first women's trade union had been organized in 1878. The WCTU, with Frances Willard as its president, was headquartered in Chicago. In 1880, Willard had announced her "do-everything policy," which extended the WCTU's concerns to women's suffrage, the hiring of women police, prostitution, and partisan politics. Both the National Woman's Suffrage Association and the American

Woman's Suffrage Association were active in Chicago. Hopkins had already experienced a predominantly female environment among the Christian Scientists in Boston. Her teacher, Mary Baker Eddy, had spoken in favor of several of the women's causes, although she had done little to implement that concern. As with Mary Baker Eddy, most of Hopkins's students and clientele were women. Hopkins probably appreciated her female environment, since after she moved to Chicago, she separated from her husband and they eventually divorced. Later, she described him as being subject to occasional psychotic episodes in which he became violent.

Hopkins's work in Chicago was an immediate success. Within a few months, she established the Emma Hopkins College of Christian Science, modeled on Eddy's Massachusetts Metaphysical College. In the summer of 1886, Hopkins offered a two-week class to train Christian Science practitioners, and she attracted thirty-seven students. After their completion of the course, these students organized the Hopkins Metaphysical Association, analogous to the Christian Science Association. On Sundays, Hopkins's office became a church, and she preached to a congregation composed primarily of her students and others attracted by her healing ministry. During 1887 she was able to hold her monthly class in three alternate locations: San Francisco, Milwaukee, and New York. By the end of 1887 she had generated a string of affiliated institutes stretching from Maine to San Francisco. She purchased a building on Chicago's South Side, and on December 1, 1887, dedicated it as her headquarters.

Hopkins's successes of 1887 were immediately followed by a near disaster. Some internal problems in the Association disrupted the work in Chicago and cost Hopkins the support of many of the institutes around the country. The disruption, which was partially about the professional status of the practitioners she had trained and the propriety of their charging for their services, led Hopkins to rethink her goals and to reorder the work she was leading.

Hopkins concluded that a mistaken image of "Christian Science" had emerged, and she began to make it clear that she was not simply training practitioners in a trade, but was guiding them into a ministry. The Hopkins College was transformed into the Christian Science Theological Seminary, and the curriculum was revised and enlarged to train people as Christian Science clergy.[20] By the fall of 1888, the restructuring of the school was complete. The recovery of the Association was progressing at a swift pace, and in September 1888 one of her students, Ida Nichols, began a new periodical, called simply *Christian Science*. The predominantly female social context within which Hopkins operated, and her Christian Science theological perspective, set the stage for Hopkins's innovative speculation that undergirded her actions in ordaining twenty-two ministers on January 10, 1889.

Emma Curtis Hopkins, Feminist Theologian

Like Mary Baker Eddy, Hopkins taught her students that God, equated with the Good, Truth, Love, Substance, Intelligence, Mind, the First Cause, the Creative Principle, was the only reality. As did Eddy, Hopkins denied the metaphysical reality of matter, as well as the reality of evil, identified as sin, sickness, and death. The solution to the human condition was found in realizing the truth of the total reality of God and the unreality of evil. While God was considered to be basically impersonal, it was quite proper to speak of God in personal terms. Again following Eddy's lead, Hopkins spoke of God as Father-Mother, but Hopkins drew major implications from that image that Eddy never developed. Like Eddy, and unlike Theosophy and Spiritualism, Hopkins attempted to operate within the larger context of ecclesiastical Christianity. She saw her teachings as derived from the Bible, and she accepted most of the central Christian symbols and used orthodox Christian language, though imbuing them with her own distinct meanings.

The clearest presentation of Hopkins's new theoretical framework appeared in an essay she wrote on the Trinity.[21] Hopkins's assertion that God, which was "the Governing Force and Law-Giver," was a "threefold Principle" consisting of Father, Mother (Holy Spirit), and Son bore a resemblance to some Gnostic formulations of the Trinity in early Christianity.[22] Referring to the millennial expectations of her day, Hopkins wrote that the people of the world were "looking for a great and mighty change of some kind to the earth and its inhabitants." Hopkins pointed to the changing roles of women as the most significant indication of the imminent new epoch. "Among all the indications of change nothing strikes the old-fashioned mind clinging to past ways, with more horror, than to see how woman, the silent sufferer and meek yoke-bearer of the world is stepping quite out of her old character or role, and with a startling rebound from her long passivity is hurling herself against the age with such force and bold decision as to make even her friends stand aghast."

Hopkins used her understanding of the Trinity to construct a vision of history progressing through three great periods, each corresponding to a member of the Trinity, reminiscent of the thought of Joachim of Fiore in the twelfth century. According to Hopkins, the first era was related to God the Father. During this time, humans created imperfect patriarchal institutions in which they attempted to embody the idea of "the guardianship of the wise and great over the weak and ignorant" masses. The second era of the Son, the "word of the Divine Mind," began with the birth of Jesus Christ. This second period was marked by a struggle against oppression, and the development of democratic structures. During this time, there was a gradual "setting free from the old idea that the people were the natural inferiors of the few in whom by birth or great physical strength was vested the administration of the law."

Hopkins identified the Holy Spirit as the "Mother-Principle," or "the Comforter, whose personified life we have scorned and put away into the silence, when we have kept the mother-voice and the sacred mother-power inactive in the world." The Holy Spirit was correlated to the Jewish concept of Shekinah, the indwelling presence of God. Hopkins elaborated that the Holy Spirit was the invisible "formless void," which is "all the time returning to us on its mysterious walls the reflections of the thoughts we have created." For example, the biblical King David thought deeply about the need for a great deliverer and teacher, and the responsive Holy Spirit returned to him revelations concerning the messiah. The Holy Spirit was "the cosmic substance" whose purpose was "to bring forth and mother and nurture the offspring of the mind."

Hopkins wrote that women's increasing worldly activity indicated that "the hour of the Spirit's exhaltation hath struck." "The personified Father-life, become the cold intellectual mind of mortal life" had lost its appeal, and the world longed for the "love, companionship, comforting, pity, tenderness" which only could come from "the mother heart of the universe." Hopkins believed that special women were being singled out to speak of the wisdom of the "Motherhood of the Life-Principle." Even though it seemed that no one listened to these women, their words were "irresistible in their power against error, and must bear wonderful fruit after many days." Hopkins saw the women she ordained, and implicitly herself, as being these messengers of the new era of the Holy Mother Spirit.[23]

Though Hopkins saw herself within the Christian tradition, two aspects of her theology clearly differentiate her from her mainstream Christian contemporaries: the assertion of the female aspect of God and the rejection of the traditional doctrine of evil and sin. In the essay on the Trinity, she described the Mother-Spirit's task as being the defeat of the idea of evil. Referring to Genesis 3:15, Hopkins asserted that the "seed of the woman" which was her "fruit-bearing word" would defeat the serpent, which represented the belief in the existence of evil, in order that all the children of the Mother be set free. Probably reflecting her own unhappy married life, Hopkins asserted that the first sign of Eden returning would be the reinstitution of "true home life, unspoiled by lawlessness or fear of evildoings." In the perfect millennial condition, there would be no more suffering or death, and there would no longer be "marrying, or giving in marriage, or giving of birth, for all shall awake to know they are as the angels of God in heaven, through the Holy Spirit's teaching them their likeness to, and oneness with the Trinity in One."

Given the strong assertion of the role of women within Hopkins's theology and her religious organization, it is not surprising to find Hopkins also encouraging involvement in women's issues in the secular realm. For instance, in the fall of 1888, Hopkins encouraged the Hopkins Metaphysical Association to join with the other women's groups in Chicago in assisting the Woman's Federal Labor Union to alleviate women's working conditions.[24] During the Columbian Exposition in Chicago in 1893, Hopkins's students organized themselves into the Columbian Congress of Christian Scientists to interact with other women's groups affiliated with the Queen Isabella Association, whose purpose was "to give opportunity to the women from all quarters of the world to meet each other socially and confer together on lines of their respective interest and advancement, professional and otherwise." Thus the women of the the Hopkins Metaphysical Association chose to participate in an exclusively women's environment at the Columbian Exposition, rather than attend the World's Parliament of Religions as did the Eddy Christian Scientists.[25]

The Emergence of New Thought

Hopkins's leadership of the school in Chicago lasted only nine years, from 1886 to 1895, after which time she continued teaching individuals while residing in New York City. In those few years in Chicago, Hopkins laid the foundations of the New Thought metaphysical tradition in American religion. New Thought literature would later refer to her as the "Teacher of teachers," a recognition that she had taught a number of New Thought leaders who became prominent in the early twentieth century. An examination of Hopkins's school records[26] and the work of her students shows that the most significant New Thought organizations, the Unity School of Christianity, Divine Science, and Religious Science, can be traced directly to her, and that with very few exceptions (i.e., several other former Eddy students who later affiliated with the movement), all of the early leaders of New Thought were either her students or her students's students. Her most important students included: Myrtle and Charles Fillmore (founders, Unity); H. Emilie Cady (Unity); Kate Bingham and Nellie Van Anderson (teachers of the founders of Divine Science in Colorado); Annie Militz (Homes of Truth); Melinda Cramer (founder, Divine Science); Clara Stocker (teacher of the founder of the Church of Truth); and Ernest Holmes (founder, Church of Religious Science). These leaders in turn taught Nona Brooks and Fannie James (founders, Divine Science, Colorado); and Albert Grier (founder, Church of Truth). Hopkins and her students brought people into classes, taught them to heal, and sent them out into the world to organize churches where others could be taught.

The key element in the development of the New Thought movement was Hopkins's mobilization and empowerment of women. For its first generation, the New Thought movement was largely composed of women, although by World War I it had developed a more even sex ratio. The explicit feminism present at its birth gradually left the New Thought movement, as did the social activism which accompanied it. The most permanent legacy of Hopkins's feminist stance is her institutionalization of female leadership, beginning with those first ordinations in January 1889. As a result, New Thought has continued to provide a space for women to develop their ecclesiastical leadership. At present (1991), women preside over four of the six largest New Thought organizations: Connie Fillmore, the great-granddaughter of Myrtle and Charles Fillmore is president of Unity School; Peggy Bassett is president of the United Church of Religious Science; Johnnie Coleman presides over the Universal Foundation for Better Living; and Judi D. Warren heads the International Association of Churches of Truth. In addition, more than half of all of the ministers and practitioners (the two professional positions) in the New Thought movement are women.

New Thought, of course, is not the ideal egalitarian religious community. The presidential post in Unity is an inherited position, and Fillmore's power is strictly limited by the board of Unity School, largely controlled by her father and the male dominated board of the Association of Unity Churches, which is in charge of the work in the field. The president of the United Church of Religious Science is largely a figurehead masking the real power of the church board, which controls the budget and appoints the president, and which is largely male in leadership. Coleman is in complete control of her foundation of which she is the CEO, but which she was forced to found because of problems within the fellowship of the Association of Unity Churches. In similar fashion, Warren, a former Church of Truth pastor, founded the International Association, and during the 1980s rebuilt a moribund denomination.

In stark contrast to most mainline Christian churches, through the twentieth century the New Thought movement has provided women with real access to all positions of power and authority, and has no theoretical restrictions to block their attainment of any professional status open to men. In practice, however, during recent decades, women have filled the great majority of posts as practitioners, the entry level professional position in the movement, while at each succeeding level of leadership the percentage of women has decreased. At the highest levels, where control of real money and property is at stake, women tend to be a distinct minority. One exception is the board of the International New Thought Alliance, which currently consists of seven women and seven men.

Hopkins in Perspective

Emma Curtis Hopkins would deserve her place in history had she done no more than found the movement to which she gave birth, and whose adherents now number in the millions around the globe. However, the women's movement in the late twentieth century has given her a new significance as the first individual to bring together several ideas which, after having become dormant in the early twentieth century, have become integral to post–World War II religious feminism. Hopkins took the idea of a female Divine, which earlier had been voiced by such diverse people as the Spiritualist Andrew Jackson Davis and the Shaker prophetess Ann Lee, and wedded it to the concerns of the nineteenth-century women's movement, in both its secular and religious phases. Neither the idea of female divinity nor the demands for equality for women was original to Hopkins, and the two ideas have no inherent necessary connection. Hopkins brought them together briefly in the 1880s and 1890s as a theological notion that was empowering to herself and the women who gathered around her.

In relation to Hopkins's theological position, it is also helpful to view her on the spectrum of other religious movements that shared her metaphysical perspective and her critique of traditional Christian theological opinions on the fatherhood of God and the nature of sin. The majority of such groups[27] were founded and headed by men and made no particular effort to offer a critique of traditional roles for women. The occult tradition, for example, had long worked on a model of the male sun and the feminine moon (which reflects the sun's light), a model that offers little assistance to feminist goals. Again and again, these religious traditions would promote very gifted charismatic women to leadership roles without drawing any connection between the leadership of, for example, a Madame Blavatsky or an Alice Bailey, and the efforts of women in general to exercise their leadership potential. The uniqueness and importance of Hopkins's movement is further highlighted when contrasted with its major competitors: Christian Science and Theosophy. Neither of these movements, which provided a place for women in leadership, possessed a professional clergy, hence neither could offer them a professional ministerial status. The Hopkins Metaphysical Association, which later became the Christian Science Association, not only welcomed women into leadership roles but explicitly recruited and elevated them into ecclesiastical positions formerly assumed by males. Unlike Christian Science and Theosophy, Hopkins uniquely moved to establish her right to ordain, and to establish the rights of her students to the social recognition and privileges (such as discounts on train tickets) enjoyed by other Christian ministers. Hopkins institutionalized the new ministerial status for women, and this was continued in the New Thought denominations of Unity, Divine Science, and Religious Science.

Situated within the women's movement in the churches of the late nineteenth century, Hopkins's movement can be seen as the logical development that completed the range of possibilities. During the 1880s, many denominations were still in the stage of trying to mobilize female members into women's missionary societies. Female-ordered communities were expanding among Roman Catholics, Episcopalians, and Methodists. A few ordained women could be found among the Methodists, Congregationalists, and Unitarians. Women evangelists were prominent but still very much in the minority among the holiness groups, which were just beginning to form separate holiness congregations and associations that would have the power to ordain.

Given this situation, Hopkins dealt systematically with the issue of women's leadership. Rather than simply accept a few women who fought their way to the top and ordain them, Hopkins established a system to recruit and train female ministers and, upon completion of that training, provide a means for graduates to gain credentials, find employment, and assume a status as professionals in the community. These actions were undergirded and motivated by the Hopkins's then-unique theological perspective, which sought to cooperate with the manifestation of the divine Mother-Principle she believed was the impetus behind the changing roles of women in church and society.

Hopkins's life and writings, forgotten for a century and still little known even within the New Thought movement, provide a vast store[28] of material for theological reflection. She was able to create a movement in which female images of God played a central role and she empowered women leaders at every level of community life. The New Thought movement created by Emma Curtis Hopkins is still growing, and women continue to play important roles in its ministry.

NOTES

1. Louisa Southworth, "Baccalaureate Address," *Christian Science* 1, no. 6 (Feb. 1889): 144–45.

2. Elizabeth Boynton Harbert, "The Right Hand of Fellowship," *Christian Science* 1, no. 6 (Feb. 1889): 141–43.

3. Before Ferne Anderson's "Emma Curtis Hopkins–Springboard to New Thought" (Master's thesis, University of Colorado, 1981), anything beyond the mention of Hopkins in passing had been limited to two biographical sketches. One was written by Margaret Cushing for *The New Thought Bulletin* 28, no. 2 (Spring 1945): 5–7; the other by Charles Braden for *Notable American Women* (Cambridge: Harvard University Press, 1971). My own research on Hopkins has been supplemented by data provided by Gail Harley in the dissertation she is completing on Emma Curtis Hopkins at Florida State University, Tallahassee. For my own more extended discussion of the course of Hopkins's life, see J. Gordon Melton, "New Thought's Hidden History: Emma Curtis Hopkins, Forgotten Founder" *META* 1, no. 1 (1993).

4. The events of the ordination were covered in the issues of *Christian Science* in the months following the event. See *Christian Science* 1, no. 6 (Feb. 1889); and *Christian Science* 1, no. 7 (Mar. 1889).

5. For example, see Gary L. Ward, "The Feminist Theme of Early New Thought," ISAR Occasional Paper #1 (Santa Barbara: The Institute for the Study of American Religion 1989), especially 18–19.

6. A helpful early chronicle of the development of missionary societies in the different denominations can be found in Isabel Hart, *Historical Sketches of the Woman's Missionary Societies of America and England* (Boston: Mrs. L. H. Daggett, 1879).

7. Carolyn DeSwarte Gifford, ed., *The American Deaconess Movement in the Early Twentieth Century* (New York: Garland Publishing, Inc. 1987).

8. Isabelle Horton, *High Adventure: Life of Lucy Rider Meyer* (New York: Methodist Book Concern, 1928).

9. On the support of the holiness movement for women in ministry, see Donald Dayton, *Discovering an Evangelical Heritage* (New York: Harper and Row, 1976); Donald Dayton, ed., *Holiness Tracts Defending the Ministry of Women* (New York: Garland Publishing, 1985).

10. Like Hopkins, Watkins is also a forgotten figure in women's history. Watkins had been a preacher on the Tunstall Circuit, an important early center of Primitive Methodism in England. With colleague William Knowles, in 1829 she initiated the Primitive Methodist work in New York. See the entry on Primitive Methodism in J. Gordon Melton, *Encyclopedia of American Religion* (Detroit: Gale Research, 1989).

11. Luther Lee, *Woman's Right to Preach the Gospel. A Sermon, Preached at the Ordination of the Rev. Miss Antoinette L. Brown, at South Butler, Wayne County, N.Y., Sept. 15, 1953.* (Syracuse, N.Y.: published by the author, 1853). This booklet is found in Donald Dayton, ed., *Holiness Tracts Defending the Ministry of Women.*

On Antoinette Brown Blackwell, see Ruth A. Tucker and Walter Liefeld, *Daughters of the Church: Women and Ministry from New Testament Times to the Present* (Grand Rapids, Mich.: Zondervan Publishing House, 1987), 279–81.

Brown completed the theological program at Oberlin College in 1850, but was not awarded her degree until 1878. After spending a couple years as a traveling speaker and sometimes preaching in churches, she was called to pastor a small Congregationalist church in South Butler, New York. Her ministry there lasted less than one year. She came into conflict with her congregation because she refused to preach hellfire and damnation, including infant damnation. She refused to condemn a young unwed mother whose infant had died, or to frighten a dying boy into conversion. In 1856 Brown married Samuel Blackwell, who shared her views on women's rights and the abolition of slavery. After raising a family and after her husband's death in 1910, she became a Unitarian minister.

12. Tucker and Liefeld, *Daughters of the Church,* 261–64; Charles Edward White, *The Beauty of Holiness: Phoebe Palmer as Theologican, Revivalist, Feminist, and Humanitarian* (Grand Rapids, Mich.: Francis Asbury Press of Zondervan Publishing House, 1986).

13. Amanda Smith, an ex-slave, was licensed to preach in the African Methodist Church. She was an itinerant evangelist who carried her work to England and India. Tucker and Liefeld, *Daughters of the Church,* 270–71; Amanda Smith, *An Autobiography* (1892; reprint, Noblesville, Ind.: Newby Nook Room 1964).

14. Phoebe Palmer, *The Promise of the Father* (Boston, 1859; reprint, New York: Garland Publishing Co., 1986).

15. Fannie McDowell Hunter, *Women Preachers* (Dallas: Berachah Publishing Co., 1905); this text is reprinted in Donald W. Dayton, ed., *Holiness Tracts Defending the Ministry of Women.*

16. Catherine Booth (1829–90) was cofounder of the Salvation Army. She wrote *Female Ministry; or, Woman's Right to Preach the Gospel* (London: Morgan & Chase, n.d.); found reprinted in Donald W. Dayton, ed., *Holiness Tracts Defending the Ministry of Women.*

17. Tucker and Liefeld, *Daughters of the Church,* 368–70.

18. On Willard, see Mary Earhart Dillon, *Frances Willard: From Prayers to Politics* (Chicago: University of Chicago Press, 1944).

19. Likewise one can have only a limited understanding of the forces operating in the suffrage movement apart from the impact of the holiness movement upon the status and aspiration of women in general.

20. This can be contrasted with the fact that although Mary Baker Eddy had been ordained by her students, and she gave clergy from other denominations roles as Christian Science ministers, she never ordained anyone.

21. "The Trinity. Isaiah 51." *Christian Science* 1, no. 4 (Dec. 1888): 77–82; "The Trinity. (Concluded.)" *Christian Science* 1, no. (Jan. 1889): 109–13.

22. The Gnostic text, the *Secret Book of John,* relates that John, the brother of James, had a vision of the Trinity as the Father, the Mother, and the Son. In the *Gospel to the Hebrews,* Jesus speaks of "my Mother the Spirit," and in the *Gospel of Thomas* Jesus explains that his true parents are his divine Father, the Father of Truth, and his divine Mother, the Holy Spirit. The *Gospel of Philip* argues that the doctrine of the virgin birth refers to the union of the Father with the Holy Spirit. Elaine H. Pagels, "What Became of God the Mother? Conflicting Images of God

in Early Christianity," in *Border Regions of Faith: An Anthology of Religion and Social Change,* ed. Kenneth Aman (Maryknoll, N.Y.: Orbis Books, 1987), 23.

23. Ward, "The Feminist Theme of Early New Thought," 17.

24. "Hopkins Metaphysical Association," *Christian Science* 1, no. 3 (Nov. 1888): 66–67.

25. Ward, "The Feminist Theme of Early New Thought," 12.

26. *Christian Science Seminary Catalogue, Year ending November 30, 1893.* (Seminary Office, 72 Auditorium, Chicago)

27. A list of contemporaneous groups would include, besides the several Hindu and Buddhist movements, the Koreshan Unity, the several churches of the New Jerusalem (Swedenborgian), the Esoteric Fraternity, the Fraternitas Rosae Crucis, the Hermetic Order of the Golden Dawn, and all of the groups that grew out of them. See entries in Melton, *Encyclopedia of American Religion.*

28. The American Religion Collection at the University of California, Santa Barbara, has a substantial collection of Hopkins materials.

Myrtle Fillmore and Her Daughters: An Observation and Analysis of the Role of Women in Unity

Dell deChant

From its modest beginning in Kansas City, Missouri, the Unity School of Christianity, which celebrated its centennial in 1989, has grown in size and impact so that today it daily touches the lives of over two million people. The attraction of Unity can be found in its interpretation of Christian faith from the viewpoint of theological idealism coupled with forms of congregational worship similar to those of mainstream denominations. Thus, Unity offers a religious alternative to mainline Christianity while retaining a sense of familiarity. As of 1992, Unity, the largest segment of the New Thought movement, has 602 churches and 166 affiliated study groups. More than four hundred thousand persons receive its monthly magazine, *Unity,* and over 2.5 million people contact its prayer ministry, Silent Unity, annually. Of its 545 active ministers, slightly more than half (287) are women.[1]

For a religious group of its size, age, and social vigor, Unity has received little serious and sustained academic attention. Moreover, the attention it has received is at times biased or incomplete. Since significant academic resources on Unity are lacking, the opportunity to evaluate the role of women in Unity also presents an important moment to introduce the Unity denomination as a whole to the academic community. To meet this twofold objective, this chapter supplies a brief sketch of the history and primary literature of Unity; surveys Unity's foundational theological assertions with special attention given to the relationship between these assertions and female leadership; discusses Unity's current institutional structure; and in conclusion, comments on the emergence of an institutional structure in Unity that seems to contradict the ideals of its cofounder, Charles Fillmore, and that calls into question the equal leadership of Unity women.

Unity History and Literature

Unity began in 1889 when its cofounders, Charles (1854–1948) and Myrtle (1845–1931) Fillmore, abandoned their secular occupations, dedicated their lives to "the study and mastery of Truth teachings," and started publishing a small periodical titled *Modern Thought*. These actions were precipitated by a number of events, perhaps the most decisive being a lecture by E. B. Weeks in 1886. As a result of this lecture, Myrtle Fillmore, who suffered from tuberculosis, discovered what she believed to be a truth as well as a principle, which would eventually restore her health. Myrtle Fillmore's truth was a sentence in Week's lecture: "I am a child of God, and therefore I do not inherit sickness." Her principle was that statements of this type, when affirmed with faith, have restorative power. Although this was a typical mind cure affirmation, and Myrtle Fillmore was representative of persons (especially women) who were receptive to the mind cure message, the impact of the ideology on her life, and consequently on her husband's life, was far more significant than for most. As one of Unity's denominational histories states, Unity emerged from Myrtle Fillmore's healing.[2]

Scholars who have studied Unity agree on its theological roots. The Fillmores were influenced by Swedenborgianism, Rosicrucianism, Christian Science, Hinduism, Theosophy, Spiritualism, New England Transcendentalism, and late nineteenth-century New Thought.[3] The dominant influence was New Thought, although the self-awareness of this ever loosely defined and loosely organized movement was decidedly undeveloped at this time. The other influences were secondary and mediated by New Thought. For example, the form of Christian Science embraced by the Fillmores was not Mary Baker Eddy's version, but the system taught by Emma Curtis Hopkins who had broken with Eddy on issues of dogma and authority. Hopkins was certainly the single greatest personal influence on the Fillmores and their early religious activities.

In 1890 a prayer ministry was formed, the Society of Silent Help—later called Silent Unity. In 1891 the Fillmores were ordained by Hopkins as Christian Science ministers, the movement was officially titled "Unity," and the first issue of *Unity* Magazine was published. The year 1893 saw the publication of the first issue of Myrtle Fillmore's brainchild, *Wee Wisdom,* which until its discontinuation in 1991, was America's longest running children's magazine. In 1894, the first lesson of H. Emilie Cady's *Lessons in Truth*[4] was published in *Unity* Magazine. These lessons written by a female student of Emma Curtis Hopkins would become Unity's first book, its best seller, and a major source of Unity's theological foundation. In 1906 the Fillmores and seven others were ordained Unity ministers; four of the seven were women. Beginning with this first ordination service, Unity has ordained women as well as men, thus affirming both the legitimacy of women religious leaders and the virtue of an ordained clergy. In 1909, Charles Fillmore published *Christian Healing,* the first of thirteen books he authored or coauthored.[5] A Field Department was established to maintain contact with the first Unity centers or churches in 1915. In 1929 the prayer ministry, Silent Unity, was moved from Kansas City to Unity Farm in nearby Jackson County. This first move began a process of gradual relocation that would see all Unity operations housed there by 1948. In 1953 the Farm became Unity Village, an incorporated area now totaling some fourteen hundred acres. Neither Myrtle nor Charles Fillmore lived to see Unity Village. In 1931 Myrtle Fillmore died at the age of eighty-six. Three years later her husband remarried, and in 1948 he too died at the age of ninety-three.

Charles Fillmore was succeeded as president of Unity School by his son, Lowell Fillmore, during whose tenure the Association of Unity Churches (AUC) was formed in 1966. Lowell Fillmore was succeeded as president of Unity School by his nephew, Charles Rickert Fillmore, in 1972. Charles Rickert Fillmore, while retaining his position as chairman of the board of Unity School, was succeeded as president of Unity School by his youngest daughter, Connie Fillmore, in January 1987.[6] Connie Fillmore currently presides over the religious movement precipitated by her great grandmother's healing over a century ago. With Connie Fillmore as president of Unity School and the titular leader of the denomination, Unity can be said to be the largest denomination in America led by a woman. However, looks can be deceiving.

In the endeavor to understand the relation of Unity's teachings to leadership roles for women, three salient considerations should be noted: 1) Unity's nature as a Christian movement whose theological principles are decidedly heretical in terms of traditional Christian norms; 2) Unity's lack of a formal doctrine and the corresponding theological freedom such a lack allows; and 3) Unity's organizational structure. These considerations affect not only the roles of women in Unity, but also the fate of the denomination itself. The first and second considerations noted are present in the discussion of Unity teachings in Part 2, and they are easily located in primary and secondary sources. The third consideration, which is discussed in Part 3, appears less frequently in both primary and secondary materials, and so an introductory explanation about Unity organizational structures is necessary.

Unity School of Christianity and the Association of Unity Churches are *related,* but they are functionally and philosophically independent. There is indeed intellectual commerce and a certain structural relationship between Unity School and the Association of Unity Churches, but the relationship is looser than one might expect. Unity School, of which Connie Fillmore is president, is a center for prayer, publication, and religious instruction. The AUC is a coordinating body for Unity churches and ministers with a rotating presidency of one-year terms. The Association of Unity Churches is really something of a misnomer because it is actually an association of Unity ministers. The ministers of the AUC are not formally bound to Unity School, and there are no formal guidelines concerning what must be taught at individual churches. In the subsequent discussion of Unity as an institution, my focus will be on the Association of Unity Churches.

The first, and effectively *only,* doctrine of Unity is the doctrine of spiritual freedom. Unity is perhaps the largest religion in the world without canon, creed, or doctrine. In principle and practice, there are no normative teachings. The looseness of Unity doctrine means that the literature of and about the movement gives only a partial picture of Unity's actual practices. Since Unity churches are fairly autonomous, and the Association of Unity Churches is only loosely affiliated with Unity School, and since there is no official canon, the teachings offered at individual Unity churches need not be confined to Unity's own literature or even its historical theological tradition. A statement from Connie Fillmore regarding Unity's "implied doctrine" suggests that Unity School does, however, have a very real interest in what is taught at Unity churches. In a letter to the author, Fillmore says: "Unity School prefers that our churches rely on the Unity teachings as their focal point. Certainly Charles Fillmore was clear in his opinion that astrology, numerology, channeling, and other psychic teachings are not appropriate for Unity centers. Unity School adheres to this same position today, although we have no direct authority in these matters."[7]

However, a recent informal survey of about 10 percent of the Unity churches in the United States reveals that a majority of the churches offer at least one class on material that either contradicts or significantly differs from Unity's traditional teachings. In most of these churches, the works of the Fillmores are rarely taught and the majority of classes and activities deal with subjects, texts, and practices not explicitly related to Unity.[8] While this survey is not a scientifically accurate poll of Unity churches, it does reveal that certain representative churches understate Unity's traditional teachings and the works of Unity's founders. Thus, as one reads Unity's authorized publications, it must be remembered that these are not considered sacred works, and neither Unity School, the Association of Unity Churches, nor individual Unity ministers and churches are formally bound to them or the teachings they contain. Unity may have begun as a religious publication enterprise, but it has never been defined by its literature no matter how extensive this literature may be. It is, however, increasingly defined institutionally by the AUC, which alone grants institutional sanction to churches and ministers.

Unity's Traditional Teachings and the Leadership of Women

Despite the tentativeness of Unity's foundational theological assertions, individual Unity leaders have never hesitated to be quite explicit about Unity's teachings. For instance, Charles Fillmore's "Statement of Faith" (1921) contains thirty affirmations[9] about God, Jesus, humanity, spiritual life, and related religious concerns. Unity School has not published Fillmore's "Statement of Faith" since 1984 due to the feeling the "writing was somewhat stilted and archaic, and did not accurately convey our Statement of Faith in Unity today."[10] Unity School has offered no new statement, although it does publish two pamphlets, *What Unity Teaches,* and *New Age/New Thought: A Unity Perspective,*[11] summarizing the general theological position of Unity. More recently, Leddy Hammock, who leads Unity's tenth largest church and its largest church led by a woman minister, has drafted her own Statement of Faith for Unity-Clearwater; V. Stanford Hampson, former AUC president, has offered twenty-one statements proposing to answer the question "Do you know what we believe?"; Connie Fillmore has offered five "basic ideas that make up the Unity belief system"; and the newly formed Unity-Progressive Council has presented forty statements under the heading of "A Progressive Reaffirmation of Unity Faith."[12]

In the context of the documents cited above, Unity's foundational theological position can be accurately captured in five assertions derived from the work of Charles Fillmore and H. Emilie Cady: 1) God (omnipotent good) is Mind/Principle, and evil (hence) has no reality in and of itself; 2) Humanity is innately divine, one with God, and individuals have direct access to God; 3) Mind/consciousness is ontologically primary and causative, and matter is secondary and the effect of mind/consciousness; 4) Persons are not spiritually bound to any religious teaching; 5) Conversely, Christian doctrine, spiritually or "metaphysically" interpreted, is normative.[13]

Unity's Theology

Charles Fillmore writes in *Christian Healing* that "God is a mind-principle whose foundation is *ideas*"; in *Prosperity* that "God is mind and His gifts are not material but spiritual, not things but ideas";[14] and definitively in

Jesus Christ Heals: "The fundamental basis and starting point of practical Christianity [Unity] is that God is principle. By principle is meant definite, exact, and unchangeable rules of action. . . . We must relieve our minds of these ideas of a personal God ruling over us in an arbitrary, manlike manner. . . . God is mind."[15]

But in Unity, God as Mind/Principle does not mean that God must remain impersonal; and when the God-concept is personalized, it is often personalized in either bisexual or female terms. For example, Charles Fillmore closes his "Statement of Faith" by saying: "Almighty Father-Mother, we thank Thee for this vision of Thine omnipotence."[16] In his interpretation of the gospel of John, we see an interesting blending of God as Mind/Principle with anthropomorphic concepts but presented so as to deemphasize the male nature of the divine. As he writes: "In the universal Mind principle, which Jesus called the Father, there is a substance that also includes the mother or seed of all visible substance. . . . Thus God is found to include both the male and the female principle."[17] Finally, Charles Fillmore did not hesitate to speak of God's female aspect in the most intimate terms. In a text coauthored with his second wife, Cora Fillmore, he observes that "prayer is more than asking God for help in the physical world; it is in its highest sense the opening up in our soul of an innate spiritual umbilical cord that connects us with the Holy Mother, from whom we can receive a perpetual flow of life."[18]

Nevertheless, in the Charles Fillmore/Emilie Cady literature, there are numerous references to God as Father and use of male pronouns to refer to divinity. These references can be attributed to the common usage of Charles Fillmore's era and our own; they are also surely a consequence of Charles Fillmore's desire to utilize traditional theological language.[19] Since Unity lacks a formal doctrine, individual ministers today may elect to use exclusively masculine terms for God. Unity texts commonly use "man" as the covering term for the human race.

Human Nature and the Problem of Evil

Since the traditional Christian doctrine of the Fall is a response to the problem of evil, Unity's position on the Fall is best understood in the context of Unity's response to this more fundamental problem. On the basis of the first assertion, that God (omnipotent good) is Mind/Principle, and evil (hence) has no reality in and of itself, the traditional Christian doctrine of the Fall stands as a contradiction of the essential nature of divinity and the fundamental principle of creation. By recognizing God as omnipotent good, Unity denies the ontological possibility of evil and its existential corollary, humanity's proclivity to sin. God is not considered the author of evil. Since God is the author of all, there can be no evil in divine creation. Even more fundamentally, since God creates by conceiving ideas, and ideas are the cause of material manifestation, and since God did not (and logically could not) think evil, evil cannot materially manifest. Not surprisingly, this "instrumentalist" response to the problem of evil (i.e., that which appears "evil" is and must be only an instrument for or portion of a greater good) at times shades into an "evil-as-privation-of-good" position. In Unity, evil has no ontological status; it is only the apparent absence of good/divinity.

The second assertion, that humanity is innately divine, one with God, and individuals have direct access to God, further mitigates traditional Christian doctrine. Unity argues that since humanity is innately divine, human beings are extensions or manifestations of divinity, and just as there is no evil in God there can be no evil, potential or actual, in humanity. The fundamental problem, then, is not evil but human error. For human beings, the existential problem is not an innate sinfulness due to a "first sin," but rather the capacity to err. The capacity to err is a necessary condition of humanity's free will.

The fifth foundational assertion, that Christian doctrine spiritually or "metaphysically" interpreted is normative, reveals how Unity can deny the reality of evil while maintaining traditional Christian symbolism and doctrinal terminology. Unity does not deny the Fall; it only denies that the Fall is a consequence of evil. In taking this tack, the scriptural story and the concept of the Fall are maintained, but its fatalistic implications are eliminated. In harmony with traditional Christian doctrine, responsibility for the event of the Fall and its consequences does rest with humanity, specifically humanity's free will.

A review of selected Unity treatments of the problem of evil and the doctrine of Fall can now be offered beginning with the preeminent teaching text in the Unity movement, Emilie Cady's *Lessons In Truth*. In her chapter on Unity's spiritual technique known as "denial,"[20] Cady offers four denials. The first is: "There is no evil."[21] Cady explains: "There is but one power in the universe, and that is God—good. God is good, and God is omnipresent. Apparent evils are not entities or things of themselves. They are simply apparent absence of the good, just as darkness is an absence of light. But God, or good, is omnipresent, so the apparent absence of good (evil) is unreal."[22]

Writing of evil in the context of denials, and in the same vein as Cady, Charles Fillmore notes: "Denial clears away belief in evil as reality and thus makes room for the establishment of Truth."[23] Denial of evil corrects the error of belief in the existence of evil. The term "evil" is used in Unity literature, but the informed reader recognizes it as a synonym for "error thought." The "punishment" for error-thought (evil) is the experience of negative material events which are the consequence of the erroneous thought. Salvation is thus found in the elimination of error-thought and the appropriation of divine ideas/good thoughts. This being so, an explanation for human error in a universe of omnipotent good must be offered. Readers will note the similarity of this explanation to the traditional free-will response to the problem of evil and the doctrine of the Fall. This similarity is evident in all of Charles Fillmore's treatments of the Genesis narrative. The following is typical: "When we are in the realm of the ideal, we are I AM; when we are expressing ideals in thought or in act we are *I will.* When the *I will* gets so absorbed in its realm of expression that it loses sight of the ideal and centers all its attention in the manifest, it is Adam listening to the serpent and hiding from Jehovah God. This breaks the connection between Spirit and manifestation, and man loses that spiritual consciousness which is his under divine law."[24]

Note that it is the "I will" that gets humans in trouble. It is the "I will" that listens to the serpent and "breaks the connection" between Spirit and matter. Writing specifically of the Fall, Charles Fillmore comments: "Man fell because he did not keep his mind on the source of life. He departed from spiritual consciousness and saw both good and evil. If he had held to the one good, good is the only thing he could have manifested."[25] Evil is mitigated by the Unity explanation that experiences and thoughts that traditionally are categorized as evil are only errors. Evil is not an ontological category although it is a theological term. The fundamental error and cause of the Fall is not recognizing divinity, and the omnipotence of good. For Unity, this error is a consequence of humanity's free will and the human capacity to posit an illusory power in opposition to God's omnipotent good.

Women in Unity

Given a theology that does not stress the exclusive maleness of God, and a view of human nature that does not blame evil on women, it is not surprising that in Unity, it is simply assumed that women and men are equally capable of religious leadership. Any position that might suggest a limited or restricted religious role for women would be thoroughly repudiated. Before summarizing the evidence on the leadership roles of women in Unity, it is necessary to comment on Myrtle Fillmore's role.

Myrtle Fillmore is atypical of the women leaders in Unity. Writing to a woman who apparently was facing difficulty finding her "right place" in a marriage, Myrtle Fillmore says:

Sometimes the very efforts of a wife and mother to go beyond the home to bring in supply and establish the social life on a higher level through such efforts, will tend to depress and discourage and to lessen the initiative and executive ability of the husband and father. Wives usually help best by standing back of the husband, and inspiring him with the feeling that his ideas are good, his undertakings worth while, the results satisfying, even though they themselves feel confident they could do better![26]

Certainly this position as stated by Myrtle Fillmore does little to encourage women to be active in leadership positions outside the home. That Myrtle Fillmore lived by this suggestion seems to be supported by the rather diminutive public role she assumed in Unity's development. Myrtle Fillmore had the healing experience that triggered Unity's beginning; she established and managed Silent Unity (née Society for Silent Help); she initiated *Wee Wisdom* magazine; and she developed what could be called the Unity style—assurance, candor, and gentle correction of the errors of others. This style is best revealed in Myrtle Fillmore's *Healing Letters*. These are important accomplishments to be sure; but in terms of Unity's public ministry and its theological development, they are eclipsed by the work of her husband. In fact, had Myrtle Fillmore's healing not inspired Charles Fillmore's spiritual commitment, the movement would never have been born. How much she directly influenced her husband and his work is debatable, and although the influence was probably significant, it was Charles Fillmore who wrote the foundational texts that helped to popularize Unity, who publicly pronounced Unity's theological positions, and who managed the institutional growth and expansion of Unity. Charles Fillmore can properly be cited as the leader, with Myrtle Fillmore following her own admonition to help best by standing back of her husband. Unity's sanctioned biography of Myrtle Fillmore corroborates this view:

Myrtle was the perfect balance necessary for Charles' metaphysical genius, spiritual devotion, and mischievous humor. She always complemented him with her quiet dignity and dedication to the Jesus Christ standard of living. While he preferred giving talks and teaching Truth courses, she enjoyed leading in prayer and meditation. While he was reluctant to write letters even to close friends, she was prolific in her correspondence.[27]

The language used above to describe the Fillmore couple is interesting. He is active: the genius, spiritually devout, and humorous. She is passive: quiet, dignified, dedicated. He gives the sermons and teaches the courses. She does the secondary work of leading the meditation and prayer, and she keeps up the correspondence, just as a "dutiful wife" would be expected to do in a traditional marriage. Such a sketch would hardly surprise us were it presented as the characterization of the wife of an early twentieth-century Protestant clergyman. I believe that this characterization of Myrtle Fillmore is essentially accurate, and she remains best defined in the context of the movement's public history as Charles Fillmore's wife.

After Myrtle Fillmore, any survey of Unity's significant female leaders, must begin with H. Emilie Cady (1848–1941). Cady was a homeopathic physician, but her fame rests entirely with a single text, *Lessons In Truth*. *Lessons* is often cited as Unity's primary text book, sometimes "next to the Bible" is added to this assertion. Cady had taught school before becoming a physician, and she apparently never married. Like the Fillmores, Cady had studied with Hopkins. Aside from her writings, Cady did not take an active role in Unity. She apparently never visited Unity headquarters and avoided the religious public.[28] Although Cady was never a public leader, through *Lessons* her influence on Unity has been enormous. Cady's affiliation with Unity was definitely a consequence of the movement's openness to women, for it was Charles Fillmore who invited Cady to write for Unity in 1891.[29]

In 1893 another spiritual teacher, Annie Rix Militz (1856–1924), published the first of many articles in *Unity* magazine. She too was a student of Emma Curtis Hopkins. Militz's special talent was scriptural exegesis from the "metaphysical" or New Thought perspective. She was a probable source of Charles Fillmore's spiritual interpretation of the twelve disciples, presented most fully in his classic text, *The Twelve Powers of Man*. Militz was affiliated with Unity from 1893–1911, yet she was ignored in Unity-authorized histories such as *The Story of Unity*, *The Unity Way*, and *Myrtle Fillmore: Mother of Unity*. During this time she wrote extensively for Unity. After the relationship with Unity terminated, she devoted herself to her own magazine, *Master Mind*, and the advance of her own, previously established organization, Home of Truth. But Militz had a significant impact on the development of Unity's theology, especially its method of exegesis, even if Unity School no longer publishes her most well known book, *Both Riches and Honor*. Like Cady, Militz's affiliation with Unity was a consequence of the movement's openness to women, since it was she who was invited to write for Unity. Unlike Cady, however, Militz's career in religious leadership far surpasses her contributions to Unity, and it was she who severed ties with the Fillmores in order to pursue her own independent work.[30]

In 1916, Myrtle Fillmore stepped down as head of Silent Unity, and she was replaced by the daughter of an important early supporter of the

Fillmores, Clara May Rowland (d. 1977). For the next fifty-five years Rowland presided over Silent Unity, which next to Charles Fillmore's years of leadership, represents the longest tenure in an executive position at Unity School. Rowland was also an author and teacher. She wrote numerous articles for Unity periodicals, and her two books, *The Magic of the Word,* and the classic, *Dare to Believe!* are still published by Unity School. Rowland is a transitional figure in Unity history. She knew and worked closely with the Fillmores and their successors as the movement grew from a small loosely organized religious enterprise into the largest New Thought movement in America with a worldwide outreach. Rowland devoted her life to Unity and the better part of it to Silent Unity. She was married three times, once to Frank B. Whitney, the first editor of *Daily Word.*[31]

The women discussed above represent only a tiny fraction of the women who have assumed leadership roles in Unity. Others of significant note include: Imelda Octavia Shanklin (author), Georgiana Tree West (author and president of the Unity ministers' association), Elizabeth Sand Turner (Bible interpreter), Catherine Ponder (prosperity teacher, author), Mary L. Kupferle (author, president of the AUC), Louise C. Beaty (field minister, church builder, and president of the Unity ministers' association), and Marjorie Kass (instrumental in the founding of sixteen churches). Women leaders in Unity today are typically field ministers in churches of less than five hundred members. Probably the majority are married and many serve with their husbands. Like their male colleagues, they are preachers, teachers, counselors, church managers, and writers.

Unity's Institutional Structure Today

If one judges by his writings, Charles Fillmore was a vigorous opponent of institutional Christianity and the traditional ordained clergy. Still, he and Myrtle Fillmore were ordained twice, and since 1906 Unity has ordained ministers. Fillmore's most sustained polemic against the institutional church is found in "Lesson Nine" of his *Talks On Truth*. The following selection indicates the severity of his opposition:

> Pure Christianity was literally killed in less than three hundred years after the Crucifixion. What is called Christianity is a combination of paganism, Israelitism, and the letter of Jesus' doctrine without the spirit. This heterogeneous mass became acceptable because it was sanctioned by kings and enforced as the church of the state. . . . The true church of Christ is never organized upon the earth, because the minute that man organizes religion, he ceases to

be guided wholly by the free Spirit of truth, and to that extent he falls away from the true church.[32]

A statement like the above introduces contradiction into Unity's ideology, especially its ecclesiology. Reading this and other similar statements leads one to ask upon what basis the Association of Unity Churches has moved to establish the clerical organization that carries the name Unity to nearly eight hundred locations worldwide. One also questions why Charles Fillmore wrote a creedlike "Statement of Faith," and why he allowed Unity churches to develop. These contradictions are underscored dramatically in Charles Fillmore's specific condemnations of the Catholic and Protestant churches and their clergy. In "Lesson Twelve" of *Talks* he observes:

> They [doctrines, creeds, and dogmas] are the work of men who had to sustain an industry known as the church, who had to provide for a privileged class called the clergy. These had become an important part of the body politic, and it was thought best to organize them according to human ideas; hence, church creed, and church government. Thus originated the Catholic Church; the Protestant churches are its offspring. All that the Protestants count dear as doctrine they borrowed from the Catholics, who had patched it together from early Christianity and from paganism. These teachings are not the pure Christianity of Jesus Christ, and He did not authorize the ecclesiastical structure called the Christian church.[33]

Nor, we note, did Jesus authorize the establishment of Unity School, or the Association of Unity Churches' extensive ecclesiastical structure. Although the Fillmores accepted ordination as a norm (probably due to Hopkins's influence), Charles Fillmore often voiced criticism of the role of the clergy in other faiths. This criticism was founded on the conviction that individuals have the capacity and responsibility to discover spiritual truth for themselves.

Unity's institutional practice today does not conform to these statements of Charles Fillmore. There is no question that Unity today, and especially the AUC, is developing a rigid institutional structure. Contemporary Unity conforms to "the clerical model of leadership" in which "the leader is a member of a professional class who monopolizes the knowledge and resources of service in a way that reduces those who are served to passive dependency" since they "lack access to specialized knowledge," and especially since they lack legitimacy.[34] Although this characterization of Unity's institutional structure would doubtless disturb Charles and Myrtle Fillmore, it seems an appropriate designation for the religion over which their theological, if not filial, heirs preside. While Unity's institutional clericalism is by no means as advanced as that which feminist critics find in Roman Catholicism, it is nonetheless present.

Given the large number of women ministers in Unity, it is somewhat surprising that Unity is devoid of a feminist critique of Unity's drift toward institutional absolutism. The absence of such a critique, and indeed any sort of organized opposition to Unity's emerging clericalism, is even more curious when one reflects on Charles Fillmore's polemic against institutional religion. Clearly the vast majority of ministers in Unity are generally satisfied with its institutional course, perhaps because of the benefits that accrue to them. Since there is no doctrine in Unity and the Charles Fillmore teachings are not authoritative, his polemic is not accepted as normative. Further, the feminist critique of clericalism grows out of the rich tradition of cultural/institutional criticism which has been a mainstay of theology especially in recent years, and since Unity ministers and educators are neither theologically literate nor conversant with the the critical horizons of the theological enterprise, they are most likely unaware of this critique. The paradox of Unity's developing clericalism can, in part, be understood as the consequence of male domination of the Association of Unity Churches. Although the majority of Unity ministers are women, and although women have historically been recognized as legitimate religious leaders, their impact on the institutional development of the AUC has been considerably less than that of their male colleagues.

Unity's emerging clericalism is best observed in terms of three institutionally relevant categories: regional representative, clergy, and laity. A brief summary of the different degrees of political and religious power granted to persons in these categories and the relationship of these categories to the Association of Unity Churches will yield a rough outline of Unity's inclination toward clericalism. Before considering the categories themselves, a further explanation of the structure of the Association of Unity Churches is in order.

As noted earlier, participation in the Association of Unity Churches, founded in 1966, is limited to ministers. Full political participation is even further limited. The AUC is bureaucratically structured, and the bureaucracy is hierarchically organized. A Board of Trustees establishes policy which is then carried out by an executive director and his staff under the supervision of an Executive Committee. The Board (as of 1992) is composed of twenty-two ministers. Board members are elected in one of three ways: by vote of the Board of Trustees, by vote of the ministers in the seven geographic regions, and by vote of the ministers present at the annual conference. The Board of Trustees appoints the members of all permanent committees. Although there is an annual conference of the full

AUC, decisions by the Board are often made without full ratification by Unity ministers. Although avenues do exist for ministers to bring motions and resolutions to the full conference body, the process is highly controlled.

The Association of Unity Churches has recently begun making inquiries into the size of churches and the personal religious beliefs of individual ministers. The placement of ministers is increasingly controlled by the AUC, and it entirely controls the establishment of new churches. Recent years have seen an increase in AUC controlled publications and programs. Suggested bylaws for churches generated by the AUC contain language stipulating membership in the AUC, leadership by an AUC minister, and acquisition of church property by the AUC in the event of dissolution of the church.

Although this is only a brief sketch of the AUC's corporate structure and policy, I believe it supports the contention that the AUC has developed and is continuing to develop a highly structured religious institution capable of perpetuating itself and controlling its member churches and ministers.[35] On the basis of this sketch, we can now inquire into the relationship of various institutional categories to each other and to the AUC.

Regional Representative

The Association of Unity Churches is comprised of seven geographic regions—Eastern, Western, South Central, Southeastern, Great Lakes, West Central, Southwest.[36] Regional representatives serve on the AUC Board of Trustees and are elected by vote of the ministers in the regions that they represent. The regional representatives have considerable power. In addition to the power associated with serving on the Board of Trustees, they serve as liaison officers between the Board and their region and represent their region in all corporate matters. They are also empowered to recommend approval or denial of membership in the AUC for churches applying for membership, and, at the request of the executive director, make recommendations regarding the placement of ministers in the region. A regional representative also has the power to recommend approval or denial of ordination to licensed ministers in his or her region. Finally, regional representatives serve on four-member boards of investigation that make recommendations regarding continued membership in the AUC for ministers/churches that have revealed evidence of noncompliance with membership requirements or violations of the Code of Ethics or bylaws of the movement. Other members of an investigation board include the executive director of the AUC, the president of the AUC, and a minister selected by the minister or church being investigated.

In principle, regional representatives serve both the Board of Trustees and the regions they represent. It must be remembered, however, that they are members of the Board that establishes and enforces the corporate policy of the AUC. Regions tend to be more loosely organized than the Board and policy committees. Regional opposition to Board decisions tends to come after policies are established or enforced. When offered, it is usually voiced by isolated individuals. At present, there exists no organized political camps that might be expected to exercise meaningful political opposition to activities of the AUC.[37] In practice, regional representatives seem more likely to project the power of the AUC into the region's activities and ministries by virtue of their explicitly stated responsibilities to the AUC and their less explicit responsibilities to the regions.[38]

Clergy

The 545 Unity ministers are the professional religious elite of the movement, and they alone possess and exercise political power in the Association of Unity Churches. Unless a minister serves in the upper levels of the AUC, his or her social/political/personal power is exercised within the confines of his or her church. Within those confines a minister's social/political/personal power can be considerable depending on such things as his or her tenure at the church, provisions in the church's bylaws, and personal magnetism. In strictly religious terms, however, the minister's power is virtually absolute within his or her church.

A minister's religious power beyond his or her church is contingent on willingness to enter the AUC system and participate in its politics. As noted previously, meaningful participation in the AUC is limited to those who have ascended to the upper levels of the hierarchy or those who serve on the more influential committees. Those who do not politically participate in the AUC have little influence on its religious or corporate policies and planning. Ordination is the necessary condition for participation in AUC politics and the possibility of exercising religious power in Unity at any level. Once ordained, a person at least can be assured of having religious power within a Unity community. Without ordination, a person has neither political nor formal religious power in Unity.

Although data indicating the scope of AUC control and influence of the clergy is not as extensive as that indicating the control and influence of regional representatives, conditions surrounding the selection of student ministers and the placement of ministers are suggestive. In the selection process for ministerial students, not everyone who is objectively qualified is allowed to enter the two-year program offered at Unity Ministerial School. Because the interview process is subjective and the interview panels are composed of a cross-section of ministers, one can only hazard a guess about the criteria used to evaluate candidates. The evaluations are supervised by a committee chaired by the executive director of the AUC and comprised of representatives from the AUC and Unity School. A prospective candidate probably would fare poorly in the interviews if he or she was less than supportive of the AUC or Unity School. Because those who make decisions on admissions to Unity Ministerial School are institutional insiders, who themselves entered the ministry through a similar process and are now fully involved in the bureaucracy and its inherent politics, it can be assumed that most of those admitted will conform to the norms of the AUC and Unity School. Given this structure, admitting potential critics of the AUC into the ministry, and eventually into the political structure, would be highly unusual.

Once credentialed, a minister relies on the AUC for information on church openings. Ministers' resumés are kept on file at AUC headquarters and released to churches at the request of ministers seeking placement, but subject to review by the Placement Committee and the regional representative. The degree of institutional interference in placement activities is impossible to judge since the process is effectively closed, but the possibility of significant interference is clearly present. Thus, the AUC tends to perpetuate conformity in the clergy, and the clergy tend to perpetuate the control of the AUC.

Laity

In Unity the laity is powerless both politically and in terms of official religious leadership. The bylaws of the Association of Unity Churches prevent the laity from voting or otherwise participating in the AUC, and only rarely are they empowered to christen, marry, or perform memorial services. They seldom preach, and they can teach officially sanctioned courses at the congregational level only if licensed as a teacher by Unity School (a rather long and demanding process). They are free to experience God in their own individual ways, find the Christ within themselves, contribute to the church, gather with others in a religious community, and attend services. The only semblance of political power that the laity does have is restricted to the congregational level, where congregational votes for church board members and ministers are typical; but even here the laity often only ratifies decisions made by ministers or church boards. In both politics and religious life, the AUC and its churches conform to a strict hierarchical structure in which participatory democracy does not exist, and the full religious legitimacy of persons is contingent on ordination.

Unity conforms to the clerical model of leadership, in which members of a professional class (clergy) monopolize knowledge and power in such a way as to disempower nonprofessionals (laity). In Unity the disempowerment of persons is predicated on their political disenfranchisement. Since only churches led by ministers sanctioned by the AUC are recognized as Unity churches, and since political power within the AUC can only be exercised by the ministers, the laity is wholly dependent on the clergy. This dependency is most obviously a political dependency since the laity has no voice in the movement beyond the voice of its clerical representatives. Political dependency broadens into religious dependency because church membership in the Association of Unity Churches is contingent on clerical leadership. One cannot be part of a Unity church, and hence a public participant in the religion, unless the church is led by a member of the professional elite of the AUC; and since this professional elite has exclusive control over formal religious activities and services, the public religious life of Unity members is dependent on their recognizing the formal religious authority of the minister who leads their church. In light of the foregoing, and in distinction to the Roman Catholic church, the disempowerment of Unity lay members is not primarily sacramental. It is primarily political, but this political disempowerment affects the religious life of the congregations.

Conclusion: How Could This Happen?

Despite Charles Fillmore's criticism of institutionalized religion, we can see in Unity the emergence of a religious institution patterned on the model of hierarchical male-dominated churches and denominations. Such institutions have historically required a professional religious elite (an ordained clergy) to maintain and perpetuate themselves. Whether one can have such an institution and not have a professional religious elite remains to be seen. Unity certainly does not stand as an exception to the rule. While there is no single reason why clericalism has developed as Unity's organizational model, the chief reason is, I believe, male domination of the Association of Unity Churches.

Clericalism is not restricted to religious institutions; it is found in virtually all social assistance institutions. Prime examples can be found in law, medicine, education, and social work. At least two central elements of clericalism, hierarchical/bureaucratic operational structures and non-democratic organizational/managerial policies, are also typical of secular corporations found in capitalistic socioeconomic systems.[39] Clericalism, then, can be seen to supply not only the organizational norms for religions and helping professions, but also those of secular business and industry.[40] The critique of clericalism in religious institutions thus conjuncts with the religious critique of corporatism in business and industry, and with the general critique of capitalism offered by feminist and liberation theologians.

Since its creation in 1966 as a nonprofit religious organization, the history of the Association of Unity Churches reveals a pattern of male dominance. The initial Board of Trustees was comprised of nine men and one woman. Since 1966 there have been eighteen male presidents of the AUC and seven female presidents. The current (1992) president is a man. In the pre-AUC years, when Unity churches and ministers were more directly affiliated with Unity School, the majority of the presidents of Unity ministers' organizations were men, but the margin was much smaller. For several years the office of executive director (CEO.) of the Association has been occupied by man. Males serve as chair or cochair of twenty of the AUC's thirty committees. Although four of the seven regional representatives are women (up from two in 1991), nearly 60 percent of the regional liaison representatives (from whom regional representatives are selected) are men. Of the ten largest churches, only one (the tenth largest with about 1300 members) has a woman as the senior minister; and of the twenty-seven largest, only seven are led by women.

The one exception to male domination is the 1992 composition of the AUC Board of Trustees. In a most interesting and important departure from the tradition of male domination in the AUC, the 1992 Board of Trustees of the Association has a female majority—thirteen women and nine men. The 1992 Board composition is the only time in the history of the AUC that there has been a female majority. In 1991 the Board consisted of eleven men and ten women; in 1990, twelve men and nine women; in 1989 and 1988, fourteen men and seven women; in 1985, fifteen men and six women.[41]

Whether the gradual increase and the current majority in female representation on the AUC Board indicates a significant departure from the tradition of male dominance remains to be seen. This situation bears close observation, especially since it presents a curious contradiction to the continuing pattern of male dominance in committee leadership, regional representative pool, the position of executive director, and leadership of larger churches. It also remains to be seen if the new female majority on the AUC Board will be perpetuated, and if any significant changes to the clerical structure of the organization occur as a result. Although we observe a female majority on the Board of Trustees for the first time, and in spite of the fact that the majority of Unity's ministers are women, the institution's controlling offices, and the movement's largest churches are for the most part controlled by men. More importantly, the institution itself remains decidedly clerical in both its structure and its practices.

Men designed the Association of Unity Churches using articles of incorporation typical of nonprofit groups, and men composed bylaws informed by the norms of corporatism/clericalism. Probably the founders of the AUC entertained no other institutional options. Their intent was to form a typical nonprofit religious institution, and this they did. I doubt that they set out to establish a religious corporation whose organization structure was similar to that criticized by Charles Fillmore, but when one forms a religious institution in America it tends to conform to normative corporate models, especially when it is formed by men who are familiar with the practical workings of such models. The AUC has grown in size and power under the guidance of other men; men for whom the Unity ministry is a second career; men who are familiar with the hierarchical corporate structures typical of the capitalistic socioeconomic system. That men dominate the AUC is hardly surprising, for men tend to advance more rapidly than women in corporate hierarchies. That these same men would, as a matter of course, establish and develop systems and policies that perpetuate the AUC and further expand its power is to be expected.

In conclusion, the religious sons of Charles Fillmore established and have perpetuated a religious corporation that bears the name Unity but that contradicts its cofounder's views on institutionalized religion. In so doing they have created an hierarchical, bureaucratic institution which affords women ministers technical equality and the possibility, though seldom the reality, of institutional power. This equality and possibility of power is contingent on their accepting the rules and regulations of the system. That men dominate the Association of Unity Churches is hardly remarkable since it conforms to the model of capitalistic institutions with which they are familiar, and in which they have learned to excel, and have greater opportunity to do so. That women seem to be making some inroads into the power structure seems to be more of a reflection of the general trend in corporate American culture rather than a significant change in the power structure itself.

And so the religious sons of Charles Fillmore have created and developed an institutional system that they share with the religious daughters of Myrtle Fillmore, but the sons have controlled the system even if the daughters have more in common with May Rowland, Annie Rix Militz, or Emma Curtis Hopkins than they do with the retiring "mother of Unity." The house of the Unity denomination was built with male hands. Unity theology in which God is seen as an "nonanthropomorphic divine principle,"[42] which can be spoken of in male and female terminology, would seem to promote inclusion of the religious leadership of women. Unity's anthropology, which reinterprets the concept of a primordial Fall and which asserts that all persons share an innate divinity, is likewise a support to women's leadership. Women have played and continue to play important roles in Unity. But although theological assertions may support the religious leadership of women, they do not assure gender-balance in the political structure of a religious institution, and they do not necessarily lead to the development of feminist institutional structures. Unity reveals that the very opposite sort of institutional structure can emerge in a religion that is nondoctrinal, and especially so when such a religion seeks to organize itself based on corporate models in a capitalistic culture that remains normatively patriarchal.

NOTES

1. For support of figures given here, see *Dictionary of Christianity in America* (Downers Grove, Ill.: InterVarsity Press, 1990), s.v. "Unity School of Christianity," by Dell deChant; and *Association of Unity Churches 1992 Year Book* (Lee's Summit, Mo.: Association of Unity Churches, 1991).

2. *A Unity Chronology* (Unity Village: Unity School of Christianity, n.d.), 4, 5; see also Charles S. Braden, *Spirits in Rebellion* (Dallas: Southern Methodist University Press, 1963), 233, 234; and Thomas E. Witherspoon, *Myrtle Fillmore: Mother of Unity* (Unity Village: Unity Books, 1977), chap. 3, pp. 37–62. The denomination recognizes 1889 as its date of inception, although the name "Unity" was not adopted until 1891. There is some conflict among sources concerning certain dates in Unity's history. The author has cited dates that appear most accurate.

3. For the Fillmores' appreciation of these and other systems, see J. Stillson Judah, *The History and Philosophy of the Metaphysical Movements in America* (Philadelphia: Westminiser Press, 1967), 235–37, 248; James W. Teener, "Unity School of Christianity" (Ph.D diss., University of Chicago, 1939), 104–12; and Braden, *Spirits in Rebellion,* 332–34.

4. H. Emilie Cady, *Lessons In Truth* (Unity Village, Unity Books, n.d.)

5. Charles Fillmore, *Christian Healing* (Unity Village: Unity Books, n.d.). In comparison to her husband, Myrtle Fillmore published relatively little, but she did write regularly for the periodicals and carried on an extensive correspondence with Unity followers. She is cited as the author of two books, *Myrtle Fillmore's Healing Letters,* ed. Frances W. Foulks (Unity Village: Unity Books, 1978), and *How to Let God Help You* (Unity Village: Unity Books, n.d.), both of which fail to give much insight into Unity's theological position. For this reason, when I discuss the literary work of the Fillmores my references will be to Charles Fillmore's work unless otherwise noted.

6. Charles R. Fillmore's older daughter is not professionally involved in Unity.

7. Letter to the author dated 27 Oct. 1987.

8. Survey conducted from Aug. 1986 through Mar. 1987 by the author. Churches were selected from all regions of the country and ranged in size from

large (one thousand or more members) to small (less than one hundred). Forty churches were surveyed by reviewing church programs and/or bulletins and categorizing the various classes, study groups, or association groups as "Unity" or "non-Unity" on the basis of the described or known content of the classes, study groups, or association groups. Those which dealt explicitly with astrology, numerology, channeling, hypnotism were classified "anti-Unity" because of the movement's historical rejection of these practices. A vast majority of churches offered classes or study groups on *A Course in Miracles,* a popular New Age scripture channeled by Helen Schucman. About 80 percent of the churches offered fewer classes or study groups based on Unity teachings or texts than they did on discernibly non- or anti-Unity teachings or texts. Classes on the works of Fillmore were rarely offered, and some churches offered no classes on Unity teachings or texts. The majority of the churches surveyed were directed by male ministers.

9. Or thirty-two affirmations, depending on date of edition.

10. Letter from Harry W. Morgan, then editorial director of Unity School, to the author dated Sept. 14, 1984. The "Statement" may have been removed from print as early as 1983.

11. Elizabeth Sand Turner, "What Unity Teaches" (Unity Village: Unity School of Christianity, n.d.); "New Age/New Thought: A Unity Perspective" (Unity Village: AUC and Unity School of Christianity, n.d.)

12. Leddy Hammock's "Unity-Clearwater Statement of Faith" is available from Unity-Clearwater, 2465 Nursery Rd., Clearwater, FL, 34624. For Hampson's statements, see V. Stanford Hampson, "Do you know what we believe?" *Vision* 2 (May/June 1990): 16. For Connie Fillmore's five basic ideas, see "New Thought/New Age: A Unity Perspective" (Unity Village, 1990), 10. The Unity-Progressive Council's "A Progressive Reaffirmation of Unity Faith" is available from the Unity-Progressive Council, P.O. Box 7753, Clearwater, FL 34618–7753.

13. These five points are developed on the basis of Charles Fillmore's theology as presented in his thirteen books, and Cady's *Lessons In Truth.* The fifth point is included as a recognition of Charles Fillmore's assertion that Unity believes in "all the doctrines of Christianity spiritually interpreted" as noted in *Unity's Statement of Faith* (Unity Village: Unity School of Christianity, n.d.), 6., and because Unity has traditionally considered itself Christian. Although not noted explicitly here, Unity does have a christology, but I believe this is implied by the fifth point. In addition to its christological affirmation, there are certainly numerous other points that could be included as Leddy Hammock, V. Stanford Hampson, and many other Unity leaders might note; but these five are, to my mind, the most definitive.

14. See Charles Fillmore, *Christian Healing* (Unity Village: Unity Books, n.d.), 92; Charles Fillmore, Prosperity (Unity Village: Unity Books, n.d.), 77.

15. Charles Fillmore, *Jesus Christ Heals* (Unity Village: Unity Books, n.d.), 34.

16. Charles Fillmore, *Unity's Statement of Faith* (Unity Village: Unity School, n.d.), 6.

17. Charles Fillmore, *Mysteries of John* (Unity Village: Unity Books, 1978), 73–74.

18. Charles Fillmore and Cora Fillmore, *Teach Us to Pray* (Kansas City, Mo.: Unity School of Christianity, 1949), 5.

19. Leddy Hammock, a former editor of Unity Books, notes that in the early 1970s an effort was undertaken and then abandoned to remove noninclusive language from the works of Charles Fillmore. The move towards inclusive language was apparently abandoned in order to maintain the integrity of Fillmore's work. Hammock's comments made in an interview with the author on June 20, 1990.

20. Denial is defined by Charles Fillmore as "the mental process of erasing from consciousness the false beliefs of the sense mind." See Charles Fillmore, *Revealing Word* (Unity Village: Unity Books, n.d.), 53.

21. Cady, *Lessons,* 44.

22. Ibid., 44–45.

23. Charles Fillmore, *Revealing Word,* 53.

24. Charles Fillmore, *Christian Healing,* 34.

25. Charles Fillmore, *Mysteries of Genesis* (Unity Village: Unity Books, 1979), 43.

26. Myrtle Fillmore, *Myrtle Fillmore's Healing Letters,* ed. Frances W. Foulks (Unity Village: Unity Books, 1978), 182.

27. Witherspoon, *Myrtle Fillmore,* 143.

28. Ernest C. Wilson, "Dr. H. Emilie Cady: Author with Authority," *Unity* 159 (June 1979): 5.

29. Braden, 245. Cady's first article was published in January 1892.

30. See John K. Simmons, "New Thought, No Thought: The Forgotten History of Annie Rix Militz and her Contribution to the Unity School of Christianity," *META* (forthcoming 1993). Dates and details on Militz's life that appear here are derived from this excellent paper.

31. Certain details of Rowland's life given here were supplied by Sharon Patterson, Unity School, Heritage Room.

32. Charles Fillmore, *Talks on Truth* (Lee's Summit, Mo.: Unity School of Christianity, 1965), 101–2, 109.

33. Ibid., 132–33.

34. Rosemary Radford Ruether, "The Women-Church Movement in Contemporary Christianity," in this volume.

35. Material for this summary of the AUC and for subsequent data on AUC offices and policies is from *A.U.C. Yearbooks* (1988, 1989, 1991, 1992) and personal studies by the author.

36. There is also a Canadian region, but this region is not represented on the Board of Trustees.

37. The one exception seems to be the newly formed Unity-Progressive Council, a Florida-based group that has no affiliation with Unity School or the Association of Unity Churches.

38. This tendency is further reinforced when one considers the requirements for holding the office of regional representative. These requirements tie the representative into the AUC's institutional structure and severely compromise the

ability of opponents of the AUC to be seated even if elected. For a list of these requirements see *A.U.C. Yearbook,* 1991, p. 3.

39. As noted by Madonna Kolbenschlag in "The American Economy, Religious Values and a New Moral Imperative" in *Cross Currents* 34 (Summer 1984): 153–70, see esp., 161. I will use Kolbenschlag's term, "corporatism," to describe the secular equivalent of "clericalism."

40. In this regard, secular corporations have been reminded of the organizational and operational virtues of clericalism by secular business authorities. See citation of the American Institute of Management study of the corporate efficiency of the Roman Catholic church, and comments by Peter Drucker in Arthur Jones, "Managing the Lord's Work," *Forbes* 135 (Jan. 14, 1985): 282–83.

41. Factual data in these paragraphs is taken from *A.U.C. Yearbooks* (1985, 1988–1992); a publication of the AUC, *Contact* 21 (June/July 1989): 10; and data in possession of the author. Although my focus has been on AUC, it should be noted that the Board of Trustees of Unity School is also male-dominated, with six of the eight positions occupied by men. Connie Fillmore, and Margaret F. Dale (wife of a male trustee) are the only women. Unity School Board members are noted on the inside cover of *Unity* magazines, for example *Unity* 172 (May 1992), inside cover facing p. 1.

42. Mary Farrell Bednarowski, "Outside the Mainstream: Women's Religion and Women Religious Leaders in Nineteenth Century America," *Journal of the American Academy of Religion* 48 (June 1980): 209.

Woman Guru, Woman Roshi: The Legitimation of Female Religious Leadership in Hindu and Buddhist Groups in America

Catherine Wessinger

The various Hindu and Buddhist groups in the United States have proved to have a significant attraction for American women who choose to step outside the religious mainstream. Some of these groups are noteworthy in that they give women the opportunity to function in important leadership roles. This inquiry will focus on the Hindu sect known as Siddha Yoga, and a comparison will be made with the International Society for Krishna Consciousness and the varieties of American Buddhism. It will be shown that women religious leaders are prominent in those groups in which the male divine is de-emphasized. The group that is strongly focused on a male deity has limited leadership roles for its women members. When an imported Asian conception of God, which de-emphasizes the masculine in some manner, meets with the growing Western expectation of the equality of women, opportunities to become religious specialists begin to open for women, and the Hindu and Buddhist attitudes that blame women for the human condition begin to fall away.

Siddha Yoga

Siddha Yoga was first brought to the United States by Swami Muktananda, who reported he was doing so at the command of his own guru. Muktananda (1908–82) made his first visit to the United States in 1970, and he made two more world tours 1974–76, and 1979–81, which included the U.S. Siddha Yoga Dham of America (SYDA) Foundation was incorporated in the United States in 1974, and acts on behalf of Muktananda's original organization, Shree Gurudev Siddha Peeth, located in Ganeshpuri, India.[1]

Before his death in 1982, Muktananda designated two successors, a sister and brother (Indians), to his position as guru. After taking vows of *sannyasa* (renunciation), the sister became known as Swami Chidvila-sananda (1954–), and the brother became known as Swami Nityananda (1962–). They ruled as co-gurus until Swami Nityananda was compelled to withdraw from the position in 1985 due to charges that he had repeatedly broken his vow of celibacy. Thus Swami Chidvilasananda, who is affectionately known as "Gurumayi" (one who is of the form of the guru) to her devotees, was left as the sole guru in the Siddha Yoga movement.[2]

The primary ashram (hermitage or retreat center) of Siddha Yoga in the United States is in South Fallsburg, New York, and the second major American ashram is located in Oakland, California. Ganeshpuri, India, remains the home base and primary pilgrimage site for Siddha Yoga devotees. Gurumayi Chidvilasananda divides her time between these locations, where devotees come to see her, in addition to traveling worldwide.

Siddha Yoga is a *sadhana* (spiritual path) that is focused on the guru, who is considered to be a *siddha* (a Master or "one who is perfected"). The goal of Siddha Yoga practice is to have a direct perception of a divine monistic universe.

Siddha methods include meditation, chanting of mantras, and *seva* (service to the guru). Siddha Yoga includes *jnana* (knowledge) since it is possible for the devotee to study the various Hindu scriptures and commentaries on which the Siddha faith is based. But Siddha Yoga is primarily a path of *guru-bhakti,* intense devotion to the guru. In meditation, one should either focus on a mantra consisting of the names of God, or on the form of the guru, and seek to become identified with her/his state. Mantras are also chanted congregationally, and the mantra is believed to be a vibrational manifestation of the unity between the devotee, the guru, and God. There is no difference between the guru and God, because the guru has the perception of unity with all things. The guru's grace causes the mantra to be effective for meditation. *Seva,* service in the ashram or in the outside world, should be done with the attitude that the guru is doing the work, not the devotee. Work done in this manner promotes constant remembrance of the guru, and a loss of the limited sense of individuality. A text known as the "Guru Gita" is chanted every morning in Siddha ashrams, and this practice further reinforces devotion to the guru.

Siddha Yoga teaches that one cannot attain the highest realization without the *kripa* (grace) of the guru. A guru is defined as a person who has the ability to transmit grace directly to the devotee and cause the experience of divine unity. This transmission, known as *shaktipat,* is described as the awakening of *shakti* (the divine power of consciousness) within the devotee. *Shaktipat* is believed to be transmitted by the guru in a variety of ways, including touch, look, or thought. The immediate proximity of the guru is not a requirement. So in Siddha Yoga, the guru is the means. The devotee seeks to surrender completely to the guru and obey her every command. The intent of this methodology is that the devotee learn to give up the limited ego to come to the experience of universal unity.[3]

Much of the Hindu tradition has been sexist, with women forbidden to study or even hear the Vedas (sacred scriptures). It has been commonly assumed that birth as a female is the result of past bad karma (actions). Women have often been considered incompetent to achieve the ultimate goal of *moksha* (release from rebirth). A woman should follow her *stridharma,* or wifely duty, and be obedient and attentive to her husband, and produce many sons. Women saints are usually found in the *bhakti* (devotional) traditions, which have been more accessible to women.[4] Women saints are seen as exceptional, and they are not regarded as models for the good Hindu wife to emulate. In modern India, it is slowly becoming more acceptable for a woman to become a *sannyasin* (renunciant) in order to pursue the spiritual goal, but this has normally been a path deemed appropriate for men.[5] Institutional religious authority has likewise been the province of men.

Gurumayi Chidvilasananda's current position is remarkable in that she combines the charisma of her ecstatic love for God (this is apparent when she chants the names of God) with the institutional authority of having been initiated as a *sannyasin* and of having been designated guru in a *parampara* (lineage of gurus). The spiritual power of her guru is believed to have been transferred to her. The institutional authority was transferred to Chidvilasananda in rituals in which women normally have no part.[6] Chidvilasananda's authority has been increased by her obvious dedication to her work, and to the power (*shakti*) that her followers perceive to emanate from her.[7]

The Siddha Yoga movement has secondary ministers in other persons who have taken the vows of *sannyasa,* and who are known by the title swami (lord). The swamis provide important teaching, counseling, and administrative services to the movement. The position of swami is open to women, although the men seem to outnumber the women.[8]

Siddha Yoga is attractive to a wide variety of people in the professions, including women. At the South Fallsburg ashram during the summer of 1989, I encountered women who were in such diverse fields as writing, medicine, law, finance, chemical engineering, psychotherapy, education, and film. At many of the congregational functions of the ashram, women outnumber men by four (or more) to one. The prominent role of women in Siddha Yoga and the equality afforded to women in the movement can be directly related to the philosophy of Siddha Yoga, which to a great extent is derived from Kashmir Shaivism. Kashmir Shaivism is a Hindu Tantric philosophy that stresses the unity of a universal "masculine" principle of spirit and a creative "feminine" principle of energy, which gives rise to the world.

Siddha Yoga and the Status of Women

Siddha Yoga is able to draw on traditional Hindu concepts, which when combined with the growing Western conviction of the equality of women, tend to promote the religious leadership of women. In the Hindu tradition, as in the Christian, there is a strong tendency to blame the limitations of the human condition on women. Traditional Hindu language on this issue is carried over into Siddha Yoga since Siddha Yoga is not explicitly feminist. Although in Siddha Yoga, male God-language is most often used, the philosophy of Kashmir Shaivism de-emphasizes male divinity in such a way that it posits the equality of the female on the divine level as well as the human. This latter influence on Siddha Yoga tends to outweigh the continued use of old Hindu language that depicts women as the cause of human suffering.

The egalitarian philosophy of Kashmir Shaivism, when combined with modern expectations of equality, opens the way for women as well as men to pursue the ultimate goal. Thus, in Siddha Yoga, women who feel called to a life-style of renunciation have the option of becoming swamis just like the men. The swamis function as the ministers of the organization, with the guru being the chief of these. In Siddha Yoga, "ordination" in the sense of an elite group of religious specialists is opened to women.[9] Although Siddha Yoga has no explicit teachings on the proper social role of women, the egalitarian relationship of the divine masculine and feminine in its philosophy, as well as the presence of women as religious specialists, strongly implies an acceptance of women in roles not confined to the domestic sphere. This is affirmed in practice by the presence of so many women professionals in the movement.

Beginning in the foundational texts known as the Upanishads, the Hindu tradition has commonly regarded the material world as *maya*. Depending on the philosophical context, *maya* can be translated as "illusion," "magic power," or "God's creative power." Whether the material world is regarded as real or illusion, the designation "*maya*" always points to the impermanence of material reality and its power to confound. The impermanent nature of *maya* is the source of human suffering. Ignorant identification with the material realm is seen as the cause of entrapment in the continual round of rebirth. *Maya* is a feminine word, and throughout the Hindu tradition, women have been identified with the temptations of *maya*. Women and *maya* have been seen as one and the same, seductive temptresses, that cause the true Self (often referred to as masculine) to forget its (his) true nature.

Since the Siddha Yoga movement has faithfully transmitted to the United States many ideas and attitudes drawn from the diverse Hindu traditions, sometimes language equating women with maya, the source of human suffering, is used. When a swami was making an announcement concerning an upcoming course on Vedanta, he stated that the course would be about *maya,* and "how we are trapped in her, and how we can escape her." Even the guru reflects her Hindu upbringing by her occasional language in this area. In a talk on July 4, 1989, in South Fallsburg, she quoted unidentified saints as saying: "One should beware of three things: women, gold, and land. These things are fickle."[10] This Hindu tendency to identify women with material objects and their fleeting pleasures, however, is tempered and outweighed in Siddha Yoga by the teaching of the absolute equality and identity of the divine masculine and feminine.

In the Siddha Yoga movement, masculine God-language is most often used. God is usually referred to as "He" or "Lord." This is an accurate reflection of the Kashmir Shaivite philosophy in which God is Shiva.[11] Shiva is at once personal and the impersonal ground of the universe. Called Paramashiva (the highest Shiva) his nature is consciousness, and he is the "Self of All."[12] The masculine aspect of the divine, Shiva, denotes the mode of God that is permanent and unchanging, which is immanent in the material world.

> He is both transcendent and immanent, the totality of the bliss of Consciousness, the constant Knower. Paramashiva is self-luminous and is the root cause of the universe. Out of His own being, He manifests this universe full of multiplicity and countless forms, yet remains the embodiment of Consciousness. He is the foundation of the world. Although the manifold universe issues forth from Shiva, His true nature undergoes no change. It neither decreases nor increases. He is supremely pure.[13]

Kashmir Shaivism and Siddha Yoga use female imagery to refer to the creative mode of God. Shakti, a feminine word, which can be translated as "power," is personified as the various Hindu goddesses. While the masculine mode of God is passive and unchanging, the feminine mode is dynamic and creative. Parashakti (the highest shakti) is the power that creates the material world. Parashakti is *chiti* (consciousness) which has the nature of *prakasha* (light). Movement of *chiti* is a contraction of Shakti whereby consciousness is limited, producing the material world and the sense of individuality. *Samsara,* the round of rebirth with its concomitant suffering, then, is the "play of consciousness." All "this" is present simply as the sport or play of Shakti.[14] Swami Muktananda quoted a Kashmir Shaivite text as saying: "The entire world is the play of the Universal Consciousness. One who sees it in this way becomes liberated while in the body."[15] The importance of this key concept, that the world is the play of consciousness, is reflected in the Hindi title of Muktananda's spiritual autobiography, *Chitshakti Vilas,* "the play of the power of consciousness."[16] This is further reiterated in Chidvilasananda's name, which means "one who has the bliss of the play of consciousness."

Chit-shakti, the power of consciousness, is manifested in all things, and it is found in the human organism as the kundalini, "the serpent energy" that lies dormant at the base of the spine in the subtle body. The kundalini must be awakened so that the awareness of the universal play of consciousness may be achieved. The awakened kundalini is described as rising through a channel in the subtle body that roughly corresponds to the spine. As it rises, various chakras or energy centers are activated. When the kundalini reaches the chakra at the top of the head, Shakti is said to have joined with Shiva in the body, and the awareness of unity is achieved.[17]

Chanting of mantras is important in Siddha practice, because the vibration of *chiti* is described as manifesting first as *nada* (sound), which consists of the *matrikas* ("mothers" or deities) of the sounds of the Sanskrit alphabet. The alphabet gives rise to language, and language produces the universe of distinctions. In order to return to the perception of the primal unity, one must still the modifications of the mind. By repeating the mantra silently or by chanting outloud, one is using a thought to focus the mind and eliminate all other thoughts. Since the mantra consists of the names of God, and the sound vibration of God's name and God are seen as identical, the mantra is the perfect vehicle to carry the practitioner to the perception of unity.[18] Muktananda asserted that there is "no difference between the seeker, the mantra, and the deity of the mantra,"[19] so the mantra is considered a natural tool to lead one to the perception of unity.

In Siddha Yoga, the ultimate way that the activation of the kundalini is achieved is through *shaktipat,* the transmission of shakti to the devotee by the guru. The devotee must make strenuous effort to achieve the goal through chanting, meditation, and *seva,* but the ultimate realization will come through the guru's *kripa* (grace).[20] The Siddha Yoga congregational chanting sessions start out at a slow pace, build to a crescendo, and then slow to a pace that leads naturally to a period of quiet meditation. This would seem to generate an openness to the reception of *shaktipat*. Chanting and meditation in the guru's presence is considered to be especially efficacious, but is not necessary for the receipt of *shaktipat*.

The ultimate goal of the Siddha path is the ending of the perception of duality. In the monistic perception, the material world is divinized and affirmed. Love for all beings and things is the natural accompaniment of the awareness of unity. A person who gains this perception is aware that there is no difference between Shiva and Shakti.[21]

> According to Shaivism, the universe is the form of Shakti, the Supreme Principle. Shiva and Shakti are one; they are not separate. A yogi who attains *sahajavidya* [natural awareness] considers the universe to be the light of his own Self, like the light produced by a flame. The knowledge of one's own true nature (*aham*, "I") and the knowledge of the universe (*idam*, "this") merge into the all-pervasive unity. This is the understanding one should have. The knowledge of "I" is like a flame, and the knowledge of "this" is like its light, which spreads everywhere equally.[22]

So the primary tendency of Siddha Yoga is to value all of creation as the divine play of consciousness. Muktananda called the monistic perception the "awareness of equality."[23] In this awareness, all persons are seen as being the same Self, so there can be no discrimination.[24] *Sannyasins*, who lead lives of renunciation, hold a place of respect in Siddha Yoga, but the life-style of the person in the world is highly respected as well. If the world is the divine play of consciousness, there is no need to try to escape the material world. Indeed, in the United States, many of the Siddha Yoga devotees seem to be doing very well in the material world.[25]

The presence of female conceptions of God in Hinduism has not been enough to ensure equality for women in the Hindu tradition. The concepts of Shakti and the goddesses are ancient, and so are the sexist attitudes cited earlier. But given a social environment in which it is accepted that women have access to education and economic independence (work outside the home), a philosophy such as that provided in Siddha Yoga can prove very attractive to women who are active outside the home.

Siddha Yoga affirms that the divine feminine and masculine are one and the same, that women are competent to achieve the ultimate goal and serve as religious specialists. Thus Siddha Yoga is very attractive to American women in all walks of life. Anyone, female or male, can achieve the perception of unity. Siddha devotees explain that since the universal Self is without sex, and that since this Self is in everyone, it makes no difference whether the guru is female or male. Yet if the dynamic power of the universe is considered female, it seems especially appropriate that her wielder and channeller, the guru, is female.

The Power of Gurumayi Chidvilasananda

As early as the Upanishads, the indispensability of the guru in attaining the ultimate goal has been acknowledged in India. The guru is regarded as having the power to make the disciple like himself.[26] A strong love-bond has normally been the basis of the guru-student relationship. The student/ disciple should serve the guru wholeheartedly, and, in turn, the guru will bestow his grace upon the disciple. The grace that is received from the guru is seen as being the grace of God.[27] The disciple is encouraged to meditate either upon the guru or God, "for this purpose they are interchangeable."[28]

Siddha Yoga is in continuity with this Hindu emphasis on the overriding power of the guru, who is seen as being able to bestow *shaktipat*. A favorite Siddha hymn implores the guru (in translation):

> Light my lamp from your lamp, O Sadguru;
>   light my lamp from your lamp.
> Remove the darkness covering my heart;
> O Sadguru, light my lamp from your lamp.[29]

While the stress on intellectual comprehension (*jnana*) that is present in some guru lineages in India is not absent in Siddha Yoga, the primary stress is on absolute love (*bhakti*) for and surrender to the guru. This surrender is expressed in obedience to the guru's command, meditation, acts of worship, and the performing of all actions as service (*seva*) to the guru. All Siddha practice is centered on the guru, who is considered equivalent to God. The "Guru Gita," a text which should be chanted in Sanskrit every morning by a good Siddha practitioner, states:

> 76. The root of meditation is the Guru's form. The root of worship is the Guru's feet. The root of mantra is the Guru's word. The root of liberation is the Guru's grace.
> 77. Salutations to Shri Guru. The Guru is the beginning (of all, but) he is without a beginning. The Guru is the supreme deity. There is nothing higher than the Guru.[30]

Every Siddha Yoga congregational program includes testimonies from devotees about their experiences of the miraculous working of the guru's grace in their lives. From these testimonies, it is apparent that Gurumayi Chidvilasananda, as the current master in the Siddha lineage, is regarded as being at one with God, and, as such, she is believed to possess superhuman powers. Her every word and gesture, no matter how mundane, are fraught with significance for her devotees. Gurumayi is regarded as being in touch with the powers of nature, even to the extent of being able to control the weather.

Devotees attribute all sorts of miracles to their guru. Examples include the conception of a child, salvation from an armed thief, protection in the 1985 Mexico City earthquake,[31] and escape from severe car accidents. The primary miracle reported by devotees is the experience of being loved unconditionally. One person relates this experience as follows:

The Intensive started bringing up old and deep feelings of unworthiness. I cried all through the chant, and when I went up on the darshan line, tears were streaming down my face. Gurumayi turned to me with a smile, but when she saw my tears, her look changed to one of compassion. * Later, a hall monitor came over and said, "You are to come and sit beside Gurumayi for the final meditation." My heart soared. I couldn't believe that such grace was being bestowed on me. * I went to the front, and I sat beside her. I was nervous and excited, thinking, *This is it! I can't believe this!* The lights went down, and Gurumayi was holding out her hand, beckoning me toward her. It wasn't a long distance, so I crawled over to her. She took my hand in hers and looked into my eyes. She was chanting, and I wasn't sure what I was supposed to do, so I just chanted and looked at her, saying to myself, *I can't believe this.* * Then she reached over to a bowl of water, dipped her fingers in it and started gently stroking my face. My eyes were closed. She did it again. Then I felt a towel softly drying my face! She took white ash and rubbed it on my forehead, and I exploded inside. All my feelings of unworthiness were completely dissolved. There was so much love and compassion in what she did, and how she did it, that I knew that she loved me unconditionally, and also that most of all she wanted me to love myself.[32]

The presence of the goddesses in the Hindu tradition helps to legitimate the religious leadership of Gurumayi Chidvilasananda. In the past, the Hindu goddesses have often been subordinated to their husbands, the gods, or the strong goddesses have not translated into models of independence for women. But with the modern expectation that women are equal to men and are competent to achieve the religious goal, the goddesses become a factor supportive of the equality of women. In the South Fallsburg ashram, pictures of Lakshmi, goddess of wealth and good fortune, are prominently displayed. It does not seem to be accidental that this particular rendering of Lakshmi bears a strong resemblance to Gurumayi

Chidvilasananda. The temple at the South Fallsburg ashram dedicated to Muktananda's guru contains images of deities, of which the female out-number the male. These deities are: Lakshmi; the divine couple, Shiva and Parvati (Shakti); Saraswati, goddess of learning and the arts; and the elephant-headed male god, Ganesha. Siddha women often prefer to use the mantra that invokes two very powerful goddesses, Kali and Durga. One woman recounted that she used this mantra while running the Boston marathon and was rewarded with a vision of Gurumayi beckoning her to the finish line. Another woman related that while in Ganeshpuri, she enjoyed doing her hatha yoga postures near the statue of Kali. Although the presence of goddesses in the Hindu tradition is not in and of itself a sufficient factor to promote equality of women, the goddesses become a strong support for the equality of women when the patriarchal structures begin to loosen and women are acknowledged as being capable of achieving important goals outside the domestic sphere, including the religious goal.

A systematic study of the types of persons who are attracted to Siddha Yoga remains to be done.[33] My observations reveal that people are attracted to Siddha Yoga primarily for the experience that it offers. Siddha devotees are serious mystics, who are looking for the very deep meditative experiences, which are described as including visions, lights and sounds, and prophetic dreams. Many experience meditation for the first time when they encounter Siddha Yoga, but many were long-time spiritual seekers before coming to the Siddha guru. The intense inner experience that is believed to be generated by the guru is the main reason that Siddha devotees return to the guru's presence again and again. Siddha devotees also reveal themselves to be highly self-disciplined. Just partially keeping the ashram schedule[34] and bringing some of these practices into one's worldly life requires a great deal of self-discipline. Finally, of course, the Siddha devotee will be a devotional type of person, willing to abandon herself or himself to the power of the congregational chanting, and ultimately to surrender totally to the guru.

Siddha devotees seem to come from all age groups and walks of life, but with a strong tendency to be upwardly mobile. It does seem that Siddha Yoga is attractive to people from a Jewish or Roman Catholic background. One Jewish woman, a physician, said that she was interested in the Jewish mystical tradition but felt excluded from it due to Orthodox attitudes toward women. She felt the need to find an alternative ancient tradition, which she believed she had found in Hinduism. Roman Catho-lics coming to Siddha Yoga will find much that is familiar to them: the veneration of saints in images; the use of a rosary (*mala*) in repeating mantras; celibate ministers who wear distinctive (orange) robes; uplifting congregational singing; elaborate and beautiful worship and places of worship; and, finally, a strong authority figure, who is more accessible than the pope,[35] and who devotees believe is able to perform miracles in response to needs. The Catholic connection is emphasized by the presence of many Mexican Catholic devotees, who regard Gurumayi as the Virgin.

The feminist observer asks whether it is mature to submit so totally to patriarchal authority, even when it is being exercised by a woman. The Siddha devotee replies that surrender to the guru is really the surrender to one's highest Self, which is the universal Self.

The International Society for Krishna Consciousness

Another Hindu sect that is now international in scope and has a significant following in America is The International Society for Krishna Consciousness. It is a faith focused on the worship of the personal male God, Krishna, and it was brought to the U.S. by its elderly guru, A. C. Bhaktivedanta Swami Prabhupada (1896–1977), in 1965. When Bhaktivedanta first arrived, his attitudes toward women reflected his traditional background, but he quickly found that in the American context, modification of teachings concerning women was necessary.

The ISKCON faith is also a *bhakti* faith, but in this case, the devotion and surrender are directed toward Lord Krishna. The guru is an important figure in ISKCON, but he (now they) is significant to the extent to which he is an exemplary devotee. The guru is the "model, preceptor, and guide," leading one to complete devotion to Krishna. "One's immediate surrender is to the guru, and through him, to God."[36]

The faith of ISKCON is typical of much of the Hindu bhakti tradition in that God is seen as a male person to whom human souls relate as females. Thus, both male and female devotees cultivate an attitude of intense love, surrender, and obedience to Lord Krishna.[37] Despite the fact that *bhakti* has been a tradition that is more open to women's participation and it often consciously seeks to cultivate "feminine" modes of thought, Bhaktivedanta initially evinced typically Hindu sexist attitudes. While teaching that the soul is spirit and all are equal on the level of spirit, since human bodies are distinguished by sex, each has different roles. Reflecting the dictums of the Hindu law codes, he taught that women are "emotionally sensual creatures" who "need to be guarded from abuse by opportunistic males."[38] Thus it is inappropriate for women to exist independent from the control and protection of men.

The normal role for women in ISKCON is the traditional one of wife and mother. Girls and boys in the ISKCON *gurukulas* (schools) receive the same education until about eleven or twelve, when the girls are directed toward the homemaking arts and the boys continue to study the sacred texts.[39]

Many ISKCON women appreciate the security and respect given to the traditional female roles,[40] yet members of ISKCON note the challenge posed to this traditional scheme by the changing values of Western society. In response, it has been accepted that a woman may have a career outside the home if she chooses.[41] ISKCON women can serve the movement in a variety of capacities, including functioning as missionaries and ministering to the spiritual needs of ISKCON women and children. According to Kim Knott, birth into a female body is not seen as an indication of low spiritual evolution, and women are seen as being just as capable of salvation as men.[42] Yet in ISKCON, women do not become *sannyasins*. Women's renunciation is informal rather than formal. Women are not gurus, temple presidents, or members of the Governing Body Commission.[43] Kim Knott suggests that there is no philosophical barrier to women moving into these roles, but perhaps the strong focus on a male deity reinforces prohibition of women's access to authoritative positions in the ISKCON movement. A recent issue of the ISKCON magazine, *Back to Godhead,* contains thoughtful statements by devotee women on their roles in the movement.[44] If women begin to move into more prominent leadership positions, Krishna's consort, Radha, may prove to be a significant theological resource for them.

American Women Buddhists

In recent books, Lenore Friedman and Sandy Boucher[45] maintain that, in contrast to women in Siddha Yoga and ISKCON, American women who become Buddhists are more consciously feminist. They are acutely aware of the opportunities women have in Buddhism for personal growth, as well as the disabilities under which women have suffered and continue to suffer. American women have great respect for the Asian Buddhist men who have come to this country as teachers, but they conclude that sometimes Asian sexist forms are being imported along with the religious teachings. Therefore, these women see themselves as being in the vanguard of the creation of an egalitarian American Buddhism.[46]

The Buddhist scriptures recount that when Gautama Buddha first founded the monastic community, only men were admitted. Five years after he began preaching, a large group of women led by Mahaprajapati, the Buddha's aunt and foster mother, applied for admission. Mahaprajapati requested three times that women be admitted into the monastic community, and each time the Buddha refused. The Buddha overcame his reluctance only when the case of the women was taken up by his close male disciple, Ananda. The Buddha admitted to Ananda that women were capable of achieving the goal of nirvana (elimination of desire that ends suffering and rebirth). The Buddha stipulated that upon entering monastic life women must agree to follow eight special rules. The cumulative effect of these Chief Eight Rules was to subordinate Buddhist nuns to the monks. Nuns must seek ordination into the monastic life from monks; they must always be supervised by monks; they must never criticize a monk; and finally, a nun, no matter how senior, must always bow to a monk, no matter how junior. This story concludes with the Buddha stating that if women had not joined the monastic order, his teachings would have stood firm for one thousand years. Since women had been admitted, he predicted that the pure religion would only last for five hundred years.[47]

Despite the limitations imposed by the monastic rules, large numbers of women joined the Buddhist monastic order. Buddhism is significant in that the admission is present from its beginning that women are competent to achieve the religious goal. Buddhist monasticism offered an alternative life-style to the traditional roles of wife and mother.

Buddhist nuns, however, never received the same degree of support—emotional and financial—as the monks. The nuns' order in India experienced serious decline after the third century C.E., whereas the monks' order in India flourished until the twelfth century C.E.[48] Women who currently follow the monastic life-style in the Theravadin countries (Burma, Thailand, Cambodia, Laos, and Sri Lanka) do not have access to full ordination as nuns and are not considered full-fledged members of the Buddhist monastic order.[49] Before 1959, Tibetan women who wished to pursue the religious goal could follow a religious life-style as independent practitioners (yogini),[50] or live in a monastic setting as novices. Full ordination into the monastic order has not been available to Tibetan women due to the requirement that twelve fully ordained nuns be present at the ordination in addition to ten monks. Full ordination has not been available to Tibetan women because they lacked the requisite number of fully ordained nuns to give ordination. Beginning in 1984, a few Tibetan women (refugees in India) have begun to travel to Hong Kong to receive full ordination.[51] In Japan, nuns in the Zen, Tendai, Nichiren, Shingon, and Pure Land schools are not fully ordained. They preserve the celibate monastic life-style, while most Japanese "monks," or more accurately, priests, are married. There are also a number of women priests who are married.[52] Full ordination into the women's monastic order is available in Hong Kong, Taiwan, Korea, and Vietnam, and the nun's order is reviving in mainland China.[53]

While part of the Buddhist tradition has acknowledged that women are capable of achieving the religious goal, a significant portion of the tradition has viewed women as sexual temptresses who embody "the limitations of the human condition, which is a continual process of suffering and rebirth."[54] The story is told that in an attempt to prevent the Buddha's enlightenment, Mara, the ruler of the realm of desires, sent his three daughters, the personifications of Lust, Aversion, and Craving, to tempt the Buddha. Women were seen by some monks as a threat to their attempt to eliminate desire, and so were identified as being the source of evil and the cause of male bondage to *samsara*.[55] A common Buddhist attitude has been that birth into a female body is the result of bad karma.

American women who become Buddhists are aware of the negative aspects of the tradition for them, yet in Buddhism they find a variety of understandings of human nature and cosmology that they find meaningful. In the various Buddhist traditions, the male divine has been de-emphasized in a number of ways. In Theravada Buddhism, there is such an emphasis on impermanence that traditional concepts of God disappear. Due to impermanence, there can be no eternal ground of being nor a permanent human self. Mahayana Buddhism contains diverse teachings on these issues, and they can be understood in a variety of ways by Western women. One example is Roshi Jiyu Kennett, a British woman who has founded a monastery known as Shasta Abbey at Mount Shasta, California. Roshi Kennett has said that "we're part, if you like, of a great central ego. We all have a spark of the Eternal." She is convinced that issues concerning the equality of women are about the acknowledgment that women have souls. She asserts that no woman will be certain she is equal "until she knows with the certainty that I know, that her own Buddha-nature, or her own soul, exists."[56] Reflecting a common Hindu/Buddhist Tantric heritage, Tibetan or Vajrayana Buddhism is most like Siddha Yoga in its androgynous depictions of the divine. Whereas in Hindu Tantra, the female principle is dynamic and the male principle is static, in Tibetan Buddhism, Upaya (skill in means) is dynamic and male, and Prajna (wisdom or profound cognition) is female, static, and associated with emptiness (*shunyata*).[57] Prajnaparamita (the perfection of wisdom) is described as the wisdom that is the Mother of all the Buddhas. Prajnaparamita as the Mother of Creation is the primordial basic ground that is neither male nor female, but is regarded as feminine for its creative potentiality.[58] Tibetan Buddhism also contains a host of female deities known as *dakinis* (Tibetan *khadro,* "sky-goer"), who represent "the everchanging flow of energy with which the yogic practitioner must work in order to become realized."[59]

Thus, the varieties of American Buddhism de-emphasize male deity so that the role of female religious specialist becomes a possibility. American Buddhism marks the meeting point of recent Western conceptions of the equality of the sexes and ancient Buddhist egalitarianism. At this conjunction, it is assumed that women can have roles other than wife and mother, and the old Buddhist identification of women with the source of evil begins to fall away. As in Siddha Yoga, the ordained religious leadership begins to become inclusive of women.

American Buddhist women exercise religious leadership in many ways. Some are informal teachers in centers; some are legitimated by the full authority of their respective traditions. Some wear the robes that denote their position as religious leader, such as Roshi Kennett; Maurine Myoon Stuart Roshi of the Cambridge Buddhist Association; Venerable Karuna Dharma, nun in the Vietnamese tradition and head of the International Buddhist Meditation Center in Los Angeles; and Bhikshuni Pema Chodron, founder of the Gampo Abbey in Nova Scotia. Some Buddhist women are authoritative teachers who do not wear special robes, sit in a special seat, or require bowing or prostrations. Examples of these types of teachers are Toni Packer of Springwater Center, New York; Joko Beck of the Zen Center, San Diego; Yvonne Rand of Green Gulch Farm in Marin County; and Annick Mahieu (Sunanda) of the Insight Meditation Society in Barre, Massachusetts.[60] Whether robed or not, these women have grappled deeply with the issue of religious authority, and have concluded that a superhuman status should not be accorded to the teacher. Maurine Stuart, Roshi, says: "People have to realize that their *practice* is their teacher. As I've said, when you depend on a person for your practice, it's not true practice. This help from a teacher is fine, and we all need one another as helpers. Everybody's a teacher, *you're* my teacher. But to put one person on a pedestal is very dangerous."[61]

Boucher reports that this examination of the dangers of religious authoritarianism has been due to revelation of the sexual activities of a number of male Buddhist teachers in America (either married *roshis* or supposedly celibate monks).[62] As a result, many American Buddhist women have turned to women teachers to avoid exploitation. An issue for these women to consider is whether they can assume that there will never be a woman religious leader who exploits her followers.

Conclusion

This examination of Siddha Yoga, the International Society for Krishna Consciousness, and Buddhist groups in America indicates that a tempering of the male God-concept can assist in the validation of women in positions of religious leadership. The history of Hinduism and Buddhism demonstrates that androgynous, neuter, or female conceptions of the divine are not sufficient in and of themselves to promote equality for women. But once there is a social expectation of the equality of women, conceptions of the divine that de-emphasize the masculine prove attractive to women and support them in legitimating their presence in religious leadership roles. Whereas in a number of other marginal groups in America, female religious leadership is affirmed in such a way that the need for an ordained clergy is denied, Siddha Yoga and Buddhism in America suggest that given the two factors cited above, specialized religious positions begin to open for women. Thus, Siddha Yoga and Buddhism have proved attractive to women who are moving into the professions, whether or not they are consciously feminist. In Siddha Yoga and American Buddhism, it is assumed that women's roles are not limited to those of wife and mother. Hindu and Buddhist ideas concerning the identification of women with the fallenness of the human condition are being abandoned. Buddhist women are consciously confronting and rejecting those texts that blame women for the human condition. The Siddha organization has not yet directly dealt with this issue since it is not an explicitly feminist movement. Yet the pressure to drop these conceptions can be seen in the fact that Chidvilasananda prefaced her July 4, 1989, remark on the deluding qualities of women, gold, and land with profuse apologies and a warning that no one should take the statement personally.

It is interesting to note that in the imported Asian religion that is strongly focused on a male deity, the International Society for Krishna Consciousness, women are totally absent in higher leadership positions. Thus this survey of female religious leadership in religions imported into the U.S. may have implications concerning the reason for the continued exclusion of women from ministry in certain Western religions, and what theological changes can be expected in those groups that do include women in ministry.

The comparison of the Siddha Yoga case and Buddhist groups in America shows that the de-emphasis of the male divine can support the religious leadership of women in both authoritarian and antiauthoritarian modes.

NOTES

An earlier version of ths essay appeared in *Gender in World Religions* 2 (1991): 37–68. In the current essay, Sanskrit words that are names or that are well known in the English-speaking world are not italicized. Diacritical markes are omitted.

1. Gene R. Thursby, "Siddha Yoga: Swami Muktananda and the Seat of Power," in *When Prophets Die: The Postcharismatic Fate of New Religions,* ed. Timothy Miller (Albany: State University of New York Press, 1991).

2. Gene Thursby's article cited above is an excellent analysis of the issues

involved in the succession controversy. This chapter will limit its scope to Chidvilasananda's religious leadership and the factors within Siddha Yoga that help legitimate a woman as guru. For the events concerning the succession, see the June/July 1982 and Dec./Jan. 1983 issues of *Siddha Path,* a magazine that has been discontinued by Gurudev Siddha Peeth, Ganeshpuri, India. See the following articles about the demotion of Gurudev Nityananda: "What Was Two Is Now One; Siddha Yoga Co-Guru Steps Down," *Hinduism Today* 8 (Jan. 1986): 1, 19; "Muktananda's Successors Embroiled in Bitter Conflict," *Hinduism Today* 8 (May 1986): 1, 10–11.

   3. The foregoing doctrines are elucidated by Swami Muktananda in his book *Siddha Meditation: Commentaries on the Shivasutras and Other Sacred Texts,* 2d ed. (Ganeshpuri: Gurudev Siddhapeeth, 1982). See particularly pp. 30, 42–46, 48, 56, 90, 92–93, 102–3, 107, 110–11, 115–17.

   4. Katherine Young gives an excellent description of *stridharma* in her chapter "Hinduism," in *Women in World Religions,* ed. Arvind Sharma (Albany: State University of New York Press, 1987), 59–103. The Tenth Anniversary Issue (Nos. 50, 51, 52, 1989) of a feminist magazine published out of New Delhi, *Manushi,* is devoted to women *bhakti* saints. This collection of articles makes the interesting point that women saints have found that love of husband and love of God were not compatible. Their families usually saw their single-minded devotion to God as distracting them from the devotion that should have been directed to their husbands. Usually women saints have had to escape their family ties in some way. For them, the personal male God is their husband, and they can have no other husband. Conversely, male saints often have the support of their wives in their pursuit of the pious life.

   5. Ursula King, "The Effect of Social Change on Religious Self Understanding: Women Ascetics in Modern Hinduism," in *Changing South Asia: Religion and Society,* ed. Kenneth Ballhatchet and David Taylor (Hong Kong: Asian Research Service, 1984), 69–83.

   6. See the *Siddha Path* issues cited above.

   7. "Muktananda's Successors Embroiled in Bitter Conflict," 19.

   8. Exact statistics on the Siddha Yoga swamis were not forthcoming from the S.Y.D.A. Foundation. A very rough count of the swamis at the South Fallsburg ashram during the summer 1989 revealed ten men and five women. Gene Thursby reports that the organization has lost quite a few swamis because of the succession dispute. About six dozen swamis were initiated into the Saraswati order during the years when Muktananda was first bringing Siddha Yoga to the West. During the transition period after Muktananda's death, about one-half of the swamis left.

   9. When there is a need for Hindu rituals, traditional Brahman priests are employed, all of whom are Indian males with the requisite training and ritual purity.

   10. Ruth Vanita notes that Eknath and Tukaram, two Maharashtran male saints who have influenced the Siddha Yoga movement, were particularly emphatic that women be equated with maya and should be avoided since they arouse worldly

attachment. Ruth Vanita, "Three Women Sants of Maharashtra: Muktabai, Janabai, Bahinabai," *Manushi* 50, 51, 52 (Jan.-June 1989): 49.

11. The pan-Hindu character of Siddha Yoga is revealed by the fact that the most commonly chanted mantras include not only their primary mantra containing the name of the Lord Shiva but also mantras that recite the various names of Vishnu and Krishna. I have heard only one mantra that calls on the goddesses Kali and Durga.

12. Swami Muktananda, *Secrets of the Siddhas,* trans. Swami Chidvilasananda (South Fallsburg: S.Y.D.A. Foundation, 1980), 100.

13. Ibid., p. 101.

14. Muktananda, *Secrets of the Siddhas,* 10, 28, 59, 76, 79, 102-3, 131, 137, 154-56, 164, 166, 177-79, 183, 189, 198, 208; Swami Muktananda, *Siddha Meditation: Commentaries on the Shivasutras and Other Sacred Texts,* 2d ed. (Ganeshpuri: Gurudev Siddhapeeth, 1977), 62-67; Swami Muktananda, *Meditate* (Albany: State University of New York Press, 1980), 36; For an excellent scholarly examination of the history and texts of Kashmir Shaivism, see Mark S. G. Dyczkowski, *The Doctrine of Vibration: An Analysis of the Doctrines of Kashmir Shaivism,* (Albany: State University of New York Press, 1987).

15. Muktananda, *Secrets of the Siddhas,* 199.

16. Swami Muktananda, *Play of Consciousness,* (San Francisco: Harper and Row, 1978).

17. Muktananda, *Secrets of the Siddhas,* 9, 12-13, 180; Muktananda, *Siddha Meditation,* 77-79.

18. Muktananda, *Secrets of the Siddhas,* 75-76, 92, 103, 169, 194-96; Muktananda, *Siddha Meditation,* 42-44, 82-83.

19. Muktananda, *Secrets of the Siddhas,* 82.

20. Ibid., 13-15, 84, 176, 189; Muktananda, *Siddha Meditation,* 114.

21. Muktananda, *Secrets of the Siddhas,* 2, 38-39, 71, 75, 166, 181.

22. Ibid., 91.

23. Ibid., 39.

24. Muktananda, *Meditate,* 46.

25. Ibid., 6.

26. Masculine language is used here since the guru has normally been male in the Hindu tradition. See William Cenkner, *A Tradition of Teachers: Sankara and the Jagadgurus Today,* (Delhi: Motilal Banarsidass, 1983), 5-6, 38. In the Sanskrit language, which has masculine, feminine, and neuter nouns, there is no word that means "woman-guru." See Catherine Clementin-Ojha, "The Tradition of Female Gurus," *Manushi: A Journal About Women in Society* 31 (Nov.-Dec. 1985): 2-8.

27. Cenkner, *A Tradition of Teachers,* 10, 18-19, 27-28.

28. Ibid., 18.

29. "Jyota Se Jyota," in *The Nectar of Chanting,* 3d ed. (South Fallsburg, N.Y.: S.Y.D.A. Foundation, 1984), p. 65.

30. "Sri Guru Gita, Song of the Guru," in *The Nectar of Chanting,* 28.

31. *Transformation: On Tour with Gurumayi Chidvilasananda,* vol. 2 (N.p.: S.Y.D.A. Foundation, 1986), 2, 30, 41, 50, 74-75.

32. Ibid., 104–5.

33. A study of the personality types drawn to Siddha Yoga such as the one done by Tommy H. Poling and J. Frank Kenney using the Myers-Briggs Type Indicator with the Hare Krishnas would be most interesting. Siddha Yoga devotees display personality characteristics similar to, but not identical with, the sensate personality that is drawn to the Hare Krishnas. See Tommy H. Poling and J. Frank Kenney, *The Hare Krishna Character Type: A Study of the Sensate Personality,* (Lewiston, N.Y.: The Edwin Mellen Press, 1986).

34. The typical ashram schedule during the summer of 1989 is given below:

3:30–5:15 A.M.	Meditation.
5:15 A.M.	Tea.
5:45–7:15 A.M.	Chanting of "Guru Gita."
7:00–8:00 A.M.	Breakfast.
8:15–11:00 A.M.	*Seva.*
11:00–12:15	Chanting in the Temple.
12:00–12:30 P.M.	Noon chant (different location).
12:30–1:15 P.M.	Lunch.
2:00–4:00 P.M.	*Seva.*
5:30 P.M.	Evening Program, concluded by *darshan* (viewing of the guru). Dinner following *darshan.*
8:30 P.M.	Evening worship in the Temple.

35. Every program at which Gurumayi Chidvilasananda is present concludes with *darshan,* the "viewing or sight" of the guru. Gurumayi shows great stamina in being able to sit for extended periods of time while her devotees come before her and bow down. She bestows a blessing by brushing them with a wand of peacock feathers. This is when the devotees may take the opportunity to say a few words to their guru and perhaps ask a question.

36. "Interview with Larry D. Shinn," in *Hare Krishna, Hare Krishna: Five Distinguished Scholars on the Krishna Movement in the West,* ed. Steven J. Gelberg (New York: Grove Press, 1983), pp. 78–79.

37. Kim Knott, "Men and Women, or Devotees? Krishna Consciousness and the Role of Women," in *Women in the World's Religions, Past and Present,* ed. Ursula King (New York: Paragon House, 1987), 112, 116.

38. Larry Shinn, *The Dark Lord: Cult Images and the Hare Krishnas in America* (Philadelphia: The Westminster Press, 1987), 114.

39. Ibid., 115.

40. Rochford notes that ISKCON offers affirmation of traditional values during a time of disruption and confusion concerning gender roles in the West. Friendships in the Krishna women's community are an important factor in the conversion of women to ISKCON. See E. Burke Rochford, Jr., *Hare Krishna in America,* (New Brunswick, N.J.: Rutgers University Press, 1985), pp. 125–37.

41. Knott, "Men and Women, or Devotees," 119.

42. Ibid., 122. This assertion by Knott is contradicted by data gathered by Susan J. Palmer in Montreal, and reported in Palmer's article, "Moon Sisters,

Rajneesh Lovers, Krishna Mothers: Women's Roles in New Religious Movements,"
Gender in World Religions 1 (1990): 19–58. Palmer interviewed a woman named
Mother Patjabali who made remarks indicating that men are spiritually superior to
women and that birth into a male body is necessary for salvation. Mother
Patjabali's remarks reflected traditional Hindu conceptions of the importance of
the retention of semen for a man's spiritual development. Women's bodies,
lacking this substance, are not as fine instruments for Krishna Consciousness.
This casts light on why only celibate men, sannyasins, are found in positions of
higher leadership in ISKCON. Concerning the desirability of being reborn a man,
Mother Patjabali remarked: "If a man becomes too attached to his wife, or too
interested in women, he is in danger of coming back in the body of a woman.
Women are often men who were attached to women in their last life. It is the
opposite for a woman. The more attached she is to her husband, the more devoted
she is to him, the more likely she is to advance spiritually and be reborn a man"
(31).

43. Ibid., p. 125. See Knott's note 23 re *sannyasa*.

44. ISKCON Community Discussion, "The Role of Women Today in the
Hare Krsna Movement," *Back to Godhead* 25, no. 1 (Jan./Feb. 1991): 40–47.

45. Lenore Friedman, *Meetings with Remarkable Women: Buddhist Teachers in
America,* (Boston: Shambhala Publications, 1987); Sandy Boucher, *Turning the
Wheel: American Women Creating the New Buddhism,* (San Francisco: Harper and
Row, 1988). It is not accurate to say that all of these women are American in their
origins. Quite a few were born in Europe and now either live in the U.S. or have
close teaching ties with the U.S.

46. For instance, see Rita M. Gross, *Buddhism after Patriarchy: A Feminist
History, Analysis, and Reconstruction of Buddhism* (Albany: State University of
New York Press, 1993).

47. Friedman, *Meetings with Remarkable Women,* 7–10. See also the follow-
ing important discussions of women in Buddhism. Nancy Schuster Barnes,
"Buddhism," in *Women in World Religions,* ed. Arvind Sharma (Albany: State
University of New York Press, 1987); Nancy Auer Falk, "The Case of the Vanishing
Nuns: The Fruits of Ambivalence in Ancient Indian Buddhism," in *Unspoken
Worlds: Women's Religious Lives,* ed. Nancy Auer Falk and Rita M. Gross (Belmont,
Calif.: Wadsworth Publishing Company, 1989); Janice D. Willis, "Nuns and
Benefactresses: The Role of Women in the Development of Buddhism," in
Women, Religion, and Social Change, ed. Yvonne Yazbeck Haddad and Ellison
Banks Findly (Albany: State University of New York Press, 1985).

48. Falk, "The Case of the Vanishing Nuns," 155–57.

49. Karma Lekshe Tsomo, ed., *Sakyadhita: Daughters of the Buddha* (Ithaca,
N.Y.: Snow Lion Publications, 1988), 105–6, 239. Other relevant chapters in
Sakyadhita include Abaya Weerakoon, "Nuns of Sri Landa," 140–44; Chatsumarn
Kabilsingh, "Nuns of Thailand," 145–49; Daw Su Su Sein, "Nuns of Burma,"
109–11.

In Thailand, women wishing to live a monastic life-style wear white and are
known as *maejis*. They take vows but are considered laywomen. They have

extremely low social status and education. They must support themselves or receive support from their families. Some are allowed to live in the temples, where they are seen as nuisances by the monks. One woman who has received full ordination in Taiwan, the Venerable Voramai Kabilsingh, is attempting to introduce the nuns' order into Thailand. See Chatsumarn Kabilsingh, "The Future of the Bhikkhuni Samgha in Thailand," in *Speaking of Faith: Global Perspectives on Women, Religion and Social Change,* ed. Diana L. Eck and Devaki Jain (Philadelphia: New Society Publishers, 1987), 148–58.

50. Tsultrim Allione's book, *Women of Wisdom,* (New York: Arkana, 1986), describes the difficulty with which Tibetan women disentangled themselves from their duties as wives and mothers to become independent practitioners.

51. Karma Lekshe Tsomo, "Tibetan Nuns and Nunneries," in *Feminine Ground: Essays on Women and Tibet,* ed. Janice D. Willis (Ithaca, N.Y.: Snow Lion Publications, 1989), 120–21. The Tibetan tradition permits a minimum of six nuns and five monks for the ordination of a nun to take place, but apparently even that minimal number of nuns was not available. Needless to say, the presence of nuns is not required for the ordination of monks. See note 7 on p. 257 of *Sakyadhita.*

Karma Lekshe Tsomo is an American woman who is a fully ordained Tibetan nun who has lived with the Tibetan community in India. She was one of the organizers of the first International Conference on Buddhist Nuns in 1987 at Bodhgaya, India. See the film *In Search of a Holy Man* by Hartley Film Foundation. An American woman, Ane Pema Chodron, helped to lead the way in making full ordination available to women in the Tibetan tradition by making the trip to Hong Kong in 1980. See Friedman, *Meetings with Remarkable Women,* 21–22, 93–110. A new international organization, Sakyadhita (daughters of the Buddha), seeks to improve conditions for Buddhist nuns. For more information, one may write to: Sakyadhita, 400 Hobron Lane #2615, Honolulu, HI 96815.

52. Tsomo, *Sakyadhita,* 106. Other relevant chapters in *Sakyadhita* include Rev. Tessho Kondo, "Nuns of Japan, Part I," 124–26; Bhiksuni Karma Lekshe Tsomo, "Nuns of Japan: Part II," 127–30. In the Soto Zen sect, the celibate life-style of nuns contrasts with the married life-style of the priests. Yet the nuns have had to struggle to gain rights to higher education, to equal authority in the transmission lineages, and to become priests. See Kumiko Uchino, "The Status Elevation Process of Soto Sect Nuns in Modern Japan," in *Speaking of Faith.*

53. Tsomo, *Sakyadhita,* 106–7. Other relevant chapters in *Sakyadhita* include Hema Goonatilake, "Nuns of China: Part I—The Mainland," 112–18; Bhiksuni Shih Yung Kai, "Nuns in China: Part II—Taiwan," 119–23; Bhiksuni Karma Lekshe Tsomo, "Nuns in Korea," 131–37; Bhiksuni Dr. Karuna Dharma, "Nuns of Vietnam," 154–59.

54. Diana Y. Paul, *Women in Buddhism: Images of the Feminine in the Mahayana Tradition,* 2d ed. (Berkeley: University of California Press, 1985), p. 3.

55. Ibid., 3–59; Nancy Falk, "An Image of Woman in Old Buddhist Literature: The Daughters of Mara," in *Women and Religion: Papers of the Working Group on*

Women and Religion 1972-73, ed. Judith Plaskow and Joan Arnold Romero (Missoula, Montana: Scholars Press, 1974), 105-12.

56. Friedman, *Meetings with Remarkable Women,* 170, 174.

57. Allione, *Women of Wisdom,* 10.

58. Ibid., pp. 21-24. See also Joanna Rodgers Macy, "Perfection of Wisdom: Mother of All Buddhas," in *Beyond Androcentrism: New Essays on Women and Religion,* ed. Rita M. Gross (Missoula, Mont.: Scholars Press, 1977), pp. 315-33.

59. Allione, *Women of Wisdom,* 25.

60. Friedman, *Meetings with Remarkable Women,* 39-133, 161-91, 193-211, 249-53; Boucher, *Turning the Wheel,* 93-99, 133-44, 151-61, 194-202.

61. Boucher, *Turning the Wheel,* 201.

62. Boucher makes the important point that secrecy in an attempt to cover up a teacher's improprieties is an expression of and perpetuates the patriarchal system. Boucher, *Turning the Wheel,* 24, 213, 225. The Buddhist improprieties are similar to the situation with the Siddha gurus. In the case of Gurudev Nityananda, he was removed from his position as guru. Similar accusations have been made in connection with Swami Muktananda, which have not been addressed. See William Rodarmor, "The Secret Life of Swami Muktananda," *Co-Evolution Quarterly* 40 (Winter 1983): 104-11.

Part 3

Contemporary Women as Creators
of Religion

Ritual Validations of Clergywomen's Authority in the African American Spiritual Churches of New Orleans

David C. Estes

One Spiritual minister in New Orleans who grew up Catholic recalls being warned as a young woman that Spiritual churches were associated with Marie Laveau, the city's legendary nineteenth-century "voodoo queen": "All I heard is don't go there. Don't get into this. They will hurt you. They will misuse you. They will trample you. And I was afraid."[1] Such warnings, with their oblique references to witchcraft, reflect the general attitude of African Americans in New Orleans toward Spiritual churches, which attract only 5 percent of the church-going black population.[2] Members are often ostracized by family and friends because of stories about occult practices that circulate by word of mouth. Negative attitudes toward women's religious leadership also inhibit membership. As one female bishop summed up the practical effects of sexism, "You're not gonna find too many men following a woman pastor." Yet many women brought up in mainline denominations decide to endure what some consider the stigma of being Spiritual for just such an opportunity. The minister quoted above, who disregarded the warnings of her family and finally became an ordained leader, recalled her first visit to a Spiritual church: "I was happy to see the women wearing the beautiful robes. . . . And I liked the way they could talk. And I didn't know a woman could do all that. I was amazed."

The negative stereotyping of African American Spiritualism exists not only in the communities where churches are located but among academics as well. Joseph Washington, Jr., for example, has called it "a business venture . . . which seeks through fears of bad luck a profit in selling good luck."[3] Yet as Hans Baer has responded in *The Black Spiritual Movement,* scholars who emphasize such generalizations distort the more complex reality. He considers its origination in the first decades of this century to be "a response to the shifting status of Blacks in American society."[4]

Spiritual churches opened first in northern cities to meet the religious needs of the many blacks emigrating from their rural southern homes. The movement expanded rapidly in the 1930s, with Chicago, Detroit, Kansas City, New York, and New Orleans becoming the centers of activity. However, New Orleans has been more influential than the others "in determining its present content," and Baer calls that city "the Mecca of the Spiritual movement."[5] Both the predominance of Roman Catholicism and the historical practice of voodoo there intensified the two characteristics that distinguish Spiritualism from other African American religious groups: its highly syncretic nature and "the emphasis on the manipulation of one's present condition through magico-religious rituals and esoteric knowledge."[6]

Women have been prominent leaders in the Spiritual churches in New Orleans from the beginning. Mother Leafy Anderson was the first person to organize a congregation in that city, after migrating around 1920 from Chicago, where she had previously established a church in 1913. Followers who led prominent congregations after her death in 1927 included Catherine Seals, Maude Shannon, and Dora Tyson, all of whom used the title mother. The list of Spiritual congregations compiled by Andrew Kaslow and Claude Jacobs indicates that there have been at least 175 in New Orleans over the years, and even though the names of pastors are incomplete or missing for 20, women led at least 60 percent of the total.[7] According to Kaslow and Jacobs, "in the first decade and a half of the churches' existence, the Spiritual religion had been almost exclusively a women's movement under women's leadership."[8] The successes of women "as individuals" did not, however, create a unified Spiritual denomination in New Orleans: "The churches as a movement remained fragmented" until "male leaders emerged" in the mid–1930s.[9] Nevertheless, women have continued to outnumber male leaders throughout the group's history. Today women are in charge of well over half of the approximately fifty active Spiritual congregations, and except in a few cases, their assistants—who are also ordained and have such titles as evangelist, minister, or bishop—have far more women than men among their ranks.

At the congregational level, then, the pattern of leadership in New Orleans differs from the national norm, as observed by Baer, that "in almost any given Spiritual temple, more of the desirable offices are occupied by males than by females."[10] Yet in another sense, his observation about gender discrimination does apply to New Orleans. The mother churches of the two national Spiritual associations headquartered there are both pastored by men. One of these bodies will not consecrate women to the office of bishop. Furthermore, the church buildings throughout the city that women occupy tend to be smaller and less expensive, all except a handful of them being simply prayer rooms established within a home. Some women leaders openly acknowledge that black Baptists are not the only ones who discriminate against them. A woman bishop said, "We have people right in our denomination that don't care nothing about women preachers. . . . A lot of the male ministers would rather you don't come in their pulpit."

Despite tensions resulting from differing ideas about the relationship between gender and leadership roles, the Spiritual church in New Orleans today perpetuates its tradition of revered African American clergywomen. Given the discrimination that they encounter from both inside and outside their church, it should not be surprising that these women validate their status as ordained ministers, in part, by emphasizing that they are carrying on the work of their spiritual foremothers. Particularly important are their stories about events in Mother Anderson's life and her continuing intervention in affairs on their behalf. Annual memorial services honoring her are formal, public contexts not only for reciting such narratives but also for invoking her spirit. Ritual feasts honoring Esther of the Old Testament are another highly symbolic way of confirming leadership roles for women. Esther's spirit, like Mother Anderson's, enters during the service to offer guidance and power in carrying out such duties. Finally, a ritual ordination publicly confers status on each woman who answers the call to ministry. Through this ceremony, she receives the title appropriate to her station, from co-worker up to archbishop. For many women, the title is important in winning respect for their work because it means they have the official recognition of the institutional church.

Preceding a discussion of rituals at these three traditional worship services that validate the authority of Spiritual clergywomen, it is helpful to look briefly at the syncretic roots of this church, noting particularly women's leadership status in several of the religious traditions that have shaped its beliefs, rituals, and organizational structures. The extreme importance of a hierarchical ordained clergy in the Spiritual tradition contradicts Mary Farrell Bednarowski's conclusion that in marginal groups the denial of traditional ordination has been necessary for the presence of female leaders.[11] The reasons for this discrepancy become clearer when one examines the eclecticism of African American Spiritualism. It has incorporated elements from Roman Catholicism; black Protestantism's wide variety of Baptist, Methodist, Holiness, and Pentecostal groups; nineteenth-century American Spiritualism; and African Caribbean religions, principally Haitian Vodoun.[12]

Spiritual people are aware that their worship services combine practices found in several different traditions and are comfortable with this fact. Bishop Inez Adams, who founded Queen Esther Divine Spiritual Temple of Christ in 1957, says that "we have a combination of Catholic, Baptist, and Spiritual. We honor the saints the way Catholics do. We dance. I've been to many Sanctified churches. They dance." Despite denominational differences, all believers are traveling to the same heavenly home, she asserts.

New Orleans has the highest proportion of black Catholics of any city in the country. Thus it is not surprising that the Spiritual churches there have been influenced by Catholicism more strongly than elsewhere. The titles and formal vestments of both men and women are similar to those used by Catholic clergymen. Also highly visible are elaborate, tiered altars with votive candles and statues of various saints, as well as the use of holy water and incense. When novena services are held for a particular saint, Catholic prayer cards may be distributed to worshipers. One church customarily concludes the Sunday morning service with all kneeling to say the rosary in unison. Although Spiritual churches arose in Chicago, New York, and Detroit around the time of the growing migration of blacks from the South, it was not until Mother Anderson introduced them to New Orleans that the elements of Catholicism became incorporated in the movement.

The typical structure of a Sunday service reflects the influence of traditional Afro-Baptist worship in both structure and style. Following the opening devotional period of altar prayers and a Scripture reading, come testimonies and then a chanted sermon, whose style reflects that of folk preachers dating back to antebellum times. Spiritual congregations share a musical tradition with other black Protestants. They sing the same jubilees and spirituals, whether solo or accompanied by musicians on electric organ, piano, guitar, and drums. The audience likewise responds vocally and physically to all that is said by the various speakers, following the call-and-response pattern of black folk culture. Frequently, they will shout or become possessed by the spirit and have to be attended by women designated as ushers or nurses. Although African American Spiritualism developed in urban centers, it maintains the folk traditions characterizing the rural southern churches from which many of its members have come.

Spirit possession characterizes black and white Holiness and Pentecostal churches. With roots in the enthusiastic style of worship predominant at frontier camp meetings, twentieth-century Pentecostals believe that speaking in tongues is evidence of one's possession by the Holy Ghost. Spiritual believers similarly tarry for the gifts of the Spirit, among which they include speaking in tongues and the interpretation of tongues. The Spiritual creed recited responsively in some congregations includes a pledge to avoid drinking alcohol and to adopt the kind of puritanical life-style typical of Holiness groups. As Baer points out, some churches through-out the country do enforce a code of behavior that separates their mem-bers from the "ways of the world." However, Spiritual churches across the country tend to take a flexible stand on such issues as drinking, dancing, premarital sex, and homosexuality, a generalization that holds true in New Orleans.[13]

Unlike the religious traditions discussed so far, both American Spiritual-ism and African Caribbean religions grant women equal leadership status with men. Yet African American Spiritual people generally deny the influences that these beliefs and practices have had on their church. Baer sees the rejection of these roots as motivated by a desire for respectability.[14]

Even though the church originally called itself "Spiritualist," the pre-ferred title among members has become "Spiritual." In testimonies, believers occasionally condemn the Yellow Pages for using the older term, which has the negative connotation of fortunetelling. Mother Anderson would certainly have disagreed with the current preference. According to a 1927 newspaper account, a white Spiritualist from Lily Dale, New York, a center for American Spiritualism, attracted a crowd when he spoke at her church, The Eternal Life Christian Spiritualist Church.[15] Spiritualism may have shaped the African American Spiritual view of God as spirit, thereby reinforcing similar ideas retained from African religions. "The Spiritualist God," according to Bednarowski, "was neither mother nor father, but Spirit, an impersonal entity."[16] One of the most frequently quoted Bible passages in these churches in New Orleans expresses the same concept: "God is a spirit, and they that worship him must worship him in spirit and in truth" (John 4:24). Spiritualists denied the image of God as a judge who expects humans to strive for perfection and likewise disputed the doctrine of the Fall. Thus they avoided an emphasis on Eve as a figure of sin and also the necessity for redemption through God's incarnation in Jesus. Mother Anderson may have fully accepted both of these implications of viewing God as a spirit. According to anthropologist Zora Neale Hurston, who researched hoodoo in New Orleans shortly after Mother Anderson's death in 1927, her members were "not allowed to call the name of Jesus . . . [because] Jesus as a man was not important—he was merely the earthly body of a nameless 'Spirit' by which name the deity is always addressed."[17] This prohibition no longer exists. Spiritual people in New Orleans frequently refer to Jesus as a personal savior in much the way that charismatic Christians and television evangelists do. So while believers proclaim God is spirit, in testimonies and sermons they simultaneously use traditional language gendering God as male. This ambivalence is only one instance of the inconsistencies attributable to the high degree of syncretism in Spiritual belief and practice. Yet even without thoroughly supplanting male images of the divine, the emphasis on God as spirit may, indeed, have contributed to making a place for African American women religious leaders during the early years of the church's development, just as Bednarowski has suggested this notion did in American Spiritualism.

Spiritualists believed in the power of mediums to communicate with spirits on behalf of the living. During the last half of the nineteenth century some of the best-known mediums were women. As Alex Owen has argued, Spiritualism was a democratic movement that offered "possibilities for attention, opportunity, and status denied elsewhere" because it "firmly held that any individual, male or female, rich or poor, could become the conduit for a dialogue with the spirits."[18] It is understandable, then, that Mother Anderson was accepted by others in this movement and that it, in turn, influenced her views and practices. For example, American Indians were popular intermediaries between the mediums and the spirits they wished to reach. Mother Anderson, likewise, was knowledgeable about the power of these spirit guides and relied on them. An announcement of a "spirit cantata" entitled "A White Man's Sin and a Squaw's Revenge" to be performed at her church in 1927 notes: "The powerful Indian guide takes control of Mrs. Leafy Anderson, as Indian squaw."[19] She had several spirit guides, but the principal one was an Indian, Black Hawk, who has come to be recognized among believers in New Orleans as the strongest of the spirit forces.[20]

Even though seances are rarely conducted these days in Spiritual churches in that city,[21] spirits do frequently appear to leaders and worshipers during services, bringing messages or prophecies that they, in turn, repeat to the appropriate individuals in the congregation. Some churches regularly hold "bless" services for healing and prophecy. Near the end of the service, ministers spontaneously deliver a message to all who come forward, or they walk out into the congregation to speak to individual worshipers as directed by the spirit. When spirits are invoked, the lights are commonly dimmed or turned completely off, and the congregation sings. Usually, only "spirit" is acknowledged as being present, but at other times the spirit of a particular saint or deceased local Spiritual believer enters and is identified by name. Messages from the spirits often state a problem the person has encountered. Sometimes they predict an event, usually one that will be favorable, but occasionally they name a misfortune, including even death. A message typically contains an injunction to perform a series of ritual actions at a certain time or place. Generally, candles, water, prayers, or Bible passages are employed to effect the appropriate outcome.

Contact with spirits occurs outside of public worship, as well. Ministers have private "clients," many of them not Spiritual, who come seeking advice or healing, which occur also under the direction of the spirit. Even though the word "medium" is not used in these churches, parallels to Spiritualist mediumship are apparent. By offering women the opportunity to speak publicly with authority, both movements have allowed them to rise to a status denied in mainstream Christianity.

Despite the prominence women achieved in Spiritualist circles in the decades immediately preceding the establishment of African American Spiritualism, the historical connection of these churches with African Caribbean religions was probably far more influential in establishing acceptance of institutional leadership status for women in New Orleans. Two waves of immigration to the New Orleans area from Haiti are important. In the years following the revolution of 1791, some planters relocated there directly from Haiti. Later, in 1809, others who had settled in Cuba followed when they were expelled upon Napoleon's naming his older brother as king of Spain. The slaves of these planters brought with them the beliefs and practices of Vodoun, which have had a marked influence on African American religious culture in New Orleans.[22] Historical links notwithstanding, because of widespread fear and misunderstanding of hoodoo, Spiritual ministers continually disavow their own association with it, calling it the devil's work. Yet they frequently condemn other leaders for practicing hoodoo and accuse them of discrediting the Spiritual church by trying to "mix oil and water," as one woman has said.

Spiritual ministers are correct in denying ties to hoodoo since they have in mind only the popular concept of it as sorcery or witchcraft. On the other hand, as the folk religion of Haiti, Vodoun is more complex than that. There is a pantheon of gods (loa), a priesthood with knowledge of the secrets for divination and healing, and a system of rituals for honoring and requesting the assistance of the loa and spirits of the deceased. Caribbean Vodoun reflects the process of creolization in its combination of Catholicism with African religions. For example, the deities from various tribes have counterparts among the Catholic saints. African elements in the ceremonies include ritual drumming, singing, and dancing as well as possession. Borrowings from Catholicism include altars, candles, and prayers. Similar creolization occurred elsewhere in the New World where the religion of the colonial masters was Catholicism, producing santería in Cuba, candomblé and macumba in Brazil, and shango in Trinidad.

Blacks in New Orleans, including Spiritual people in this century, have undoubtedly incorporated elements of Catholicism directly into their religious folk life just as happened elsewhere. However, the historical influence of syncretic religions from the Caribbean complicates the heritage of African American Spiritualism in New Orleans. During the years under the colonial rule of France and Spain, New Orleans had political, economic, and cultural ties with the Caribbean. The effects persist to this day in its African American folk traditions, which differ in many ways from those in the rest of the South. In the twentieth century, Spiritual churches have institutionalized some of the syncretic worship, divination, and healing practices introduced by Caribbean slaves and passed down as popular or folk religion.

The initiation of women into leadership roles is customary in all African Caribbean religions,[23] and it was continued by slaves shipped to New Orleans. From the 1830s to the 1880s, the two Marie Laveaus, mother and daughter, became the most renowned priestesses there. Although hoodoo in America is no longer the highly developed worship cult found in Haiti, its continuing influence in New Orleans goes beyond the magic with which it is generally associated. Its practice there during the eighteenth and nineteenth centuries firmly established the tradition of ritually initiating women possessing spiritual powers to serve as religious leaders. Thus, although Mother Anderson would have found her contemporaries fearful of hoodoo, her status as ordained clergywoman was in line with a long-standing folk religious custom among blacks there.

The preceding overview of religious traditions syncretized in the Spiritual churches suggests an important point not previously emphasized by scholars: female leadership in this twentieth-century movement continues a practice dominant in its eclectic heritage. Nevertheless, cultural history does not reveal how Spiritual women today go about affirming their status in response to challenges on the basis of gender from inside and outside the church. As one might expect, they readily explain that their roles are confirmed by Biblical authority and cite passages on which clergywomen in a wide spectrum of denominations similarly rely in making a theological defense of their position as ministers. Spiritual ministers do not, however, point to precedents of female leadership in the non-Christian roots of their church. Because of the predominant negative stereotype of hoodoo, acknowledging any indebtedness to the family of African Caribbean religions would not enhance pride in either their gender or ethnicity. Yet Spiritual women are not without a sense of history, and in traditional ways, they recollect and celebrate historical women as one important means of validating their own positions. Various worship rituals provide mutual confirmation and renewed determination. At the three kinds of services mentioned above, female leaders remind themselves of spiritual ancestresses, affirm their own divine calling into ministry, and publicly receive the sanction of both the spirit as well as the institutional church.

The first of these public worship rituals is the memorial service for

Mother Anderson, which Bishop Inez Adams sponsors annually on the anniversary of her death, 12 December. In some years, it is in conjunction with regular Sunday worship; in others, it is a series of special services up to four evenings in a row. She places Mother Anderson's picture, surrounded by white flowers and candles, on a table in front of the main altar. A Bible on the table is open to one of her favorite chapters, John 14, which begins "Let not your heart be troubled." This memorial service is an occasion for recounting important incidents in her life and sometimes for welcoming her spirit's return. Mother Anderson's last words were "I am going away but I shall come back and you shall know that I am here."[24] Hurston reported that in the late 1920s at Mother Anderson's church "on Monday nights there is a meeting presided over by a woman, which the spirit of Mother Anderson (now dead) attends."[25] Although less frequent now, ceremonial gatherings in the founder's memory continue to reflect the syncretism of American Spiritualist and African ideas about the spirits of the dead, which Hurston noted. Aware that some might think such a service inappropriate within a Christian church, Bishop Adams instructed those present in 1988: "We not worshiping her. We just thank the Lord for she came here and taught us the way. She is a good teacher, and I declare if you want to learn, you seek God, that spirit will help you." Yet testimonies by others emphasize Mother Anderson's "doing" rather than "teaching" because they narrate her active interest in the crises in their lives. In keeping alive the memory of Mother Anderson, the services at Bishop Adams's church do more than offer a lesson in church history; they introduce worshipers to a female spirit on whose power they may confidently call for assistance.

A folk biography of Mother Anderson can be constructed from the stories related in testimonies and sermons at these annual events, as well as from time to time at regular worship services. Newspaper accounts of her death at the age of forty in 1927 report that she was born in Balboa, Wisconsin, and came to New Orleans from Chicago.[26] Oral tradition, however, does not always agree. "She came from Norfolk, Virginia," a female bishop said at one memorial service. "And they tell me she didn't come in a car. She didn't come in a train. She didn't come by plane. She walked from Virginia all the way down to New Orleans, Louisiana, carrying, spreading the Word, being a missionary for the Lord." Another leader says that one of her parents was black and the other was a Mohawk Indian.[27] Stories emphasize her battles against racial, sexual, and religious discrimination in New Orleans. According to Bishop Adams at one memorial service, the charges are the same that she herself and other leaders must face: "Children, she came here and suffered for us, and all they did, they called her everything. Called her Beelzebub. They say she was a man disguised as a woman. She was a hoodoo. She was two heads [a conjuror]. Oh bless God, children. They be saying all that about you. They say it about me." In an interview conducted during the late 1930s, one of Mother Anderson's associates and Bishop Adams's own leader, Mother Dora Tyson, contradicted rumors associating the founder with transvestism: "Taint true all de things ya hear er bout Mother Anderson. She was as much woman as I is. . . . Ise know case I nursed her when she was sick. She had a breast lak mine. . . . In de street she wore deep neck dresses to let people see her brest."[28]

Alongside stories about Mother Anderson's suffering from unjust accusations are other accounts of her fearless defiance in contrast to the timidity of others. At one service a male bishop explained that before her arrival, Spiritual people "had their little churches. They was hiding them all in little rooms, and going through the back doors. And all this time no one wanted to step out bold, standing up for what we believe in. Martin Luther King say if you don't believe in something to die for it, then you don't believe in it. See, this was a bold woman in God. She wanted to make the world know what God was doing for her." Here Mother Anderson is depicted as a liberator of her people. On account of her courageous acts, they no longer needed to worship secretly, fearful of religious persecution. They could come out into the open and take the name Spiritual.

How Mother Anderson accomplished this transformation is the subject of the most frequently told story: her arrest and subsequent release from jail after her prophecy to the magistrate proves accurate. The most commonly stated reason for the arrest is that she lacked a permit for leading her barefoot people in an outdoor march with lighted candles. According to some, she was guilty of preaching on the street. Bishop Adams was told that

> while she was in jail, she had a prayer service in the jail, and the walls cracked. When they brought her before the judge, she prophesied to the judge about his invalid child he had at home, and he had them to check on his child. The child was sick. And when they checked on the child, it was true that the child had run into some kind of seizure or something. She told him so many true things about the child, that's how he could turn her loose, made them turn her loose and told them don't arrest her no more.

Although details of the legend vary from one person to another, it always ends with the same point: the grateful judge made it possible for Mother Anderson to obtain a state ministerial license, thus establishing the precedent so that all women may obtain this important certificate upon ordinaation. This document legitimizes leaders and their churches in the eyes of the law, thus protecting them from the harassment and oppression Mother Anderson endured in establishing her ministry. In remarks delivered on 19 March 1992 at an annual feast honoring St. Joseph, the sponsoring minister pointedly reminded her congregation that Mother Anderson's prophecy is the source of their freedom to worship without fear of interference from civil authorities: "So many people wondered why Mother Anderson was a woman that she could prophesy to the judge as she did. She prophesied to the judge. She said, you trying to worry about me. She said, but pick up that phone and call home and you'll find that your son is dying. He picked up that phone, called home, and his son was dying. And sure enough from that day they left Spiritual religion alone." According to such traditional oral accounts as these, Mother Anderson's clairvoyance and her timely warning about the child in danger won official recognition of her leadership status. Taken out of context, however, the legend might imply that she had used or had threatened to use witchcraft to endanger the child, thereby intimidating the fearful judge and father. Yet such a reading would contradict the tellers' emphasis on Mother Anderson's exemplary compassion and his gratitude to her.

The Spiritual believers who know this legend see it not only as a woman's successful battle for legal status in the community as a religious leader. They also understand the dramatic courtroom confrontation to be a protest against racial discrimination. The male bishop quoted above conveyed this idea by alluding to Martin Luther King when he described Mother Anderson's boldness. At one service Bishop Adams underscored the racial barriers the founder overcame in her legendary encounter with the judge: "[Mother Anderson] came into this land—this terror-ridden and segregated land—and stood up in the courthouse and prophesied to the Caucasian judge. When Negroes were saying, Guess what? Get ready. Oh praise God! She came in and told him." By retelling the events of Mother Anderson's life, women not only respectfully perpetuate her memory but also challenge themselves to follow in her footsteps by protesting racial, sexual, and religious discrimination.

During memorial services, worshipers occasionally speak about times when Mother Anderson's spirit has assisted them. Their remarks suggest, however, that stories of her life encourage two contradictory modes of behavior. At the same time narrators moralize about boldly protesting against injustice, the narratives themselves invite believers to rely on her spiritual intervention in situations they lack the power to influence. Among these are court cases, in which Mother Anderson's spirit is supposed to specialize. One woman stood at a service to testify that during a friend's trial she walked up and down the block four times, praying and asking the Lord to back up the spirit of Mother Anderson. The man was set free, and she came to the service to thank the deceased leader for intervening. Other times Mother Anderson's spirit acts on behalf of people needing strength to carry them through crises. One woman saw Mother Anderson's spirit in church while she was pregnant with her first child and took a picture of the founder with her into the delivery room. Although her mother, a minister, could not see the spirit, she felt "vibrations" when her daughter talked about the experience, thus validating belief in Mother Anderson's abiding power on behalf of believers.

The memorial service Bishop Adams conducts concludes with the ritual lighting of seven-day candles beside the founder's picture displayed on the special altar. Worshipers file to the front, place their donation in a basket, and then light a tall candle. One year Bishop Adams directly linked herself to the woman being honored by explaining that she had put a candle on the altar for her own leader Mother Tyson, who "came from under" Mother Anderson. Thus the altar with its burning candles can symbolize not only the direct bond each worshiper feels with this respected leader but also the particular heritage of female leadership from which Bishop Adams derives spiritual strength. As congregational singing continues, the spirit of Mother Anderson, or of other deceased male and female leaders, sometimes appears to the robed ministers with messages for those in the assembly about their problems and instructions for rituals they should perform privately for assistance. Contributing to the shared, intimate feeling of Mother Anderson's presence, which worshipers have come hoping to find, is their quiet singing of "In the Spirit World," repeating over and over the single line of lyrics in each stanza: "She's in the spirit world," "We're gonna meet up again," and "Mother Anderson's here."

Ritual feasts, distinguished by elaborate temporary altars displaying a variety of foods, are a second traditional type of service at which female spiritual power is honored. Feasts for the Virgin Mary and Esther are structured similarly to others in the annual cycle for such popular saints as Anthony, Joseph, and Michael and for Mother Anderson's own spirit guide Black Hawk.[29] Worshipers attend out of devotion to the spirit or in hope of a particular blessing. Near the end of the service, following testimonies about the saint's assistance and remarks by visiting clergy, they file up to the altar and deposit a donation in exchange for blessed candles, incense, oils, and other items to be incorporated into their devotional rituals at home. At the conclusion of the service, ushers put the cookies, candy, apples, oranges, bananas, lemons, and other fruits displayed on the altar into small bags and distribute them to each person seated in the congregation. Other helpers take the cakes to the kitchen where they are sliced and put onto styrofoam plates along with a meal that is often fried chicken or fish, baked macaroni, potato salad, and peas.

Kay Turner and Suzanne Seriff's analysis of the traditional food altars Sicilian-American women erect to St. Joseph provides insights applicable to these altars in Spiritual churches, which are similarly prepared almost exclusively by women. Paying particular attention to the symbolic display and gift of food, Turner and Seriff argue that the altars are ritual enactments of "the reproductive labor" of women: "At the heart of this labor is the supreme gift of all womankind: the gift of life."[30] At feasts dedicated to female spirits, then, such altars of spectacular abundance appropriately symbolize female spiritual power, which is at the core of the celebration.

Although several churches sponsor a feast for the Blessed Mother, Bishop Adams is currently the only leader holding one for Queen Esther, after whom her church is named. The celebration draws many Spiritual leaders and members from throughout the city, who fill the building. Esther, one of Mother Anderson's spirit guides, is a symbol "of protest and empowerment" for female Spiritual ministers in New Orleans,[31] and many women consider this feast to be a significant ritual for affirming their own status in the church. Esther was the beautiful virgin whom the Persian king Ahasuerus selected to replace his unsubmissive wife, Vashti. Because of Esther's position in the court, she was later able to plead with him to spare her Jewish people from the annihilation planned secretly by one of his advisors. A correspondence to Mother Anderson's speaking to the judge is apparent. In addition to the meaning this feast has for Spiritual women in general, for the sponsor Bishop Adams, it is a ritual display of the source of her personal spiritual authority because Esther is one of her spirit guides. Furthermore, it is a ceremony through which she publicly prepares her intended successor, a woman called into the ministry by a spiritual encounter with Esther, to assume greater authority.

Preceding the feast, which varies in length from one to three nights, is a series of novenas held every Friday evening from January through March. In contrast to the crowded culminating service, novenas are usually attended by only ten to fifteen women and children. Although the organist is frequently a man, rarely are men in the congregation. Because of the small numbers, all have an opportunity to testify, and many witness to the power of Esther in their lives. Some thank her for giving them money or a job. Others rely on folk metaphors, calling her "a way-maker, a mind-regulator, and a heart-fixer," abilities typically ascribed to Jesus. Frequently, she is characterized as a sympathetic intermediary to God who "will intercede for you, just as she interceded for her people." Like Mother Anderson, she is an inspiration to women to be courageous. In contrast to the biblical account, read chapter by chapter over the three months, which attributes her success in saving the Jews to the influence of her beauty on the king, these women emphasize Esther's courage in going before him without the required invitation. Testimonies, such as the following one by a woman who used to cry when people condemned the Spiritual church, often present Esther as a model for exemplary behavior that is necessary but difficult to achieve: "Truly I'm just so proud . . . for the many years that I have known her [Esther] and known that she was bold and courageous. She stood up for what was right. Truly tonight this is what we come for. To ask the Lord to give us boldness so that we might be able to stand up to our foes because when you are on the Lord's side, Satan is going to strike on every hand. But if we continue to do as Queen Esther, just stand up, stand tall and be bold, I know that everything is going to be all right."

Minister Geraldine Coleman, secretary of the congregation, conducts the novena services. She is called the Instrument because her role is to "let the spirit of Esther use her," as Bishop Adams phrases it. The spirit that worshipers feel in these services is not, however, always specified as Esther's, even though they do acknowledge that by "getting into the spirit" they learn more about her and how she can bless them. A rhinestone tiara, scepter, and pink robe mark Minister Coleman as the embodiment of the royal Esther's spirit. In order to fulfill the demands of this role, Minister Coleman fasts the day of each novena, just as the Bible says Esther fasted for three days while the Jewish people feasted. After the opening devotional and the testimonies, Minister Coleman comes down from the ministers' seating area into the congregation to lead the "bless" section of the service, the spiritual high point of the evening. She begins a congregational song, often "I'll Be Somewhere Working for the Lord," during which she often circles the room counter-clockwise with incense. Singing and dancing may continue for anywhere from ten to thirty minutes until she feels that the spirit is high enough for her to continue. Then worshipers come forward in turn to light seven-day candles on a small altar dedicated to Esther. After so doing, each one kneels before it, and Minister Coleman prays over her. Sometimes blessed objects are included in this ritual to assist people in receiving the gifts Esther intends for them. One week, for example, Minister Coleman directed each person to touch her scepter and make a wish. Some evenings, if the spirit has so directed, she brings messages to individuals in a quiet voice. Despite the emphasis on female spirituality throughout the service, this section concludes with a prayer directed to "God, King of the Universe." All recite it in unison with their hands joined, making a circle around Minister Coleman and the special altar to Esther. In this ritual action, the worshipers follow the model of Esther as intercessor, taking the needs of themselves and others before God much as their foremother went before the king.

Bishop Adams served as the Instrument for many years, but in the mid-1980s appointed Minister Coleman to the role, in part because Esther is the spirit guide who called her assistant into the ministry. Minister Coleman occasionally narrates that personal experience at these public services as a means of verifying the reality of Esther's spirit. In so doing, she simultaneously validates her own spiritual authority. At the feast in 1988, for example, she told the congregation how the call came one day at the day care center she directs: "And I heard that knock [raps on pulpit]. There was a young child in the room with me who said, Miss Coleman you want me to go see who that is at the door. I said, no baby, because I knew he wouldn't understand. But I knew that was my calling. Those of you that can accept it, accept it." In remarks at the close of each novena and feast, Bishop Adams frequently emphasizes her pleasure in the work Minister Coleman is doing through the direction of Esther's spirit, further confirming her status.

In one sense, the Queen Esther services are a training ground for Minister Coleman, who is a generation younger than her leader. By learning more about Esther's spirit and by using that knowledge to help worshipers receive the blessings they seek, she will merit increased respect and authority in the future. At a novena service in 1989, Bishop Adams announced for the first time that she wants Minister Coleman to succeed her as leader of Queen Esther Temple, even though others on the ministers' board are her seniors in age and in length of affiliation with the congregation: "Thank God for Minister Coleman. . . . I know God sent her to me for I'd been praying and praying for God to send somebody that meant Jesus every step of the way . . . Now I don't know when I'll leave. But I'll tell you what. If it is in my power, she'll get my mantle . . . It belong to God, and sometime you got to give it to who God want you to. But if I have a say about it, Coleman will get mine. She's proven herself." The transfer of leadership, alluded to here through the Scriptural image of a mantle, can create jealousy and may even split a congregation, particularly when membership is based on personal attachment to a charismatic minister, as is generally true in Spiritual churches. Thus Bishop Adams was not merely politely complimenting her associate. Her statement established the hierarchy of authority within the congregation and derived its force not only from her own respected status but also from the context: worshipers had themselves just witnessed the effects of Minister Coleman's spiritual power in the rituals of the "bless" section of the service.

The Queen Esther novenas and feast are, then, aesthetically rich ceremonial occasions at which a woman can be prepared to assume more authority within the institutional church. In addition, they are times for celebrating a tradition of female leadership, petitioning a female spirit for assistance, and displaying the sponsor's personal bond with a reliable spirit guide. As is customary in African American Protestant churches, Bishop Adams annually holds a pastor's anniversary service in which the monetary gifts and testimonies by members attest to her authority over them. However, the elaborate and richly symbolic Queen Esther feast much more dramatically exhibits why she merits her stature as a spiritual leader.

As explained above, the Spiritual church's syncretism of Catholicism and African Caribbean religions probably accounts for its hierarchy of ordained clergy. Spiritual women today feel that ordination is essential for them, as one minister explained in an interview: "You're not recognized unless you are ordained. They [both members of Spiritual churches and private clients] don't have that much respect for you if you don't have no papers. They respect you more with the title. A lot of them are hung up on those titles, robes, and things like that.... The most important thing [i.e., reason I was ordained] was to be recognized in order to do the work. Not that I couldn't work without it, but just in order to get recognized. The respect, to earn that respect." Given such sentiments as these, it is not surprising that women with a wide variety of gifts—healing, prophecy, teaching, and preaching—seek the official recognition of church and state by undergoing a ritual ordination. The variety and complexity of ordination services preclude a full discussion of them here. However, those in which women are ordained by other women deserve consideration as a third type of worship service where rituals validate female leadership.

Ordination in the Spiritual church usually follows a vision that the believer interprets as a call into the ministry. Many clergywomen say that the experience was troubling and that they sought their pastor for an explanation. Candidates can be ordained as missionaries, evangelists, or ministers, depending on what they and their leader understand their particular gifts to be. Few men or women hold the rank of bishop, and only one woman in New Orleans has been named an archbishop. The duties of a missionary vary widely, but they are generally commissioned to visit the sick and needy and to help with such chores as cooking and cleaning. Yet they might also be called to preach. Evangelists go out to visit churches, where they preach and teach. Most of the ordained clergywomen hold the rank of minister. Nowadays, they seem to prefer being called "reverend," in contrast to "mother," which some of the elderly leaders still use.

Ministers can reach their position by formally advancing from one rank to the next or by being ordained to that position initially, according to the spirit's direction. The various titles suggest a hierarchy of spiritual authority that does not always exist in practice, in part because there is no direct correlation between a title and leadership of a congregation. While one church might be pastored by a minister with other ministers below her, the head of another might be a bishop with boards of bishops and of ministers beneath her. It is common for men and women with the title bishop not to have their own church. Further confusing the issue are the many prayer rooms established in homes. Sponsored almost exclusively by women, these often lack a formal membership but do have a core of regular worshipers and a designated head, the occupant of the house. Titles do not consistently correspond to leadership positions within a congregation. Nevertheless, those who have been ordained enjoy increased status and prestige, as indicated at worship services by their liturgical vestments and by the reserved seating for them in the front.

Ordained clergy also have increased responsibilities. Thus many delay accepting the call. In extemporaneous remarks to the congregation at her ordination in 1989, a woman who had to rear a family alone after the death of her husband spoke of why she resisted what she knew was the Lord's will: "I know that I was called to the ministry in '78. That's a long time. And I knew I should have been a minister long ago. But I'll tell you why I delayed it. I've seen ministers have such hard times with their children. Look like when you pick up the banner and carry it to be a minister, your children begin to pull away. . . . So I kept praying Lord is that [the ministry] what you want me to do? And I would look at them. And then I had to make up my mind. I had to put God first." Some women tell stories about problems they encountered during the years they refused to answer their call. Bishop Adams could be speaking for many in this personal reflection: "When there's a calling upon your life, I don't know about nobody else, but I know for myself that everything went wrong and there was a void that couldn't be filled until I submitted to God and started doing what I was supposed to be doing."

At regular worship services, prophecies from other female ministers will occasionally encourage the hesitant to join the clergy. For example, one evening at Prudential Spiritual Church, Bishop Victoria McSwain grabbed a woman's elbow, pulled her into the center of the church, lifted up her arms, and struck the outstretched palms twice with her own right hand. Bishop McSwain told the worshiper that she "had work to do." In an interview after her ordination, the woman explained that the spirit had at that moment revealed her gift of healing to the bishop. The woman already knew about her powers, but public confirmation through the leader's prophetic insight helped strengthen her resolve to become a minister. A month before her ordination, the bishop offered further encouragement by speaking these words for all to hear during the prophecy portion of a regular Sunday service: "You getting on the right track now, baby. You gonna be talked about. . . . But that's all right. Stay there. Don't let nothing move you. . . . I had it hard too, and I know how it is. God gonna fix it up for you. . . . Thank God for the Spirit 'cause he uses you. . . . Some don't want to see you go, but you going. . . . You going on out there for Jesus. And that's quite all right. . . . Get about your father's business." Such moments as these, in which women urge a sister to become a minister, occur time and time again during worship services. By publicly validating the individual's personal sense of being called, clergy-women not only encourage the candidate but also prepare the church to accept the newly ordained woman.

Ordinations take place when both leader and candidate agree that she or he is ready. Although no formal instruction is required, some attend weekly spiritual development classes to deepen their knowledge of Scrip-ture as well as of meditation and healing techniques. Leaders conduct these classes from time to time, whenever they have a group of interested candidates willing to undergo the required regimen of fasting and praying. In the 1920s, Mother Anderson ordained candidates after they had partici-pated in such a series of classes. In testimonies, women generally speak appreciatively if not reverently of their teachers. Some, however, claim independence, asserting that their spiritual power has come through no human intermediary. One woman told me that her leader "had a couple classes, but it wasn't that many. I didn't get my learning from her. I got my learning from the Lord. . . . Everything I learned came from the Holy Spirit and watching, observing other people, going to different Spiritual churches watching them doing what they were doing."

When the time comes, a bishop will frequently perform ordinations during an annual district or national convention of Spiritual churches in the same association. In some ways, these are like a revival, with nightly services throughout the week. Sometimes as many as twenty ministers will be sponsored by pastors from different congregations. At these large services, ministers might also be consecrated as bishops.

For a variety of reasons, many candidates schedule an individual ordina-tion service in their home church. Such celebrations are more personal be-cause family and friends are called in turn by a mistress of ceremonies to honor the candidate with a solo, an extemporaneous speech, or possibly a prepared devotional verse. This opening portion of the service, during which all those present are encouraged to speak, lasts several hours, depending on the number present. The remarks praising the candidate's character and religious devotion are meaningful expressions of support to the minister, who anticipates confronting rejection from many people in her new role. They serve also as testimonies to the church in general about the candidate's worthiness for spiritual leadership. At the ordination and for several weeks preceding it, she herself must remain "in silence" during services, forbidden to sing, preach, prophesy, or heal. Thus an ordination differs from the memorial and feast services discussed above because the candidate is unable to validate her position herself by publicly working with her spirit guide. She must rely on those who attend to speak as her witnesses.

Frequently, the candidates, male and female alike, wear white robes and march to the front of the church holding a burning white taper or white flower. In contrast to this custom, Edmonia Caldwell, the presiding bishop at Prudential, continues the tradition, practiced since at least the 1930s, of having women dress as brides for the occasion.[32] The clothing is brought to the church ahead of time to be blessed. Then before the service, several women ministers and bishops gather to clothe the candidate. They repeat the Lord's Prayer as each article is put on—the dress, the veil, and finally the rosary worn as a necklace. Carrying white flowers, the candidate is escorted down the aisle by the bishops at the beginning of the service and sits on a chair placed in the center facing the congregation, with the train and veil swirled around her feet.

Following the many testimonies and solos, and sometimes even a sermon, Bishop Caldwell conducts the final stage of the ritual. She stands face to face with the candidate, encircled by the other ministers, all robed in black. At one ordination, she began with a charge to avoid the gris-gris bags, powders, and buried charms used by hoodoo practitioners: "I don't give you no bags [gris-gris] to use. I don't believe in nobody sprinkling behind nobody door. . . . See, bags don't get it. Digging pits don't get it. 'Cause if you dig one pit, you gotta dig two, and if you don't dig them two, that same pit gonna fall on you. So you gotta tell Jesus. He the pit digger." Next she offered a traditional chanted prayer, petitioning God the Father and Jesus to bless the candidate. In one section of this strongly rhythmic prayer, she metaphorically reclothed the woman in "the whole armor of God" by alluding to Ephesians 6:

> I want you to preparate her feet, huh
> With the preparation of the gospel
> Girdle her with gird of truth, huh. . . .
> And while you talking with her tonight Jesus
> Put the helmet of salvation upon her head
> Please sir have mercy Lord

An ordination conducted by Bishop Caldwell concludes with four visible symbols, which she presents in variable order at each occasion: a wedding ring, a new Bible, a cup of water from which all ministers in attendance drink as a sign of their unity, and a certificate of ordination signed by her. At the ordination described above, she placed the gold band on the woman's finger and said: "When man forsake you, when your children forsake you, when your friends turn they back on us, let everybody know you been married to Jesus, and you don't need nobody else. Just call Jesus."

By enacting the bride of Christ metaphor, what does a traditional ordination suggest about the status of clergywomen in the Spiritual church? Although the ritual calls to mind both the role ascribed nuns in the Catholic church as well as the mystical marriages in Vodoun between *loa* and humans, male and female alike,[33] it should be read in the context of this church's own tradition of female leadership. Ordinations of men, in contrast, do not play out the same metaphor, one of many indications that notions of a patriarchal God persist alongside images of God as a genderless spirit in the Spiritual churches. The idea that this marriage is between unequal partners—the passive wife subordinated to a powerful husband—cannot be ignored, particularly when women, such as Bishop Adams in the quotation above, refer to accepting their call as "submitting." It is not uncommon for female ministers, like their male counterparts, to acknowledge a desire for the selflessness that comes from being guided totally by the spirit. The submissive wife of patriarchal society is, then, an image they find congruent with one part of their spirituality.

Nevertheless, the marriage trope is richly paradoxical in this context where, as the services described above demonstrate, the community believes that intimacy with spirits enhances status. Mystical oneness with them, traditionally dramatized in the ordination as a wedding, confers power that the ministers intend to use to change conditions in the world. Bridal imagery does not imply to these women that a woman remains incomplete without a man. That sexist notion does not square with their own experiences in life, many of them having survived numerous hardships independently. Rather, they believe that all humans are powerless without the spirits. Ministers intimate with spirits possess such gifts as preaching, prophecy, and healing, with which they combat the practical problems their people face. Thus the bridal gown in which a woman receives her official ministerial papers is ritual garb appropriately symbolizing her complex power relations in the spiritual and terrestrial worlds.

Like the memorial services for the founder Mother Anderson and the feasts honoring the spirit guide Esther, ordinations are public celebrations of the female leadership that has predominated in the African American Spiritual churches in New Orleans since their founding. Responsible for church buildings, finances, instruction, and rituals, Spiritual women have openly directed their religious lives for over seventy years. They have done so despite the stigma of assuming roles traditionally reserved for men. They have withstood condemnation from outsiders who mistake their beliefs and practices for black magic. And they have persisted in the face of charges of charlatanism. Through the traditional rituals described above, these women publicly demonstrate their spiritual power and, hence, their worthiness for positions of authority within the institutional church. A large number of African American women in New Orleans find the Spiritual church, with its heritage of female leadership, to be a refuge from denominations that allow them to worship but not to lead. One bishop voiced the feelings of many when, looking back over her religious life, she remarked that the various Protestant congregations in which she grew up "didn't give you [women] opportunity. The Spiritual church gave me a closer walk with God by being active."

NOTES

1. Unless otherwise noted, all quotations from Spiritual ministers are taken from interviews conducted during 1989. I wish to thank Nancy Gamble for assistance in documenting the Queen Esther feast in 1988. The fieldwork for this chapter has been supported by an NEH Fellowship and by grants from Loyola University and the New Orleans Jazz and Heritage Foundation.

2. Andrew J. Kaslow and Claude Jacobs, *Prophecy, Healing, and Power: The Afro-American Spiritual Churches of New Orleans* (New Orleans: Jean Lafitte National Historical Park, 1981), 19.

3. Joseph R. Washington, Jr., *Black Sects and Cults* (Garden City, N.Y.: Doubleday/Anchor, 1973), 115.

4. Hans A. Baer, *The Black Spiritual Movement: A Religious Response to Racism* (Knoxville: University of Tennessee Press, 1984), 11, 1.

5. Baer, *The Black Spiritual Movement,* 18, 22.

6. Ibid., 9.

7. Kaslow and Jacobs, *Prophecy, Healing, and Power,* 105–18.

8. Claude F. Jacobs and Andrew J. Kaslow, *The Spiritual Churches of New Orleans: Origins, Beliefs, and Rituals of an African-American Religion* (Knoxville: University of Tennessee Press, 1991), 183.

9. Kaslow and Jacobs, *Spiritual Churches,* 184.

10. Baer, *The Black Spiritual Movement,* 166.

11. Mary Farrell Bednarowski, "Outside the Mainstream: Women's Religion and Women Religious Leaders in Nineteenth-Century America," *Journal of the American Academy of Religion* 48 (1980): 209.

12. For helpful discussions of African American Spiritualism as a syncretic religion, see Jacobs and Kaslow, *Spiritual Churches,* 49–95, and Baer, *The Black Spiritual Movement,* 110–59.

13. Baer, *The Black Spiritual Movement,* 136–39.

14. Ibid., 152–54.

15. Untitled article, *Louisiana Weekly,* 22 Jan. 1927, p. 8.

16. Bednarowski, "Outside the Mainstream," 214.

17. Zora Neale Hurston, "Hoodoo in America," *Journal of American Folklore* 44 (1931): 319. Although "voodoo" may be an appropriate label for African-influenced black religion in New Orleans through the first decades of the nineteenth century when contact with Haiti was immediate, Hurston has argued that "hoodoo" should be used when referring to contemporary manifestations of the religion, which differs markedly from Haitian Vodoun.

18. Alex Owen, *The Darkened Room: Women, Power and Spiritualism in Late Victorian England* (Philadelphia: University of Pennsylvania Press, 1990), 4, 5.

19. Untitled article, *Louisiana Weekly,* 22 Jan. 1927, p. 8. The important influence of American Spiritualism in Leafy Anderson's work is indicated by the special drama that closed the 1926 "national meeting of Christian Spiritualists," held at her church. The performance was entitled "'The Life of Mrs. Leafy Anderson—Mortal and Immortal,' in three parts—The Woman, the Medium and the Mother. The singing of Mrs. A. Price Bennett captivated the audience. . . . The play opened with a night scene in Chicago, then the home life of Mrs. Anderson was shown, her call to spiritualism, and her works. Mrs. Anderson played the leading role." See "Eternal Life Church Presents Play," *Louisiana Weekly,* 11 Dec. 1926, p. 5.

20. See Claude F. Jacobs, "Spirit Guides and Possession in the New Orleans Black Spiritual Churches," *Journal of American Folklore* 102 (1989): 45–56, 65–67.

21. Kaslow and Jacobs, *Prophecy, Healing, and Power,* 40.

22. Paul F. LaChance, "The 1809 Immigration of Saint-Dominque Refugees to New Orleans: Reception, Integration and Impact," *Louisiana History* 29 (1988): 112. For an overview of Vodoun's influence in America, see Albert J. Raboteau, *Slave Religion: The "Invisible Institution" in the Antebellum South* (Oxford: Oxford University Press, 1978), 75–87. For information on the practice of voodoo in New Orleans, see Jessie Gaston Mulira, "The Case of Voodoo in New Orleans," in *Africanisms in American Culture,* ed. Joseph E. Holloway (Bloomington: Indiana University Press, 1990), 34–68.

23. The only books devoted entirely to female leadership in African Caribbean religions are Ruth Landes, *The City of Women* (New York: Macmillan, 1947), a study of *candomblé* priestesses in Brazil, and Karen McCarthy Brown, *Mama Lola: A Vodou Priestess in Brooklyn* (Berkeley: University of California Press, 1991).

24. "Mother Anderson Dies, Followers Await Her Spirit," *New Orleans Morning Tribune,* 15 Dec. 1927, p. 20.

25. Hurston, "Hoodoo in America," 319.

26. "City Shocked by Death of Spiritualist," *Louisiana Weekly,* 17 Dec. 1927, p. 1.

27. Michael P. Smith, *Spirit World: Pattern in the Expressive Folk Culture of Afro-American New Orleans* (New Orleans: New Orleans Urban Folklife Society, 1984), 43.

28. WPA Federal Writers Project Files, The Robert Tallant Collection, New Orleans Public Library.

29. Jacobs and Kaslow provide a helpful description of the feast service and also suggest the possibility of its historical connection to voodoo rituals (*Spiritual Church,* 177–21, 208).

30. Kay Turner and Suzanne Seriff, "'Giving an Altar': The Ideology of Reproduction in a St. Joseph's Day Feast," *Journal of American Folklore* 100 (1987), 454. For a discussion of this tradition in Spiritual churches, see David C. Estes, "Across Ethnic Boundaries: St. Joseph's Day in a New Orleans Afro-American Spiritual Church," *Mississippi Folklore Register* 21 (1987), 9–22.

31. Jacobs, "Spirit Guides and Possession," 66.

32. Jacobs and Kaslow, *Spiritual Church,* 110–12.

33. Alfred Métraux, *Voodoo in Haiti,* trans. Hugo Charteris (New York: Schocken Books, 1959), 212–19.

Twentieth-Century Women's Religion as Seen in the Feminist Spirituality Movement

Cynthia Eller

Contemporary religious expression in the United States provides a rich field for examining the role of women spiritual leaders. In addition to women's traditional haven in alternative religions, we are now beginning to see women leaders in mainstream religions. We might usefully imagine a spectrum, with alternative religions created and led by women at one end, mainstream religions with ordained women clergy at the other end, and various alternative religions in the middle, which, while not created by women, do allow for female spiritual leadership. On this spectrum, the feminist spirituality movement occupies the territory on the far left, and gives us a contemporary example of what women appropriate and what they invent when they set their hands to the task of creating religion in a realm largely free of the restraints of tradition. Though some women active in Jewish or Christian feminism consider themselves part of the feminist spirituality movement, for ease of discussion, I will restrict myself to post-Christian manifestations of feminist spirituality.[1] The broadest of definitions will suffice: whatever religious expressions maintain both a feminist viewpoint and a stance outside normative religions can be regarded as feminist spirituality.

Feminist spirituality, though sometimes inclusive of men, caters primarily to the spiritual needs of women through the offices of women leaders, writers, teachers, and healers. Overarching hierarchy and authority are utterly lacking in feminist spirituality; it is less a religious group than a spiritual movement. In fact, many women who see themselves as part of the feminist spirituality movement have never participated in the kind of communal worship that is often taken to be the hallmark of organized religion. Perhaps they have attended a workshop or read an influential book; perhaps they have had conversations with friends or spiritual experiences of their own that led them to identify themselves as spiritual feminists. Perhaps they continue to maintain other religious affiliations alongside their participation in feminist spirituality. Whatever their degree of participation, every woman who identifies herself with the movement is seen as at least a potential leader, and in fact, most women find opportunities to exercise this leadership in one fashion or another.

What draws the many diverse forms of feminist spirituality together is their shared devotion to examining women's spiritual experiences and presuming them valid. It is assumed that women have access to an unperverted spirituality, one that can prove revolutionary not only to women, but to the world. In locating spiritual truth, feminist spirituality is arch-pragmatic: spiritual experiences and practices are deemed valid if they work to make one stronger, as a person and as a woman.[2] Thus a tremendous variety of beliefs and practices are subsumed under feminist spirituality, ranging from astrology and divination to homeopathic medicine and Goddess worship. Feminist spirituality is also syncretistic, borrowing freely from the myths and religions of many cultures, always seeking symbols and stories that can be transformative for women. The resulting pastische differs from woman to woman. One woman may worship the Hindu goddess Kali, attend Native American sweat lodges, and use the Tarot to guide her actions; another may identify herself with the Greek goddess Artemis, worship the Earth as a living female entity, and rely on the *I Ching* for spiritual advice; another may do all of the above and more.

Within this variety, there are a number of salient themes, the most prominent of which are Goddess worship and what might be called feminist spirituality's "sacred history": a version of Western history that argues that prehistorical societies were at least Goddess-worshipping, and perhaps matriarchal as well, that these peaceable societies were destroyed by the rise of patriarchal forces, and that we now stand at a crossroads where we will either reclaim the values of the ancient matriarchies or destroy ourselves. Not all spiritual feminists worship a Goddess or believe there were ancient matriarchies, but most do, and many of the other beliefs and practices of feminist spirituality can be seen as derivative from these two themes.

The Historical Development of Feminist Spirituality

Feminist spirituality emerged in the United States some twenty years ago at the confluence of several streams of feminist thought. The radical political feminism of the 1960s, increasing frustration among feminists within traditional religions, and an ongoing concern with alternative worlds of meaning provided the raw material on which the early feminist spirituality movement fed. Together these three factors gave birth to America's most recent "women's religion."

Like all of the political movements of the 1960s era, the women's liberation movement in America eventually faced a split between those of its members who favored the development of cultural alternatives to the present order and those who opted for more traditional forms of political action.[3] There was extensive overlap between these two groups, and most feminists played down the potential divisiveness of this difference. Nevertheless, broad understandings of the methods and goals of feminism formed into two centers of gravity within the movement: "political" feminism and "cultural" feminism. Where political feminism tended to focus on the disequilibrium of social power and material goods between men and women, to cite specific instances of sexism and to seek to remedy them by law, cultural feminism hoped to create values and institutions nurtured by a feminine vision of the good. From the viewpoint of political feminism, cultural feminists were hopelessly naive about the realities of political power: they threatened to make themselves irrelevant to the struggle against sexism by becoming enamored of regressive notions of the "feminine" and by building a semiprivate feminist utopia that could do nothing to alleviate the sufferings of the great majority of women. Cultural feminism, on the other hand, saw political feminists as fighting symptoms without an adequate appreciation of the underlying disease. If sexism is grounded in biological predispositions, religious worldviews, or the structure of our language—cultural feminists argued—the relatively narrow political gains of the feminist movement could not uproot it, and sexism would merely emerge in new, and perhaps more insidious forms.

At the same time that the feminist movement found itself increasingly split between cultural and political factions, feminists within the Christian church were facing their own set of challenges. Christian feminism initially took the form of agitating for inclusive language and equal opportunities for women for participation and leadership in the life of the church. But sexism proved quite intractable. Biblical bases for sex discrimination were expounded by feminism's opponents, and feminists found themselves faced with a hard wall of authority and tradition that justified placing women in subordinate positions. As the problem appeared deeper, feminists moved their analysis to a deeper level: now it was not only that the church failed to respect women's talents, but that the church was not likely to so long as God was conceived of as male. The ever-deepening cycle of feminist critique continued, until eventually a number of women felt that they could never change traditional religions or make their peace with them, and so were compelled to leave them behind.[4]

Unchurched cultural feminists and disaffected Christian feminists shared an analysis of women's predicament that saw sexism stemming from deep sources, at least one of which was mainstream religion. Implied in the critique was a desire for meaningful alternatives, alternatives that could be enlivening for women in a way that current religious worldviews and practices never could be. This search for alternatives was further fed by a desire to give support and value to spiritual experiences that fell outside the norm prescribed by mainstream religions. Since mainstream religions were overwhelmingly male in image, myth, and symbol, it was difficult to make sense within them of experiences of the divine as female, or of spiritual experiences that centered on those things traditionally associated with the "feminine" and devalued in mainstream religion (e.g., nature, cyclical time, the body as sacred, immanence).[5]

A hunger for feminist spirituality can be established from this complex of social factors, but the specific form that feminist spirituality took when it first emerged on the American religious scene is a fascinating study in religious syncretism. Basically, feminist spirituality began by adopting a preexisting alternative religion—neopaganism or witchcraft—and then adapting it to its own needs. Neopaganism claims for itself a long history, tracing its roots as far back into prehistory as we can see by means of archaeological remains. Apart from this broader claim of being heir to a quasi-universal "Old Religion," neopaganism sees its specific genealogy as European.[6] According to its apologists and to some historians of religion, paganism in Europe was not entirely eradicated (or appropriated) by Christianity, but continued throughout the Middle Ages as the secret practice of witchcraft.[7] Having survived centuries of persecution by the church, paganism is now able to "go public" in a climate of relative religious toleration. This recent resurgence of paganism (termed "neo-paganism") was first popularized in the mid-twentieth century by Gerald Gardner, a British witch who brought paganism to public attention after the repeal of the last of Britain's Witchcraft Acts in 1951.[8] Some neopagans claim to be hereditary witches (having learned witchcraft from parents, grandparents, or other older friends or relatives who handed the tradition on to them), but most claim no exposure to witchcraft before its renaissance in the past few decades. Rather, they see themselves as part of an effort to piece together and revive European paganism for the modern era.[9]

There are great variations among neopagans, and the "traditions" of modern witchcraft have proliferated greatly since Gardner announced the return of the Old Religion. Some traditions are dedicated to discovering and recreating what they believe to have been the medieval, or even premedieval, practice of witchcraft. These groups often operate under hierarchical clergy and prescribe rigid rules for ritual, initiation, and celebration. Other traditions are eclectic, acknowledging the existence of historical paganism, but feeling free to create their own practices out of such diverse sources as Asian and Native American religions, science fiction and fantasy, and their own imaginations.[10] Though incredibly diverse, neopagan groups unite around belief in a primary Goddess; belief in other deities both male and female (sometimes including a Horned God paired with the primary Goddess); ritual coinciding with planetary events such as solstices, equinoxes, and full moons; and the practice of magic.

That feminists in search of a spirituality liberating to women should have fastened upon neopaganism is not too surprising. To begin with, neopagans were already worshipping a Goddess as primary (seeing other deities as having been born from her, being other names for her, or being various aspects of her). Neopagans believed that pre-Christian societies were Goddess-worshipping, if not always matriarchal. In their understanding of medieval witchcraft, neopagans allowed for images of women that were powerful, even threatening to the established order. Most neopagan groups focused on gender at some level, and showed an interest in recovering "the feminine." All of these characteristics were naturally attractive to women committed to finding alternatives to male-dominated religions.

But feminism and neopaganism came together not only for ideological reasons, but for sociological ones as well. In the early phase of the women's movement, before there were women's studies departments on every major college campus, feminism was explored and spread through consciousness-raising groups: small groups of women discussing their experience as gendered individuals. The witchcraft coven was similarly a small group sharing a concern with gender and dealing with one another on a personal level.[11] In addition, both consciousness-raising and neopaganism shared a tradition of seeing the political illuminated through the personal. It was through consciousness-raising groups that feminists first began to understand and deplore religious justifications of sexism, and through feminist spirituality that religious alternatives were created.

The first group to explicitly bring the two worlds of feminism and neopaganism together was WITCH, a politically activist collective of women formed in 1968 in New York. The acronym originally stood for "Women's International Terrorist Conspiracy from Hell," but as collectives sprung up in various cities across the United States, the title changed to accommodate the different targets of their political actions, becoming "Women Infuriated at Taking Care of Hoodlums," "Women Interested in Toppling Consumption Holidays," and "Women Incensed at Telephone Company Harassment," to name a few.[12] Though not connected to the neopagan revival in America (probably even unaware of it), WITCH was the first group of feminists to call themselves "witches," and in their original manifesto they anticipated some of the motifs of the feminist spirituality movement which was to follow. Their manifesto reads:

WITCH is an all-women Everything. It's theater, revolution, magic, terror, joy, garlic flowers, spells. It's an awareness that witches and gypsies were the original guerrillas and resistance fighters against oppression—particularly the oppression of women—down through the ages. Witches have always been women who dared to be: groovy, courageous, aggressive, intelligent, nonconformist, explorative, curious, independent, sexually liberated, revolutionary. (This possibly explains why nine million of them have been burned.) Witches were the first Friendly Heads and Dealers, the first birth-control practitioners and abortionists, the first alchemists (turn dross into gold and you devalue the whole idea of money!). They bowed to no man, being the living remnants of the oldest culture of all—one in which men and women were equal sharers in a truly cooperative society, before the death-dealing sexual, economic, and spiritual repression of the Imperialist Phallic Society took over and began to destroy nature and human society.

WITCH lives and laughs in every woman. She is the free part of each of us, beneath the shy smiles, the acquiescence to absurd male domination, the make-up or flesh-suffocating clothing our sick society demands. There is no "joining" WITCH. If you are a woman and dare to look within yourself, you are a Witch. You make your own rules. You are free and beautiful. You can be invisible or evident in how you choose to make your witch-self known. You can form your own Coven of sister Witches (thirteen is a cozy number for a group) and do your own actions.

Whatever is repressive, solely male-oriented, greedy, puritanical, authoritarian—those are your targets. Your weapons are theater, satire, explosions, magic, herbs, music, costumes, cameras, masks, chants, stickers, stencils and paint, films, tambourines, bricks, brooms, guns, voodoo dolls, cats, candles, bells, chalk, nail clippings, hand grenades, poison rings, fuses, tape recorders, incense—your own boundless beautiful imagination. Your power comes from your own self as a woman, and it is activated by working in concert with your sisters. The power of the Coven is more than the sum of its individual members, because it is *together*.

You are pledged to free our brothers from oppression and stereotyped sexual roles (whether they like it or not) as well as ourselves.

You are a Witch by saying aloud, "I am a Witch" three times, and *thinking about that.* You are a Witch by being female, untamed, angry, joyous, and immortal.[13]

The connection between feminism and witchcraft was further strengthened by radical feminists who researched the persecution of witches in Europe during the Middle Ages, describing this as yet another—though particularly terrifying—manifestation of the misogyny of Western culture. Andrea Dworkin, in her 1974 book *Woman Hating,* was the first to describe the witch burnings as "gynocide"; this was followed in 1978 by Mary Daly's *Gyn/Ecology,* which included an account of the witch burnings as an instance of the patriarchal "Sado-Ritual Syndrome." In addition to arguing that the European persecution of witches was actually the persecution of women, Daly claimed words like "witch," "hag," "crone," and "spinster" as feminist self-descriptions.[14]

WITCH and radical feminists like Dworkin and Daly helped to create an intellectual climate in which women could see themselves in solidarity with witches of the past, but it remained for others to draw more fully religious connections between feminism and neopaganism. The two most influential women in bringing about this convergence were two California witches, Zsuzsanna Budapest and Starhawk. Certainly there were women who were both neopagans and feminists before Budapest and Starhawk began their work, but it was these two who developed a neopaganism that was explicitly feminist at its base and spread it to the feminist community through books, newsletters, lectures, and word of mouth.

Zsuzsanna Budapest, a Hungarian immigrant, describes herself as a hereditary witch. She claims to have learned witchcraft from her mother, Masika Szilagyi, who in turn learned it from an elderly woman who worked in her parent's house as she was growing up. After immigrating to the United States, Budapest became deeply involved in the feminist movement, and eventually sought to integrate her training in witchcraft with her commitment to feminism. In 1971, she and a group of friends founded the Susan B. Anthony Coven No. 1 in southern California. Like other neopagan groups, they celebrated the equinoxes, solstices, cross-quarters (holidays falling midway between the equinoxes and solstices), and the full moons. But unlike other neopagan groups, they did not admit men or refer to male deities, and they described the direct aim of their spirituality as the overthrow of the patriarchy. The Susan B. Anthony Coven No. 1 coined the term "Dianic Witchcraft" (from the Roman goddess of the moon, Diana) for their new tradition of neopaganism dedicated to the worship of women's mysteries. They engaged in active outreach to the feminist community, sometimes attracting as many as 120 women to their rituals.[15] They issued their own manifesto, which read:

We believe that Feminist witches are wimmin[16] who search within themselves for the female principle of the universe and who relate as daughters to the Creatrix.

We believe that just as it is time to fight for the right to control our bodies, it is also time to fight for our sweet womon souls.

We believe that in order to fight and win a revolution that will stretch for generations into the future, we must find reliable ways to replenish our energies. We believe that without a secure grounding in womon's spiritual strength there will be no victory for us.

We believe that we are part of a changing universal consciousness that has long been feared and prophesized by the patriarchs.

We believe that Goddess-consciousness gave humanity a workable, long-lasting, peaceful period during which the Earth was treated as Mother and wimmin were treated as Her priestesses. This was the mythical Golden Age of Matriarchy.

We believe that wimmin lost supremacy through the aggressions of males who were exiled from the matriarchies and formed the patriarchal hordes responsible for the invention of rape and the subjugation of wimmin.

We believe that female control of the death (male) principle yields hummin evolution.

We are committed to living life lovingly towards ourselves and our sisters. We are committed to joy, self-love, and life-affirmation.

We are committed to winning, to surviving, to struggling against patriarchal oppression.

We are committed to defending our interests and those of our sisters through the knowledge of witchcraft: to blessing, to cursing, to healing, and to binding with power rooted in womon-identified wisdom.

We are opposed to attacking the innocent.

We are equally committed to political, communal, and personal solutions.

We are committed to teaching wimmin how to organize themselves as witches and to sharing our traditions with wimmin.

We are opposed to teaching our magic and our craft to men until equality of the sexes is a reality.

Our immediate goal is to congregate with each other according to our ancient womon-made laws and to remember our past, renew our powers and affirm our Goddess of the Ten-thousand Names.[17]

Starhawk first discovered neopaganism through nonfeminist channels. It was Budapest who introduced Starhawk to specifically feminist witchcraft in the early 1970s. Budapest describes their meeting as follows:

> One day Starhawk was driving down Lincoln Boulevard in Santa Monica, wondering why feminism and witchcraft hadn't found each other yet. Just as she thought this, she drove past the Feminist Wicca and the name caught her eye. She stopped her car and came into our candle shop for the first time. I happened to be staffing that day, so I told her about the Susan B. Anthony Coven No. 1, and invited her to our upcoming Spring Equinox Festival. Starhawk attended her first ritual with us, and the impact on her life was glorious proof of why we should never close circles to anyone new. She quickly became a great teacher and priestess.[18]

Starhawk, raised as a religious Jew and trained as a therapist, explored a number of neopagan traditions before settling on the Faery tradition of "the Little People of Stone Age Britain" (though certainly she is not slavishly devoted to this tradition and experiments freely).[19] Starhawk's covens are not separatist (i.e., men are allowed to participate and be initiated), but her writings are insistently feminist, and it is clear that she regards witchcraft's attitude toward women and the female to be among its greatest strengths. A frequent public speaker, Starhawk has also written several widely read books on witchcraft, including *The Spiral Dance* and *Dreaming the Dark,* and continues to be active politically. She is the preeminent thealogian[20] of feminist witchcraft, having a fully elaborated theory of the Goddess and her political and spiritual significance. Starhawk's "Kore Chant," one of the most frequently used Goddess chants, reads:

> Her name cannot be spoken,
> Her face was not forgotten,
> Her power is to open,
> Her promise can never be broken.
>
> She charges everything She touches, and
> Everything She touches, changes.
> Change is, touch is; Touch is, change is.
> Change us! Touch us! Touch us! Change us!
>
> Everything lost is found again,
> In a new form, In a new way.
> Everything hurt is healed again,
> In a new life, In a new day.[21]

All leaders in the feminist spirituality movement are quick to say that they are not leaders, or that if they are, all women in the movement are equally leaders. There is a tendency, following the feminist movement generally, to be antihierarchical, to try to guarantee that each woman receives a hearing and an opportunity to lead. Nevertheless, both Budapest and Starhawk are somewhat ambivalent on this score. Certainly both are aware of their unique gifts as leaders and do not hesitate to use them, but both make an effort to downplay their leadership (at least in writing) and stress the equality of all women involved in feminist witchcraft.[22] Starhawk reflects on her ambivalence about being a leader in *Dreaming the Dark* when she describes a trance she experienced in which she committed herself to being a teacher of spirituality and magic. In this trance, she agreed to this commitment only on the condition that she have "equal companions." Starhawk reflects:

> In raising the question of equal companions, I showed that I really didn't feel equal. If I had, it would never have occurred to me that companions could be anything else. Although consciously I believed firmly in equality and collectivity, my unconscious identity was still that of the precocious child, the smartest kid in the class. Now I created situations in which I could remain one step above as the teacher, the focal point. Yet being central, keeping others peripheral, is a very lonely position.[23]

Of course, the feminist spirituality movement, as all religious movements, does depend on its leaders. Particularly in the case of ritual, leaders fill an important role in orchestrating events. But more significantly, it could be that spiritual feminists, being on the margins of religion as it is ordinarily practiced in the United States, have a persistent need to have someone transform their tentative spiritual inclinations into certainties. One sometimes gets the feeling in feminist rituals that the main function of the leader is to help navigate the participants away from feeling silly about dancing or chanting or lighting candles and toward experiencing these acts religiously. It is the leader's confidence in what she is doing, her belief that it is legitimately *religion,* that communicates itself to the participants and allows for the transformation from awkward play-acting to sacred ritual.

Central Elements of Feminist Spirituality

The feminist spirituality movement has now grown far beyond its genesis in feminist witchcraft. Many women who identify themselves as spiritual feminists claim no interest in or connection to witchcraft or neopaganism.

The feminist spirituality movement as a whole is even more eclectic than feminist witchcraft, more free to adopt symbols and practices from other religious traditions, and less likely to form itself into ongoing religious groups. Particularly in the last five years, the influence of Native American religions and the New Age movement on feminist spirituality has been marked.[24] Still, the primary characteristics of feminist spirituality remain similar to those that were in place when the movement first emerged over twenty years ago. The four that I will examine here are the Goddess, sacred history, ritual, and magic.

Goddess

The Goddess is a central figure for almost all spiritual feminists. She is conceived of in a number of ways that appear contradictory at a superficial level, but which are not felt as contradiction by her worshippers. She is often referred to as the Great Goddess, the Great Mother, the Creatrix—all of which give rise to an impression of Goddess monotheism. It is rare to find Goddess worship without this ultimate monism. Yet the Goddess is also worshipped—indeed is far more frequently worshipped—in terms of her various polytheistic aspects. One prevalent version of the Goddess's aspects is trinitarian: she is virgin (or maiden), mother, and crone, a division meant to illustrate that she is not merely a fertility goddess or a wise old woman, but a goddess who manifests characteristics of all the phases of a woman's life. Most common, however, is to refer to the Goddess by her names, and these are legion. Any name given to female divinity in any culture is fair game for spiritual feminists, who quite happily take neopaganism beyond its European roots. And because there have been an abundance of goddesses in the history of the world's religions, the individual seeking a particular sort of goddess is generally able to find one to suit her needs. A woman may choose to worship the Greek goddess Demeter to connect with the concept of motherhood, or with Artemis to grow in strength and independence. She may call on Pele, the Hawaiian goddess of the volcano, or Kali, Hindu goddess of destruction, if she is working through feelings of rage. Nearly every ritual includes a recital of some of the Goddess's many names as invocation, chant, or meditation.

The Goddess is a radically immanent deity, present in all things and accessible through all things.[25] It is frequently remarked that the Earth is the body of the Goddess, and that women connect with the Earth through their experiences of their own bodies and their experiences of nature. The Goddess *is* nature, and nature is sacred: she celebrates her sexuality, and gives birth to everything. Like the natural world, the Goddess is conceived of as constantly changing, ever-renewed, moving endlessly through the cycles of the seasons and the ages. The quality of belief in this Goddess is thus significantly different from that of belief in the transcendent God found in most Western religious traditions. Spiritual feminists stress time and again that it is not necessary to have faith in the Goddess because one can experience her directly. Starhawk responds to the question "do you believe in the Goddess?" as follows: "People often ask me if I *believe* in the Goddess. I reply "Do you believe in rocks?" It is extremely difficult for most Westerners to grasp the concept of a manifest deity. The phrase "believe *in*" itself implies that we cannot *know* the Goddess, that She is somehow intangible, incomprehensible. But we do not *believe* in rocks—we may see them, touch them, dig them out of our gardens, or stop small children from throwing them at each other. We know them; we connect with them."[26]

Sacred History

The sacred history of the feminist spirituality movement begins with a long-dead golden age in which whole cultures worshipped the Goddess—and nature through her—and lived in peace with themselves, their environment, and their neighbors. It is mythically reconstructed as a time when women had social power, were revered as a reflection of the divine, and when "female" values (nurture, cooperation) held sway. Writing, mathematics, and agriculture are all believed by spiritual feminists to have been developed under the beneficent rule of the Goddess's worshippers. The assumption seems to be that matriarchy[27] was a worldwide phenomenon, though discussion of matriarchal societies is almost always limited to Mediterranean, southern European, and Middle Eastern cultures.

The golden age of the matriarchies ended around 3000 B.C.E. according to spiritual feminists, when the patriarchy prohibited Goddess worship and enslaved women. That the patriarchs and their "male" values triumphed over the nearly utopian matriarchies presents spiritual feminists with a formidable problem: who would want to destroy paradise? The patriarchal revolution is sometimes thought to have been masterminded by disaffected males within the Goddess-worshipping cultures, but much more commonly it is believed to have been the result of invasions from outside the matriarchies, specifically invasions by nomadic patriarchal tribes whose original homelands were in the North Eurasian steppes.[28] The invading patriarchs were eager to establish the existence of paternity and to assert their control over it, and it was primarily for this reason that they oppressed women.[29] The demise of Goddess worship was necessary for the success of the patriarchs' mission, spiritual feminists argue, because women who knew they were living reflections of a powerful Goddess would never have assented to having their lives controlled by men.

Yet as noted earlier, spiritual feminists believe that Goddess worship was not entirely destroyed, and that even under the patriarchal religions of Judaism and Christianity it continued to exist as a minority religion among the peasant populations of Europe. According to feminist spirituality's sacred history, Goddess worship was persecuted as witchcraft by both the Catholic and Protestant churches. The figure typically given by spiritual feminists for the number of men, women, and children burned as witches in Europe during the Middle Ages is nine million, the great preponderance of these being women.[30] However, spiritual feminists are quick to add that not all of those persecuted for witchcraft were actually practitioners of paganism or Goddess worship (in this they follow the analysis given by Dworkin and Daly). Most are seen as the victims of the patriarchs' need to consolidate their power. Women who did not fit neatly into the categories allotted to them under male domination were accused of witchcraft and then murdered for their supposed crimes, so that the potential revolution of women could be contained and patriarchal rule secured. Thus the "Burning Times" stand for spiritual feminists as the single most egregious case of misogyny in Western history.[31]

The understanding of spiritual feminists is that we continue to live in the patriarchy today, and if women are no longer burned as witches, it is due more to luck and persistent rebellion than to any reform on the part of the ruling patriarchs or the ordinary men who carry out their mission. However, the final installment in feminist spirituality's sacred history is not the present, but the future. Spiritual feminists look forward to a time when society will be returned to the life-loving values of matriarchy, to the worship of nature as the Goddess and of women as her representatives. However, happy anticipation of utopia is frequently overshadowed by a dread of planetary catastrophe brought on by the abuse of the environment through technology and the abuse of women, children, and minorities by ruling males. We hover at the edge of apocalypse, and the days of the present order are numbered: either the patriarchy destroys us all, or we are able at the last moment to extricate ourselves from the bonds of male domination and give birth to a new matriarchal (or equalitarian) golden age.

Ritual

The practice of feminist spirituality consists of either ritual or magic, or a combination of the two. Feminist witches conduct regular rituals according to the lunar and solar cycles of nature. The esbats, or full moons, are celebrated each month, while the sabbats (solstices, equinoxes, and cross-quarters) are marked by ritual eight times per year. Feminist witchcraft's "Wheel of the Year" begins at Candlemas or Yule (the winter solstice) and ends at Hallowmas or Samhain (our Halloween), and is ritualized as a cycle of birth, life, death, and rebirth. Rituals differ depending on the season: winter is a time for looking inward while summer is a time for dance and revelry. Most feminist witchcraft rituals exhibit the same basic structure, beginning with the opening of the circle and ending with its closing. Often an altar is constructed in the middle of the ritual space, covered with flowers, candles, fruit, seashells, crystals, figurines of the Goddess, and any other objects that participants consider important to them. The ritual begins as all participants stand in a circle. The priestess (or several priestesses) go to each of the four compass points, beginning with the East and moving counter-clockwise, and with a ritual object in hand (usually a wand or a knife), she invokes the goddesses associated with each direction. Once the circle has been formally cast, no one leaves it until it is formally closed. The ritual progresses with a series of songs, chants, readings, meditations, and dances. At some point there is usually an effort to "raise energy" by holding hands, breathing together, and chanting or singing with increasing tempo and volume until it is felt that the energy has reached its peak. The energy is then "sent" to its desired object (the end of the patriarchy, the health of mother earth, healing for a sick friend) and grounded (participants place their hands on the ground and gradually relax their breathing). Often participants will go around the circle, with each woman lighting a candle and announcing a wish to the group, with wishes ranging from "an end to the oppression of women" to "a new lover" and "money to pay the rent." Wishes are answered with shouts of "blessed be!" from the other participants. The circle is closed in the opposite direction from which it was opened, and the goddesses are thanked and dismissed. After the circle is closed, participants usually share a meal, discuss the ritual, and catch up on the changes in each other's lives since they last met.[32]

The broader feminist spirituality movement is less cohesive and more embracing of religious elements that are not strictly pagan than is feminist witchcraft, but when spiritual feminists do rituals (say, for example, at workshops or in discussion groups), they tend to follow patterns similar to those described above. Those elements seen as more extreme, more "witchy," are frequently dropped: trance, nudity, and cauldrons are rarely seen outside feminist witchcraft. But the classic patterns of circle, song, and candles are found throughout feminist spirituality.

Magic

Some spiritual feminists remain suspicious of the term *magic,* finding it too laden with occult associations to suit their self-image. But for others, magic is a subset of feminist spirituality's ritual (indeed, for some spiritual feminists, ritual is defined as magic, and vice versa). When feminist witches send healing energy to mother earth, when they light a candle for a successful job interview, or when they hold hands and call down the Goddess's judgment upon rapists, they practice a form of magic. Magic is also practiced alone, often in the form of creating protective charms or binding the powers of one's enemies so that they cannot cause one harm. Many enterprising spiritual feminists make their living selling candles, oils, herbs, salts, and other magical provisions, and others earn their keep by writing the recipe books that instruct practitioners in how to achieve their ends through magic.

The mechanisms of magic are explained differently by different individuals in the feminist spirituality movement. The most straightforwardly psychological interpretation of magic offered by spiritual feminists is that it works by triggering the subconscious mind. Magic, and the material devices it relies upon, operate to focus one's thoughts and energy on the desired event so that it is more likely that it will be brought to pass. For example, a woman may sew a red heart-shaped charm, fill it with herbs and place it under her pillow, in the belief that it will bring love into her life. When love does come into her life, she may say that it could just as well have happened had she sewn a green rectangular charm, and that if the red one was more efficacious, it was only because her mind has been trained for years to associate red with love. What really produced the desired result was her determination to have it.[33]

Another interpretation of magic given by spiritual feminists, this one with a cosmological base, suggests that magic works because it moves patterns of energy in accord with the practitioner's desires. According to this view, everything in the universe is connected by energy, consists of energy. And though it may seem to the conventional Western mindset that there is no way for someone to protect her house from a tornado if it happens to be in its path, feminist spirituality answers that the energy of the tornado and the energy of the individual mind are composed of the same substance, and may therefore communicate with one another. Again, the focus is on one's mind, and not on the magical props used to trigger it, but the idea that the mind has powers to control not only one's own behavior but also other people and objects by virtue of their interconnection, is superadded in this view of magic.[34]

A third understanding of magic among spiritual feminists is that there are actual causal connections between the magical props used and the ends sought. Thus if a woman wants love, a green rectangular charm will never do, but neither will a red heart-shaped one unless it is filled with the proper herbs and oils and charged with the proper ritual actions. It is not that the practitioner has become more receptive to love because she has focused her subconscious mind on it or that she is sending out energy to attract love, but that she has physically created a charm which will bring her lover to her. For those who understand magic in this way, it is the actual magical act, and not merely the intention behind it or the changes it creates in one's consciousness that effects the desired result. To illustrate, one feminist witch told me that she had made a charm to keep the police away and placed it in her freezer. For over a year, the police gave her no trouble, but one day a highway patrol officer pulled her over and gave a speeding ticket. Puzzled and confused, she drove home, only to find that her refrigerator had failed and everything in her freezer—including the charm—had thawed out.[35]

Feminist Spirituality as Women's Religion

Feminist spirituality is the late twentieth-century cultural creation of a small group of predominantly white, middle-class feminists in their thirties and forties, a significant proportion of whom are lesbians. These women have come together to create feminist spirituality in the quest for a religion that will not oppress women, but rather free them to fulfill their utmost potential, a religion that will value the female experience and incorporate it into its vision of the social good. What can we learn by examining its history, its beliefs, its practices? How does it differ from other alternative religions created and/or led by women? As Mary Farrell Bednarowski makes clear in her 1980 article "Outside the Mainstream," this is not the first time women have embarked on the project of creating a religion auspicious for women, nor the first time that women have created religions they hoped would be agents for widespread social change in every area from gender relations to international relations to divine-human relations. Is feminist spirituality merely the twentieth-century echo of the nineteenth-century religions that Bednarowski discusses, or does feminist spirituality represent some advance over its feminist forerunners? Or is feminist spirituality a regression, an eddy outside the mainstream where feminist dreams and visions are hoarded like the miser's gold and never put into the hard coin of political action? These questions are of paramount importance both for women inside the feminist spirituality movement and those outside trying to assess the movement's significance for feminism as a whole.

First, it must be granted that the feminist spirituality movement provides a close fit to Bednarowski's profile of religions sympathetic to female leadership.[36] Feminist spirituality's deity is not exclusively masculine; human beings (or at least women) are presumed to be good, not flawed by original sin; clergy is not traditional or hierarchically structured; and certainly there is an openness to women having nontraditional roles. More striking, however, than the four characteristics detailed in Bednarowski's profile is a fifth characteristic that is prominent in all of the nineteenth-century movements, but which is notably absent—in fact reversed—in feminist spirituality. This is antimaterialism, the elevation of mind or spirit over body, a denial of either the reality or the ultimate significance of the material. This is an especially conspicuous theme in Christian Science and Shakerism, but the Spiritualists and nineteenth-century Theosophists also wish to keep the body secondary and to focus their attention on transcendent realms. Spiritualist mediums frequently attained their calling only after a severe mortification of the flesh, not self-imposed, but nevertheless painful; and though Theosophists denied that the body was sinful, it was part of one's "lower nature" that had to be controlled and managed in service of the higher designs of the soul.[37] Why should antimaterialism be a common theme among the women's religions of the nineteenth-century, only to be superseded by a twentieth-century religion that worships the material and revels in the miracle of the body and nature?

A denial of the ultimate significance of nature and the body is a reasonable strategy for women with feminist sensibilities to take. Women have long been believed to have closer ties to nature, to bodiliness. Different societies and historical periods have interpreted these ties differently— some maintaining that women's bodies are what stand between men and their personal salvation, others that women's relationship to nature is an important part of the cultural balance—but most say these ties between women and nature exist. In her article "Is Female to Male as Nature is to Culture?" Sherry Ortner asserts that it is this presumed affinity between women and nature, and the parallel association of men with culture, that is responsible for the "pan-cultural fact" of women's secondary status.[38] If these are the true roots of women's oppression, it seems only sensible to deny the connection of women with nature and the body and to claim for women the full association with culture and transcendence that has formerly been the province of men.

This appears to be the strategy taken by nineteenth-century women's religions. When Mary Baker Eddy says that the body is an illusion and only spirit is reality, when Annie Besant describes bodies as outer garments on which existence is not dependent, when a spiritualist medium regards her body as a frail vessel through which the spirit world can speak, or when Ann Lee advocates celibacy as the proper relation between men and women, the time-honored connection between women and nature is being severed.[39] If women are not unbreakably bound to nature, they are free to claim what men have always had and what they as women have been denied: an autonomous will, the free use of intellectual gifts, and the ability to transcend bodily existence in communion with the divine.

This same strategy—of denying a necessary connection between woman, nature, and the body—appears outside the strictly religious circles of the Shakers, Spiritualists, Christian Scientists, and Theosophists in the nineteenth century. The entire Victorian denial of women's sexual drive (in contradistinction to a still earlier belief in women's extreme carnality) can be read as an effort to acquire a higher, firmer ground for women where they might gain social respect for their intellectual and spiritual qualities, and not their reproductive ones alone. In "Passionlessness: An Interpretation of Victorian Sexual Ideology," Nancy Cott makes this argument:

> Passionlessness served women's larger interests by downplaying altogether their sexual characterization, which was the cause of their exclusion from significant "human" (i.e., male) pursuits. The positive contribution of passionlessness was to replace that sexual/carnal characterization of women with a spiritual/moral one, allowing women to develop their human faculties and their self-esteem. The belief that women lacked carnal motivation was the cornerstone of the argument for women's moral superiority, used to enhance women's status and widen their opportunities in the nineteenth century.[40]

If it is true that women's association with the body and nature has been to their detriment, what can be the possible advantage in celebrating this connection, as the feminist spirituality movement does? Why should the nineteenth-century attempt to invalidate the link between women and nature give way to a twentieth-century attempt to reinforce it? Can such diametrically opposed strategies both be termed "feminist"?

There are a number of possible answers to these questions. One is to suggest that antimaterialism was well-suited to the feminism of nineteenth-century America, but that social conditions have changed such that it is no longer necessary or beneficial to the feminist cause to separate women from their bodiliness. According to this view, elaborated by Nancy Cott, a denial of women's carnality gave women significant leverage in a social system that was stacked against them. In an era where women were almost wholly dependent upon men for economic support, commodifying their sexuality by denying their own need for it gave women something to sell in the marriage market, as well as giving them cultural and ideological backing for the refusal of sex (which was their only reliable means of birth control).[41] As women's opportunities for economic independence (though not economic parity) have grown in the twentieth century, women are freer to desire men sexually as they need them less economically. And with advances in contraceptive technology and the legalization of abortion, heterosexual women are able to express their sexuality with less dire consequences.

Yet the turn in feminist spirituality toward *worship* of nature and the body is a much more dramatic shift than can be accounted for in terms of these changes in social conditions. Twentieth-century feminists continue to see women's association with nature and the body as a major source of their oppression under the patriarchy; why then would not the tactic of denying this association continue to be as valid now as it was in the nineteenth century? The answer is that it *is* still valid, and it continues to be used by twentieth-century feminists (and even by feminists within the feminist spirituality movement, at one level). But a second tactic is used as well: that of glorifying women's traditional association with nature, of accepting and revaluing it. These are, after all, the two major strategies available to any group that suffers social oppression: one is to argue that the cultural assumptions that support the oppression are ill-founded, that one's oppressors are simply wrong in their diagnosis of one's group, and that therefore the oppression is illegitimate. The other is to agree with the cultural assumptions of the oppressor, but to insist that they have been wrongly valued, that what has been called evil is in fact good, that what has been called worse is actually better. The two strategies that appear to be polar opposites are rather two sides of the same coin.[42]

Feminism, whether secular or religious, political or cultural, historic or contemporary, shifts between these two modes of reasoning, sometimes leaning more heavily on one, sometimes on the other, often striving to strike a balance between them. Nineteenth-century women's religions, for example, with their antimaterialist bias, tend to proceed by denying key cultural assumptions regarding women: women are not merely the female bodies that the patriarchy has chosen to denigrate; they are spirit as well (or spirit only). Twentieth-century feminist spirituality tends to take the other tack: yes, the patriarchs are right, women are closer to nature and more in touch with their bodies; however, this is not a failing, but a strength.

Neither brand of feminism is exclusively tied to one form of reasoning at the expense of the other. One of the characteristics Bednarowski notes among nineteenth-century women's religions, that of the denial of the doctrine of the Fall or of human depravity, shows this clearly. For there is no reason why feminists could not have chosen to exaggerate the doctrine of the Fall, to bring out its implication that if women are fallen, beset by the burdens of body and nature, then men are equally so. And yet nineteenth-century feminists chose to emphasize the opposite, that neither women nor men operate from a position of crippling original sin. This is particularly true of Theosophy and Spiritualism, as Bednarowski notes in her article "Women in Occult America." As one Theosophist writes, "sin does not consist in fulfilling any of the functions of nature."[43] Nineteenth-century women's religions deny that women are rightly seen as more enmeshed in the material than men, but they also claim that nature and the material are not inherently contaminating, so that even if women *were* more closely tied to nature this is not sufficient reason to discriminate against them.

The feminist spirituality movement is similarly committed to both strategies of dealing with women's oppression. Most prominently, the patriarchal association of women with nature and the body is taken to be true by spiritual feminists, but rather than being treated as a reason for maintaining women's secondary status, it is seen as an epiphany of the divine, and as a reason for elevating women to a position of cultural leadership so that all might learn to appreciate our shared human dependence on nature. Yet spiritual feminists never try to argue that women lack intellectual talents or that they should abandon the tasks of culture creation to men and get back to the far more important business of celebrating nature and bearing children. If the cultural assumptions of patriarchy regarding women are adopted on one level, they are denied at another: women's connections to nature and the body do not imply passivity, irrationality, or cultural irrelevance, as the patriarchy has claimed, but leave ample room for aggression, intelligence, and social power.

However, the choice twentieth-century feminist spirituality has made to embrace women's traditional association with nature and the body is not accidental. As noted above, that association is no longer as punishing as it was in the nineteenth century, now that women have a measure of economic independence and reproductive control. Furthermore, there is a greater openness on the part of society generally to hear the gospel of nature, materiality, and the flesh. Technology no longer seems to hold every key to the successful manipulation of nature for human ends, and increased urbanization has brought a renewed longing for the cycles and seasons of the natural world. For early American colonists, nature was a foe, and the divine was sought in civilization. As Rosemary Radford Ruether remarks of the Puritans: "The city set on the hill represents the elect of Zion raised to redemption through divine grace. But all around, unredeemed nature bears the face of death, sin, and the devil."[44] By the nineteenth century, the sacred center was no longer the city, the pinnacle of civilization, but the home: sacred suburbia, if you will.[45] Now, in the twentieth century, when the principal products of the city seem to be poverty and crime rather than culture and freedom, and when the suburban home provides no safe haven from these social ills, the sacred is sought in nature, in the contemplation of nature's beauty, order, and self-renewal. Feminists are able to capitalize on this trend, to see in the turn to nature an opportunity for women to assert their historic association with this realm and to glorify it. Thus the feminist spirituality movement retains at least the possibility of social relevance, while giving undeniable strength and solace to the women who turn to it for spiritual sustenance.

NOTES

1. Christian women who have become heavily involved with the Goddess-worship, neopagan, or witchcraft elements of the feminist spirituality movement typically end by repudiating Christianity. In both the literature of the movement and in interviews I conducted, formerly Christian women are critical of Christianity, often viewing it as irredeemably patriarchal. For this reason it is fair to describe the movement as post-Christian. Jewish women seem less inclined to view their involvement with feminist spirituality as necessitating a break with their Jewish heritage. I will not here speculate on the reasons for this difference and will restrict the following discussion of normative religions to Christianity.

2. See, for example, Hallie Austen Iglehart, *Womanspirit* (San Francisco: Harper and Row, 1983), xii.

3. For a description of this phenomenon in other movements of the 1960s, see Steven M. Tipton, *Getting Saved from the Sixties* (Berkeley: University of California Press, 1982).

4. Accounts of feminist breaks with traditional religions can be found in Carol P. Christ, *Laughter of Aphrodite* (San Francisco: Harper and Row, 1987); Mary Daly, "The Qualitative Leap beyond Patriarchal Religion," *Quest* 1, no. 4 (1975): 20–40; and Naomi Goldenberg, *Changing of the Gods* (Boston: Beacon Press, 1979).

5. Robert Ellwood sees an interest in feminine spiritual leadership and feminine divinity as a long-standing hallmark of the alternative religious tradition in the United States. See his *Alternative Altars* (Chicago: University of Chicago Press, 1979), 40.

6. Margot Adler, *Drawing Down the Moon* (Boston: Beacon Press, 1979), 42; Starhawk, *Truth or Dare* (San Francisco: Harper and Row, 1987), 7.

7. Starhawk, *The Spiral Dance* (San Francisco: Harper and Row, 1979), 5–7; Margaret Murray, *The Witch-Cult in Western Europe* (Oxford: Oxford University Press, 1921); Mircea Eliade, *Occultism, Witchcraft, and Cultural Fashions* (Chicago: University of Chicago Press, 1976), 69–92.

8. Adler, *Drawing Down the Moon,* 60–66.

9. Ibid., 84–91.

10. Ibid., 92–132.

11. Ibid., 177.

12. Robin Morgan, *Sisterhood is Powerful* (New York: Random House, 1970), 538–39.

13. Ibid., 539–40.

14. Andrea Dworkin, *Woman Hating* (New York: E.P. Dutton, 1974), 118–50; Mary Daly, *Gyn/Ecology* (Boston: Beacon Press, 1978), 178–222.

15. Zsuzsanna Budapest, *The Holy Book of Women's Mysteries* (Berkeley: Wingbow Press, 1989), xi-xviii, 258–62; Adler, *Drawing Down the Moon,* 76–77, 181–84.

16. Alternative spellings of "woman" (womon), "women" (wimmin, womyn), and "human" (hummin), are used by some feminists to avoid the inclusion of the root words "man" and "men" in language referring to women alone or to people in general.

17. Z. Budapest, *The Holy Book of Women's Mysteries* (Oakland, CA: Susan B. Anthony Coven No. 1, 1979), 9–10. The 1989 edition of *The Holy Book* has a revised version of the manifesto. Traditional spellings of "woman" and "women" are employed, the death principle is no longer parenthetically termed "male," and the phrase, "We teach 'Pan' workshops today and work together with men who have changed themselves into brothers," is appended to the second-to-the-last statement in the manifesto [*The Holy Book* (1989), 2–3].

18. Budapest, *The Holy Book* (1989), xiv. Starhawk's account of their meeting can be found in the second edition of *The Spiral Dance* (San Francisco: Harper and Row, 1989), 3.

19. Starhawk, *Spiral Dance,* 11.

20. Spiritual feminists commonly use the spelling "thealogy" to indicate that they are reflecting on the divine as feminine, substituting the Greek root "thea," the feminine form of the word "god," for the traditional "theos," which is masculine. An account of the development of this neologism in feminist circles can be found in Emily Erwin Culpepper, "Contemporary Goddess Thealogy: A Sympathetic Critique," in *Shaping New Visions: Gender and Values in American Culture,* ed. Clarissa W. Atkinson, Constance H. Buchanan, and Margaret R. Miles (Ann Arbor: UMI Research Press, 1987), 51.

21. Starhawk, *The Spiral Dance,* 88–89.

22. Budapest, *The Holy Book* (1989), xv.

23. Starhawk, *Dreaming the Dark* (Boston: Beacon Press, 1982), 50.

24. In fact, some varieties of feminist spirituality seem to owe more to New Age thought than to feminist witchcraft and can probably be more accurately interpreted as the feminist wing of the New Age movement than as a diffusive manifestation of feminist witchcraft.

25. Starhawk, *Dreaming the Dark,* 9.

26. Starhawk, *Spiral Dance,* 77. This sentiment is frequently echoed by spiritual feminists when in the course of interviews I ask them whether they believe in a Goddess.

27. I use the term *matriarchy* for convenience. Some spiritual feminists object to the term as denoting inappropriate power relations and prefer to describe these societies as *gynocentric, matrifocal, gylanic, partnership,* or *equalitarian.*

28. Archaeological findings generally support the claim that these migrations took place, but scholars disagree on their cultural significance. Feminist archaeologists such as Marija Gimbutas [*The Goddesses and Gods of Old Europe* (Berkeley:

University of California Press, 1982)] interpret these invasions as a patriarchal revolution, and it is to these sympathetic archaeologists that spiritual feminists most frequently appeal.

29. It is sometimes claimed that under matriarchal rule there was no understanding of the connection between sexual intercourse and conception.

30. The 9 million figure is ubiquitous in feminist references to the European witch burnings. Apparently this figure was first claimed by Matilda Joslyn Gage in *Woman, Church and State,* originally published in 1893 (reprint edition [Watertown, Mass.: Persephone Press, 1980], 106–7). Medieval scholars' estimates are more conservative, some as low as 100,000 (E. William Monter, *European Witchcraft* [New York: Wiley and Sons, 1969], 73). However, it is generally conceded that the majority of those persecuted as witches were female (Jeffrey B. Russell, *Witchcraft in the Middle Ages* [Ithaca, N.Y.: Cornell University Press, 1972, 279–84]; Pennethorne Hughes, *Witchcraft* [London: Longmans, Green and Co., 1952], 71–74; Richard Kieckhefer, *European Witch Trials* [Berkeley: University of California Press, 1976], 96; H. R. Trevor-Roper, *The European Witch-Craze of the Sixteenth and Seventeenth Centuries and Other Essays* [New York: Harper and Row, 1956], 91–92). Certainly the stereotype is female, since all these authors use feminine pronouns when speaking generically about witches, in contravention of the usual practice of using either male or gender-neutral language when speaking generically.

31. Medieval scholars agree that to whatever extent there were pagan survivals in medieval Europe, this factor in the witch burnings was clearly outweighed by the need of the Christian state to purge the social body of imagined threats to its monopoly of power. Feminist scholars name the threat as female; other scholars have seen the threat as Protestant or Catholic, rebellion of the lower classes, or deeply-rooted psychological fantasies (Trevor-Roper, *European Witch-Craze;* Jules Michelet, *Satanism and Witchcraft* [New York: Citadel Press, 1939]; Norman Cohn, *Europe's Inner Demons* [New York: Basic Books, 1975]).

32. This description is based on my observations of feminist witchcraft groups in southern California. A written account of feminist witchcraft ritual can be found in Starhawk, *Spiral Dance,* 55–75.

33. This view of magic is common among spiritual feminists who are strongly influenced by New Age philosophies, particularly the New Age concept of the omnicausal agent: that each person is completely responsible for what happens to her or him and has chosen these experiences (sometimes before birth) in order to learn important spiritual lessons.

34. This view of magic is probably most common among feminist witches and has a long and illustrious history in the New Thought, Christian Science, and Theosophical movements of the nineteenth century. Starhawk gives a basic introduction to this understanding of magic in *Spiral Dance,* 18.

35. Anonymous witch, interview with author, 1983. Marcello Truzzi discusses this and the previous understanding of magic under the term *extra-scientific technology* in his article, "Towards A Sociology of the Occult," in *Religious Movements in Contemporary America,* ed. Irving I. Zaretsky and Mark P. Leone (Princeton, N.J.: Princeton University Press, 1974), 630–31.

36. Mary Farrell Bednarowski, "Outside the Mainstream," *Journal of the American Academy of Religion* 48, no. 2 (1980): 209.

37. Mary Farrell Bednarowski, "Women in Occult America," in *The Occult in America,* ed. Howard Kerr and C. L. Crow (Urbana: University of Illinois Press, 1983), 184; R. Laurence Moore, "The Spiritualist Medium," *American Quarterly* 27 (1975): 215.

38. Sherry B. Ortner, "Is Female to Male as Nature is to Culture?" *Feminist Studies* 1, no. 2 (1972): 5.

39. Bednarowski, "Outside the Mainstream"; Annie Besant, *Man and His Bodies* (London: Theosophical Publishing House, n.d.), 5–8; Moore, "The Spiritualist Medium," 202; Sally L. Kitch, *Chaste Liberation* (Urbana: University of Illinois Press, 1989).

40. Nancy F. Cott, "Passionlessness," in *A Heritage of Her Own,* ed. Nancy F. Cott and Elizabeth A. Pleck (New York: Simon and Schuster, 1979), 173.

41. Ibid., 172–73.

42. Nancy Cott discusses how these strategies have been at work in the first and second waves of feminism in the United States in her article "Feminist Theory and Feminist Movements," in *What is Feminism?* ed. Juliet Mitchell and Ann Oakley (New York: Pantheon Books, 1986), 49–62.

43. Bednarowski, "Women in Occult America," 187.

44. Rosemary Radford Ruether, *Sexism and God-Talk* (Boston: Beacon Press, 1983), 81.

45. See Colleen McDannell, *The Christian Home in Victorian America* (Bloomington: Indiana University Press, 1986).

The Women-Church Movement in Contemporary Christianity

Rosemary Radford Ruether

The Women-Church movement has emerged in contemporary Christianity, especially from Roman Catholicism, in direct response to the frustration that feminist Christian women feel toward the clerical, patriarchal church institution and leadership. Since Women-Church is not an organization and has no official leaders or spokespersons, one cannot make a definitive statement of what its views are. Yet there are enough commonalities in the basic patterns out of which it operates that some working definitions are possible. Indeed this deliberate looseness of structure, leaving the definition of its thought and way of operating up to whatever the local communities wish, fits very much into one of the salient characteristics of women's religion, according to Mary Farrell Bednarowsk, namely, anticlericalism.

History of Women-Church

Women-Church advocates often claim that their vision of the church is in better keeping with the original Christian vision of a community of equals. One of those who would claim that Women-Church is a reclamation of the original Christian vision is Roman Catholic feminist New Testament scholar, Elizabeth Schüssler Fiorenza, who coined the term the *ecclesia* of women or Women-Church.[1] Yet, however much Christian feminists may seek to lay claim to normative tradition, both the idea and the acting out of the idea of church as a feminist liberation community begins historically in American Catholicism in the 1970s, with the rise of both feminism and liberation theology.

American Catholicism appropriated the ideas of church renewal initiated by the Second Vatican Council with particular zeal. For many American Catholics the shift to the idea of Church as "people of God" appealed to their democratic culture. Many became disappointed by the unwillingness of the hierarchy of make more radical reforms in the direction of a participatory church. They began to experiment with "house-churches" or more informal, egalitarian forms of liturgical community.

At the same time, liberation theologians in Latin America were developing the "base community" as a similar kind of small, egalitarian Christian community for Bible study and worship, aimed at providing the motivational base for committed action for social justice in society. The base community was defined by its theoreticians, not simply as a substructure of the parish, but as the more authentic expression of church or Christian community. The people at the grass roots, particularly among oppressed classes, were claiming the right to reinvent the church.[2] These ideas influenced North American Christians sympathetic to the liberation movements in Latin America.

Thirdly, a feminist movement in American society was having its impact in the Christian churches. Between 1956 and 1975 there was a rapid increase in the number of churches that began to ordain women. The 1970s also saw a continual rise in the numbers of women undertaking advanced theological degrees in seminaries, reaching an average of 35 percent in the mid–1980s. Liberal Protestant seminaries often had 50 percent or more women students, while even more conservative denominations that did not ordain women, such as Roman Catholicism, saw an increasing number of women seeking theological degrees.

Some of these Catholic women went to more liberal Catholic seminaries run by religious orders, such as the Jesuit seminaries in Berkeley or Cambridge, Massachusetts, while other Catholic women found their way into Protestant seminaries, particularly less denominationally affiliated ones, such as Harvard or Yale Divinity Schools. The Catholic women began to teach in religious studies faculties and in Protestant and Catholic seminaries and to write books. They laid the basis for a new Catholic feminist intelligentsia that could challenge traditional patriarchal Christianity on its own ground of scripture, historical tradition, and theology.[3]

Another source of feminist ferment in Roman Catholicism came from the renewal of women's religious orders, also the fruit of the Second Vatican Council. In the 1950s, American Catholic nuns had been engaged in a struggle with the hierarchy to improve their educational levels, a struggle that implied a more independently thinking type of religious woman. When the Second Vatican Council invited nuns to renew themselves by reexamining the charisms of their founders, many American religious orders took this as a mandate to radically democratize their orders, modernize, or discard altogether the religious habit that set them apart from lay women and to move into ministries to the poor no longer under the control of the church hierarchy.[4]

Feminist consciousness grew among those sectors of religious orders most engaged in this type of renewal, especially when they experienced the repressive backlash from the hierarchy against what they saw as their best and most authentic efforts of renewal. Many of the most progressive of these nuns left their orders, often pursuing further theological study and/or more autonomous grass roots ministries. Others have remained in their orders, but in such a way as to make these orders a base for a more autonomous way of living in women's communities oriented to social justice for oppressed people, especially poor women.

In 1974 the struggle in the American Episcopal church over the ordination of women caused a temporary rift, when a group of retired bishops decided to ordain eleven women "irregularly." Two years later this conflict would be resolved by the Episcopal church accepting the ordination of women. This conflict in a church with a priestly tradition similar to Catholicism sparked a parallel movement for the ordination of women among Catholics.

In 1975 the first gathering of the Women's Ordination Conference took place in Detroit, Michigan. The planners of the Detroit conference defined their goals, not simply as the inclusion of women in priestly ministry as it had been traditionally defined, but also as the "renewal of priestly ministry," by which they meant a substantial redefinition of the clerical pattern of priesthood to bring it more in line with a more participatory understanding of the church as community. They saw the traditional priesthood as symbolically and socially patriarchal and misogynist. This contradicted what these feminist women saw as the authentic nature of Christian ministry and community. It also made it impossible for women to be authentically included in it without a fundamental revision of the way it was imaged and functioned.[5]

This Detroit gathering resulted in the organization of the Women's Ordination Conference as a national movement, with both a central office and local chapters. A second national conference of the Women's Ordination Conference in Baltimore in 1978 saw an increasing doubt as to whether ordination should be the priority goal of Catholic women. In October 15, 1976, the Vatican had released an official statement claiming that the ordination of women was inadmissible because women, by their very nature, were incapable of "imaging Christ."[6] Although this declaration was widely rejected by both theologians and grassroots Catholics, it raised the question for feminists about whether their focus should not be on the renewal of community, with ordination to follow only after a major process of shaping an alternative way of being church.

In the 1970s there also emerged a variety of Catholic feminist organizations independent of the hierarchy: the National Assembly of Religious Women (which came to include lay women in its membership), the

National Coalition of American Nuns, WATER (the Women's Alliance for Theology, Ethics and Ritual); Chicago Catholic Women, the Institute for Women Today, *Las Hermanas,* Catholics for a Free Choice, among others. These groups formed a coalition called the Women of the Church Convergence. In November 1983 they put on a major conference in Chicago called "Woman Church Speaks." At this conference ordination was put on the backburner, and Women-Church was launched as a movement.

The second major Women-Church conference, organized by an even larger coalition of Catholic church groups, was put on in Cincinnati in 1987. These conferences were basically liturgical in character, although there were a wide variety of workshops that canvassed the whole spectrum of Catholic feminist concerns, sexual, spiritual, and social. At the Chicago gathering, under the category of "spirituality," there were workshops on such topics as feminist theology, counseling, retreat work, spiritual guidance and liturgical communities.

Under the topic of sexuality were considered topics such as sexual life-style; marriage, celibacy, divorced women, lesbians, single women, reproductive rights, rape, incest, pornography, and prostitution. Under the category of "survival" there were workshops on women with children alone and poor, women on welfare, church workers, aging women, refugees, militarism, unemployment, networking, and organizing. The conferences attempted to be bilinqual in English and Spanish and multiracial.

But, above all, the conferences sought to be a collective experience of what it meant to be Women-Church. Women-Church signified a new stance of feminists toward the institutional church, no longer petitioning the male leadership for "permission" to enter canonical leadership, but defining church for themselves. For most of these women this did not mean an attempt to form a women's denomination. Women-Church is seen as an exodus movement within the Christian community, but no longer defined or confined by its institutional boundaries, laws, and forms. By implication, the patriarchal church is seen as a falsification of the true message of Christian community and Women-Church its authentic expression.

The second half of the 1980s has seen an increasing globalization of feminist liturgical communities, whether or not the term Women-Church is adopted to express this reality. In England, Holland, Germany, and Scandinavia, Christian feminists typically develop feminist liturgies as their way of expressing their vision of the celebration of women's spiritual and social redemption from patriarchy at their gatherings. In England such gatherings have been sponsored by groups such as the Catholic Women's Network and the Women In Theology group. In Holland the lead in feminist liturgical gathering has been taken by the Grail, a lay noncanonical Catholic women's religious movement that was founded in the 1930s.

Asian Catholic and Protestant women have also founded strong feminist networks regionally, nationally, and internationally. They have gathered international conferences under the aegis of the Women's Commission of the Ecumenical Association of Third World Theologians and the Asian Women's Resource Center for Culture and Theology.[7] Feminist liturgy and scriptural exegesis is a regular part of such gatherings. Examples of feminist prayer, liturgy, and exegesis, as well as feminist theology and analysis, is published through the Asian Christian feminist journal, *In God's Image*. [8]

The Women-Church movement is a strong exemplar of all the characteristics of women's religion lifted up by Mary Bednarowski. In the case of Women-Church there is no debate about whether this movement happened to have these characteristics and thus attracted women, or whether it was women who developed it with these characteristics. Clearly the latter is the case. Women with an explicitly feminist agenda set out to create religious community to express redemption from patriarchy. The critique of clericalism, the rejection of a pessimistic anthropology that blames women for sin, openness to a plurality of sexual life-styles, and a view of God that is no longer defined by the male gender exclusively are all taken for granted as elements in this understanding of community. I will treat these four points of women's religion as they appear in Women-Church.

Clericalism versus Community

Clericalism is seen in Women-Church as an organizational pattern modeled after the patriarchal relation of the *pater familias* over his wife, children, and slaves. Clericalism is the extension of the *pater familias* model of relationships of domination and subordination into service relations between adults. This model of relationship is fundamentally antithetical to true liberation and community. In the clerical model of leadership the leader is a member of a professional class who monopolizes the knowledge and resources of service in a way that reduces those who are served to passive dependency.

Those who are served are forbidden to exercise these functions for themselves, by lack of access to specialized knowledge, but especially by lack of legitimacy. This lack of legitimacy may be defined legally, as well as culturally. Lay people are defined as both incapable and legally forbidden to exercise these functions themselves. Only those ordained (empowered by God) and/or licensed (permitted by the laws of the organization) may exercise these functions.

Clericalism pervades not only institutionalized religious leadership but also many "helping" professions, such as doctors, lawyers, psychiatrists, professors and social workers. Characteristic of the clerical mode of helping is that those who are served are rendered unable to help themselves. They are disallowed and disempowered from healing themselves, teaching themselves or organizing themselves to solve their own social problems. They are taught to believe that they must depend on the professional to solve their problems. Thus clericalism is based on the disempowerment of the people. Clericalism creates and perpetuates a constituency dependent on receiving help from the professional, without ever becoming able to learn to do these same things through this relation to the professional.

In my book, *Women-Church,* I analyzed this disempowerment of the people by ecclesiastical clericalism in terms of sacramental life, education and administration.[9] For the church, the core of lay disempowerment is sacramental, although in the areas of teaching and administration, lay participation is also rendered dependent on the clergy. Clerical sacramental disempowerment of the people means taking the life symbols of the community's relation to God and claiming that the divine power and efficacy of these symbols belongs to the clergy alone, through a special infusion of this power from God that takes place at ordination.

Any attempt by an unordained person to exercise this role, by blessing the bread and wine or making the signs of forgiveness of sins, would be not only invalid (legally unpermitted) but also impotent. In effect, nothing would happen. No divine power of blessing, divine presence or forgiveness would be transmitted, because the lay person does not possess this divine power and so cannot transmit it.

Teaching and administration is also controlled by the clergy, but primarily by institutional monopoly, rather than by claims that they alone possess divine efficacy. However, in the Roman Catholic system the claim that only the Pope and, through association with the Pope, the episcopal magisterium can teach infallibly comes close to this same assertion of a divine validity that sets the clerical elect decisively apart from those who lack this holy power.

Catholicism also insists that only clergy can preach, that clergy are the preferred teachers of doctrine in Catholic seminaries and colleges, and that both priests and theologians should take an oath of allegiance to the Pope in order to exercise their teaching and preaching office. Particularly the recent effort to impose an oath of allegiance on Catholic teachers manifests a more exaggerated effort, under the pontificate of John Paul II, to tie all Catholic teaching to this papal claim to a power to teach that is error-free.[10]

The capacity to administer the property and resources of the church is tied to the apex of the clerical hierarchy in Roman Catholicism by such devices as defining the bishop as a corporation sole who owns the property of the diocese. Priests as well as laity administer this property only under the corporate ownership and final decision-making power that rests in the hands of the bishops.

By monopolizing the appointment of bishops, the Vatican has attempted to tie the resources of the local dioceses and national churches to the papal administrative center. Under the pontificate of John Paul II, there has been an effort, not only to reverse the democratizing tendencies unleashed by the Second Vatican Council but even to cancel traditions of local and national self-rule that come down from medieval tradition, in favor of a strictly monarchical system of church government.

Women-Church represents a radical dissolution of this whole theory and practice of clerical hierarchical control over sacraments, teaching and administration. This is seen most centrally in the appropriation of the power to do Eucharist by the people. The bread and wine of the Eucharist are understood, not as magic fetishes, but as simply the ordinary food and drink of daily meals of the Mediterranean world. Translated into religious symbols, they represent our ordinary life transformed and restored to its potential for goodness. This goodness is wholistic and communal; it means physical, psychical, and spiritual health that finds its locus in a loving and mutually affirming community.

By celebrating our ordinary life redeemed from alienation and evil, through the symbols of bread and wine, we are put back in touch with the fullness of our life, rooted in the divine life from which we are sprung and are continually renewed. This divine life-giving power is not off some-where else in "another world," removed from this present one. Therefore it does not need to be "brought down" to this present world by a rite of ordination available only to an elite. Rather it is the ground of being of our human life in its authenticity. The community, by entering into its authen-tic biophilic potential, puts itself in touch with this redemptive Spirit that is under and around us all the time.

This means that the Eucharist, above all, must be a participatory and communal act. As much as possible, the whole community that celebrates it together should be involved in doing it, by blessing the food and drink together and passing it from one to another. There may be particular leaders of the community with the expertise to put together satisfactory dramatic forms for this celebration, in words, music, and gesture. But this, in no way, means that these people have some special power to make the divine present. The divine is made present precisely through the depth of the participa-tion of the community in expressing its intention to be together in love.

Having dismantled the heart of the clerical claim to special divine magical power, unavailable to the people, it is less difficult to deconstruct other clerical claims to monopoly on teaching and administration. Here the key question is how power and skill is exercised. Is it exercised in such a way as to make the community dependent on the teacher and leader? Or is it exercised in such a way as to widen the circle of participation and imbue more and more people with a share in the skills of teaching and leadership?

The critique of clericalism does not result in anarchy. There is no denial that there are people with distinct gifts and training that are better fitted to teach, to do interpretation of symbols and social relations, and also to organize and administer programs. But the exercise of these roles needs to be organized in such a way as to engender participation rather than dependency. Teachers need to teach in such a way as to draw the learners into becoming teachers in training. A teacher-learner community is formed that increasingly becomes one of mutual learning. Members of the learning community are formed to become new teachers of new circles of learning.

In a similar way those with the mandates of program organizing and administration need to draw around themselves people with a variety of skills. They need to find ways of both sharing this role and creating "understudies" that can take over part of the work. A key issue here is the distinction of salaried and volunteer workers. The salaried person(s) typically come to be seen as the ones who are "supposed" to do the work and the others become consumers of the work of this "professional." This issue has yet to be fully faced by Women-Church. By and large, its organizations tend to have one or more paid administrators. These administrators draw around themselves a circle of others with particular expertise in various areas who participate as volunteers.

Women-Church understands leadership as a ministry of function, rather than of clerical caste. Such an understanding of ministry can allow the true variety of the needs of particular communities to be defined and addressed. It can draw on many people in the community who have skills and gifts and activate these skills and gifts as ministries. Community life needs a variety of enablers. Lumping all ministry into one ordained caste has meant that many of the community's needs go unmet, because no one person possesses all these skills and capacities.

A religious community needs enablers in at least five areas: (1) liturgical creators—poets, artists, musicians, choreographers, who can help the community bring forth in creative expression its symbolic life; (2) teachers who know the history of religious thought systems and their relation to social systems and can help the community reflect on and reconstruct its inherited symbols; (3) administrators, organizers, in some cases a lawyer, who can oversee the material resources of the community; (4) social justice experts who can critically analyze different structures of social oppression, the interface of poverty, sexism, racism and militarism, and help the community focus its energies and resources on some particular areas of action; and (5) spiritual counselors who have a wisdom in the inner life and its relation to life in community and can be guides in this journey of psychic-spiritual development.

Few Women-Church groups will be rich enough to pay all such people. Most of the ministry must be seen as familial obligations and expressions of creativity that are unpaid. This presupposes a redefinition of the modern capitalist definition of the relationship of job and life.

Anthropology, Good, and Evil

It can be surmised, from what has been said about the revisioning of sacramentality, that Women-Church operates on a nondualistic view of ontology or of the nature of reality. Nature, is not set apart from God as something evil. Nature is that continually reforming manifestation of the underlying wellspring of life that is called God or Source of Being. Nature, as the continual coming to be and passing away of divine creativity, shares in divine goodness. It is, as the Scripture says, "very good" (Gen. l:31) by its nature and the source of its life. Original Blessing is its foundational reality. Women-Church affirms a creation-centered spirituality.[11]

Evil also exists. But here we must distinquish transience and mortality, which sadden us, but belong to the good nature of things, and sin. Sin is perversity. Sin is possible because humans, and only humans, are sufficiently free to be able to pervert the life-giving relations that bind them to each other, to the community of other beings around them, and to the Source of life. Humans set up distorted relations of domination and exploitation. Such distorted relations express the competitive power principle that aggrandizes one side of the relation at the expense of the other. Slavery, class-hierarchy and patriarchy are examples of such distorted relationality.

Sin is fundamentally systemic and relational. It does not reside in some natural part of reality, such as sexual impulses, as evil. Rather it resides in turning life-giving into death-dealing relations, by organizing relations so that one side monopolizes the work of the other and gains its fruits, while reducing the others to poverty, bondage, and denigration of their humanity. Those in control over the lives of others typically back up this control by a violence that spills over into sadism. The final sanction of sinful relations is victim-blaming ideology.

Victim-blaming ideology blames the oppressed for their own oppression. It is said that it is their nature to be subordinate, but they got out of their place at some primal moment. Therefore, the coercive power that is used to keep them down is justified to punish them for this sin and put them back in their place. It is they and their insubordination that is the cause of evil in the world. The myth of Eve and the Fall is the classic example of this victim-blaming ideology. It not only justifies women's subordination but also mystifies and covers up the real nature of evil as sexism and patriarchal relationships.[12]

Women-Church rejects completely this Biblical-Christian myth of women's natural inferiority and subordination, with its reinforcing claim that woman caused evil to come into the world by getting out of her place. It affirms women's natural goodness and equivalent worth. It defines sin, not as women's insubordination, but rather as the system of subordination, of which patriarchy is a primal expression. It sees redemption as exodus from patriarchy, and from all relations of domination and exploitation, and the restoration of relations of life-giving mutual affirmation.

Redemption also is relational. It is the overcoming of distorted relations of domination and subordination, and the creation of new relations of mutual empowerment. This must be both a psychic-spiritual and a social-systemic conversion. We must convert both our minds and hearts and our social systems from relations of domination to relations of mutuality.

Sexuality and Life-style

Women-Church does not canonize one particular sexual life-style. It affirms a variety of life-styles, vowed and unvowed celibacy, heterosexual marriage and lesbian and gay relations. It regards reproduction as a decision that must be freely chosen, not forced upon women as their destiny and the definition of their fulfillment as women. This does not mean that it is tolerant of exploitative uses of sexuality and has no moral norms about good and bad sexual relations.

Fundamentally it sees moral or immoral sex in the context of the morality of relations, rather than in terms of one prescribed and legitimate life-style. Relations between people, whether of different or the same gender, whether of life-long or shorter term commitments, are moral to the extent that they are imbued with qualities of faithfulness, accountability, truthfulness and mutual support in growth and fulfillment of human potential. Relations are evil to the extent that they transgress these norms. Lying, betrayal, psychic and physical violence, exploitation of the labor, and denial of development of human potential for the benefit of the other, without reciprocity—all these are hallmarks of immoral relations.[13]

Many of these patterns of immoral relationship have been sanctioned under the aegis of patriarchal marriage. This does not mean that hetero- sexual marriage is rejected as a potentially good relationship, although some lesbian separatists in the feminist community have tended in that direction. But there is a recognition that mutuality between men and women is difficult, because patriarchal relations remain in force, both in our psychic and cultural socialization and in the way in which marriage is institutionalized in legal and economic relations.

However, celibate community can also be exploitative and psychically violent. Celibate women in religious orders have been engaged in a struggle to transform their communities from hierarchical patterns to patterns of peer mutuality. They are often impeded in their progress by the male church, which has attempted to reinforce the older system of hierarchical control both within and over the religious community.[14] Lesbian relations can also be exploitative and nonreciprocal. The shaping of biophilic relationships, and the decisions about how to use sexuality to express biophilic relations, is part of the larger process of creating redemp- tive relationality. Sexual relations as loving and life-giving are the critical arena for overcoming evil as distorted relationality.

Women-Church celebrates giving birth to children and women's capac- ity to create life, but as one of women's creative works among others. It is not the sole type of creativity for which women are destined. It must be freely chosen. It should also be part of a rhythm of life that is balanced with other kinds of growth and fulfillment. The good life for women, as for men, should be a good interaction of life-giving to others, including to children, and self-affirmation of one's own life and growth. Women- Church thus rejects the gender stereotypes that assign altruism to women and the right to self-affirmation to men. Women's right to reproductive choice is an essential element in women's ability to balance life-giving service to others with their own rights to life and growth.

Gender and God

It goes without saying that Women-Church rejects the patriarchal con- cept of God. This concept of God is based not only on imaging God exclusively as male but also on imaging God as a patriarchal male, as the source and sanction of a patriarchal system of domination. Such a con- cept of God is not only false but evil. It functions as the sanction for an evil system, by assigning the authorship of this system to God.

The tendency of Women-Church spirituality and worship is to explore primarily female or women-centered images of God. But this is not an attempt to substitute matriarchy for patriarchy. Rather it is an effort to release symbols that affirm women's own experience as related to God. Although there has been no effort to define this matter definitively, the basic tendency of Women-Church is to explore images of God that are immanentist, female, and relational.

God is the source and ground of that mode of life-giving relationality that is blessing, and not curse; biophilic, not necrophilic. Therefore whatever images of human experience, including those that involve men, that affirm life-giving relationality are of God and are appropriate to God. It is images of God drawn from power relations of domination and subordination that must be thrown into question.

Women-Church spirituality is also ecological. It therefore must go beyond the anthropomorphic God, who is the ground only of human relations, and include the whole of being in its understanding of community. Human life cannot exist apart from its embeddedness in the community of all the other beings of earth around us. The human sins of distorted relations also devastate the earth, torture animals, pollute the waters, air, and soil. Therefore redemption must include the whole of nature. It must mean a turning, not only to other human beings but also to the whole community of life around us, in life-affirming rather than death-dealing ways of living together.

Images of God must be drawn from our relations with the whole earth and draw us into biophilic relations with the whole earth. God is personal but not limited to human personhood. God is the personal heart of all things in community. Our ways of naming God, therefore, have to allow us to hail our sisters and brothers, the animals, plants, planets, and oceans, as members of our community and manifestations of the divine.

Women-Church: Christian or Post-Christian?

A potentially divisive conflict hangs over Women-Church. Is it primarily a reform within the Christian tradition or is it on the way out of the Christian tradition into post-Christian or goddess religion? This author recently attended a feminist liturgy sponsored by a Catholic group at an ecumenical center of women of faith. They were celebrating the anniversary of the birthday of Margery Tuite, a Catholic nun who had committed her life to justice for women and for the Nicaraguan people.

In this liturgy the remembrance of women was all drawn from the Western Christian tradition, Catholic and Protestant. But the rite defined as Eucharist was a blessing and sharing of apples and apple-juice that referred back to the pre-Christian religion of the goddess in Ireland. It was designed to reject the Christian myth of Eve. Reference to Christ was absent in the Eucharistic prayer and in the liturgy as a whole. Its spirituality was referred to as women-centered.

The participants were ecumenically Christian, and most appeared comfortable with this mix, which has become typical of Women-Church liturgy. But one woman was clearly upset and confessed to difficulty participating in the apple-Eucharist. The blessing and sharing of apples was, for her, not Eucharist. Authentic spirituality for her was Christ-centered, not woman-centered. She asked for clarification on these issues. Clarification was left to private conversations after the liturgy, and it is doubtful that these conversations resulted in adequate clarity on either side.

This tendency to span Christian and goddess religion is not only found in feminist circles in North America and Western Europe. In Asian, African, and Latin American feminist circles there is also some ambiguity about whether religious symbols remain confined to the Christian tradition. For most Western women, references to the goddess are to a mythical world they have never really experienced as living religion. For third-world women pre-Christian religions are still living religions.

Some of these religions are clearly as patriarchal as Christianity, such as Confucianism, Hinduism, and even, to some extent, Buddhism. But some Asian, African, and Latin American women find feminist potential in the shamanistic and nature religions of their cultures. They are beginning to explore the ways in which their contextual theology, as both women and as third-world people, might include aspects of these non-Christian religious traditions.[15]

As is clear from the above account, Women-Church has not made a decision to be either confined to Christianity or to move out of Christianity completely. It finds some Christian symbols reclaimable for feminism and others unredeemable. It is engaged in creating a new synthesis between the symbols it finds good in Christianity and symbols drawn from goddess religions. Its genius may lie in refusing to be forced into one side or the other of the boundaries that divide Christianity from other religions—especially from nature religions—but in reaching for a new synthesis across this divide. The theological rationale for this synthesis must be clarified if an explosive misunderstanding is to be avoided. Perhaps it can only be as the Woman-Church movement tests the ability of the Christian churches to relate to its message that the movement can begin to clarify its historical identity and role.

NOTES

1. Elizabeth S. Fiorenza, *Bread Not Stone: The Challenge of Feminist Biblical Interpretation* (Boston: Beacon, 1984), lff.

2. Leonardo Boff, *Ecclesiogenesis: The Base Communities Reinvent the Church* (Maryknoll, N.Y.: Orbis Press, 1986).

3. Marie Augusta Neal, *Catholic Sisters in Transition, From the 1960s to the 1980s* (Wilmington, Del.: Michael Glazier Press, 1984).

4. Mary Jo Weaver, *New Catholic Women: A Contemporary Challenge to Traditional Religious Authority* (San Francisco, Calif.: Harper and Row, 1985).

5. *Women and the Catholic Priesthood: An Expanded Vision: Proceedings of the Detroit Ordination Conference,* ed. Anne Marie Gardiner, S.S.N.D. (New York: Paulist Press, 1976).

6. Congregation on the Doctrine of the Faith, "Declaration on the Question of the Admission of Women to the Ministerial Priesthood," 15 Oct. 1976; see also Leonard and Arlene Swidler, eds., *Catholic Priests: A Catholic Commentary on the Vatican Declaration* (New York: Paulist Press, 1977).

7. For the major papers and final reports of the Asian, African and Latin American conferences and the global conference of the Women's Commission of EATWOT, see *With Passion and Compassion: Third World Women Doing Theology,* ed. Virginia Fabella and Mercy Amba Oduyoye (Maryknoll, N.Y.: Orbis Press, 1988). The complete papers of the November 1987 conference in Singapore of the Asian Women's Commission of EATWOT has been published under the title, *Asian Women Doing Theology* (Hong Kong: Asian Women's Resource Center, 1989).

8. *In God's Image* is published by the Asian Women's Resource Center, 566 Nathan Road, Kiu Kin Mansion 6/F, Kowloon, Hong Kong.

9. Rosemary R. Ruether, *Women-Church: Theology and Practice of Feminist Liturgical Communities* (San Francisco: Harper and Row, 1985).

10. James Coriden, "Report on the Holy Office: Inflating the Oath," *Commonweal,* 8 Sept. 1989, 455–56.

11. Matthew Fox, *Original Blessing* (Santa Fe, N.Mex.: Bear and Co., 1983.

12. Rosemary R. Ruether, *Sexism and God-Talk: Toward a Feminist Theology* (Boston: Beacon, 1983), 159–83.

13. For an effort at a revised ethic of human sexuality, based on relationality, see A. Kosnik, et al., *Human Sexuality: New Directions in American Catholic Thought* (New York: Paulist Press, 1977).

14. See Madonna Kolbenschlag, *Authority, Community and Conflict* (Kansas City, Mo.: Sheed and Ward, 1986).

15. This reclaiming of non-Christian themes in third world theology has been discussed under the rubric of indigenization. For some questioning of how helpful African indigenous religions are for African women, see Mercy Amba Oduyoye, *Hearing and Knowing: Theological Reflections on Christianity in Africa* Maryknoll, N.Y.: Orbis Press, 1986), 120–37. Reclaiming shaman traditions for Korean feminist theology has been explored particularly by Chung Hyun Kyung. See her article, "Han-pu-ri; Doing Theology from Korean Women's

Perspective," in *We Dare to Dream: Doing Theology as Asian Women,* ed. Virginia Fabella and Sun Ai Park, eds. Hong Kong: Asian Women's Resource Center, 1989), 135–46.

Widening the Banks of the Mainstream: Women Constructing Theologies

Mary Farrell Bednarowski

Many contemporary theologians speak of the work they do as constructive in nature. It involves not only the passing on of a tradition and its interpretation in light of the issues of a particular time in history. Theology, they contend, also requires creativity, what Gordon Kaufman calls "the creativity of the human spirit, attempting to find its way in the face of ever new problems and crises arising in life."[1] The work of the theologian, says Kaufman, is imaginative work. It is not merely the application of old doctrines to new situations.

This spirit of construction, creativity, and imagination informs the theological work of many women in a variety of traditions who have chosen to remain within the religions traditions that have shaped them, often since childhood. "Reformer" is not the best term by which to characterize these women, although many may see themselves in this role, and conversations about whether to reform or to leave a tradition have been intense and sometimes acrimonious since the late 1960s. These women might better be looked upon as artists whose medium is the theology of their own particular tradition—its doctrines and symbols and rituals. Like poets or painters or musicians or sculptors, these women choose to accept on their own terms what might be called "the conventions" of the tradition. They claim grounding in the tradition, but they are insistent on the freedom not just to respond to it but also to shape it out of their own experiences.

In this theological work, contemporary women share many continuities with their nineteenth-century sisters, particularly in their awareness that images of God or ultimate reality and human nature in a tradition drastically affect how women are seen and how they see themselves. On the other hand, there is a growing confidence among contemporary women that "the mainstream" of a tradition is a constructed reality; its banks can be widened and, if the water is living, it can be made to flow in new directions. Whereas Mother Ann Lee, numerous Spiritualist mediums,

Mary Baker Eddy, and Helena P. Blavatsky constructed their systems outside the theological mainstream of nineteenth-century America, many women theologians at the end of the twentieth century choose to do otherwise.

In this essay, I am concerned with the theological work of contemporary women in Mormonism, Roman Catholicism, and Theosophy. Like their sisters in the nineteenth century—but, it appears, with more self-consciousness—they are engaged in constructing theological systems that push at the limitations on women's self-understanding and social roles imposed by their various religious traditions. They address the same broad issues about deity and woman's nature and women's roles that concerned women in the nineteenth century.

They address these issues within the theological, historical, psychological, and anthropological complexities of their own religious systems. The particular issues they face concerning deity, women's nature, and women's roles are articulated differently. Thus, not only as women but also as Mormons and as Catholics and as Theosophists, they look for new ways to image the divine, for ways to define and interpret women's nature, women's bodies and women's unique gifts; they claim that their experiences of the tradition have been different from men's; and, until their voices are heard, the tradition has no hope of achieving wholeness. By their particularities, then, and also in what they share by way of issues, the women in these three traditions provide insights into some of the theological concepts that emerge when women claim for themselves the work of shaping a theological system.

Mormonism

The belief system of Mormonism would seem to be particularly conducive to promoting the leadership of women. It offers not only a Heavenly Father but also a Heavenly Mother. Its theology of human nature holds that men and women can achieve divinity; they can become gods and goddesses, priests and priestesses, kings and queens. Mormons are not dogged by the stain of original sin—they are held responsible only for their own sins, not for Adam's. Mormons do not denigrate the physical body as a prison of the spirit. To "fall" into mortality and to take on a physical body allows the individual to make the moral decisions during the earthly life that are required to earn divinity.

In reality, Mormonism has circumscribed women's roles both in the church and in the world. Mormonism's optimistic doctrine of human nature and its rejection of the power of original sin does not appear to apply to women in the same degree that it does to men. As Jan Shipps, a historian of Mormonism, has pointed out, "LDS women continue to suffer the curse of Eve and consequently are assigned to all the tasks associated with eternal motherhood."[2] The priesthood is reserved for worthy males, and a woman's spiritual standing is dependent upon the standing of the male, usually husband, to whom she is attached. Motherhood has been elevated to the highest office a woman can hold. The church has taken an official stand against the ERA amendment. And the concept of Heavenly Mother remains largely undeveloped. Devotion to her is not churchwide but individual in nature, particularly among women.

In response to the women's movement and in an attempt to sort out reasons for the church's stance against the ERA, many Mormon women have taken on the task of assessing the theological and social reasons that account for the circumscribing of their roles. Their most pivotal argument has been that Mormonism has come to operate as though priesthood and motherhood were ontological categories of parallel function—separate but equal—and that these roles are eternally inherent in the nature of the universe. That this is the case becomes very clear in recent church responses to questions about the priesthood: "Why should God give his sons a power that is denied his daughters?"[3] Traditional church theologians have offered a threefold answer: God has ordained that the sexes play two different roles in the church—the principle of complementarity; womanhood is an eternal principle, not just an incidental quality of the mortal life; and during the time of preexistence women chose to be mothers rather than priests.

"God has decreed," says Elder Robert L. Backman, "that man may hold the priesthood and woman may become a mother, and thus they are dependent upon one another. Neither can achieve exaltation and eternal life without the other."[4] Oscar McConkie claims that, "Woman had an existence long before there was a woman on earth," and not only womanhood but motherhood as well will endure into eternity.[5] Backman suggests further that gender roles are a matter of choice made previous to the taking on of a physical body: "Since we chose to come to this earth to gain bodies and enjoy earth's experiences, we must have known of our individual roles and consequences of our being man or woman."[6] For women, this meant voluntarily giving up the power of priesthood, supposedly for the higher office of motherhood: "Faced with an alternative— partnership or priesthood—did you, Sister, pass up priesthood? Did women by their own free choice choose to be the family heart rather than the family head?"[7] In addition, both Backman and McConkie make use of the argument familiar to women of the Victorian era that women are somehow more spiritual than men. Therefore their role is not to wield priestly power but to make sure that the males to whom they are attached do not abuse it.

Many Mormon women have not been accepting of these arguments about eternal differences between men and women and the accompanying need for different roles. They have responded at a visceral level, one by saying that she had only heard the argument about eternal differences offered by men. The first time she heard the phrase, she said, "It raised the hair on the back of my neck."[8] Another woman expressed her conviction that, "A parallel between motherhood and priesthood makes no logical sense, it makes no historic sense, it makes no biological sense. It's so patently illogical that I wonder people can continue to make it." She pointed out that one of the worst consequences of this kind of parallelism is that it "take[s] out of the equation any value to be assigned to the value of fatherhood."[9]

Mormon women have gone beyond visceral responses to refute the notion that priesthood/motherhood complementarity is imbedded in the foundations of the universe. Meg Wheatly-Pesci, a management consultant, employs a combination of knowledge gained from her profession and theological argument to make the claim that withholding the priesthood from women is not only bad for the church but it is also a distortion of Mormon beliefs. Wheatly-Pesci suggests that the organizational structure of Mormonism communicates messages about the inequality of women. She claims that "the range of contributions open to them is quite limited compared to that of men, simply because of the priesthood requirement. No matter what role they serve in, women are further circumscribed by organizational rules that require that all decisions be approved by priesthood authority." She indicates that she has "seldom seen women with more titular power and less real power than in the present women's auxiliaries." She concludes that the experiences of women in the church are very different from those of men—that women have lower self-esteem as well as fewer aspirations.[10]

Wheatley-Pesci sees the situation as contrary to Mormon theology and wonders "whether an organization which believes in the perfectibility of its members, and teaches that we are all equal in the sight of God should feel content with a structure that communicates such disparate messages to men and women?" She considers it a "special irony" that women should experience such a lack of opportunity in a church that teaches that men and women are potential gods and goddesses. Her practical suggestion is for the church to become more clear about what the priesthood actually is, to separate priesthood from purely administrative functions, "to sort out spirit-centered needs from bureaucratic exigencies."[11]

Mormon women have also sought to untangle priesthood/motherhood parallelism by means of research into the early years of the church. They are discovering the extent to which accommodation to Victorian and middle-class American values resulted in the gradual glorification and romanticization of motherhood. This development was intensified by Mormonism's belief that motherhood exists in the afterlife, a belief which "includes not only mothering one's mortal children but having 'millions' more. Motherhood, as many church leaders have noted, is as eternal and endless as is godhood."[12]

Historical research has also revealed that in the early years of the LDS church there was widespread exercise of spiritual gifts—speaking in tongues, healing, washing, and anointing the sick—by women. In fact, at one time there was little difference between men's and women's exercise of them. Linda King Newell points to conflicting opinions among church authorities during the nineteenth century as to the conditions under which women could heal and anoint the sick, but it is clear to her that women healed and anointed with the consent of the church hierarchy. These functions, she concludes, did not compel women to sacrifice their role as mothers, nor were men's priesthood gifts diminished by women's exercise of spiritual gifts. By the beginning of the twentieth century, these gifts were regarded primarily as priesthood powers and thus to be exercised only by men. They "are seldom spoken of among LDS women today."[13]

All of these factors taken together no doubt help to account for the failure of Mormonism to develop images of Heavenly Mother in ways that might contribute to greater empowerment of women and the expansion of their roles within the church. But that is another of the tasks in which Mormon women are engaged. The history of the origins of Heavenly Mother is not clear, according to Linda P. Wilcox, but credit is often given to Joseph Smith and to the poet Eliza Snow, one of Smith's wives.[14] What little development occurred in the nineteenth century emerged by a theological method very much in keeping with Mormonism: "inference and commonsense extension of ordinary earth-life experience."[15]

In the twentieth century, Wilcox identifies three different time periods: the turn of the century when Heavenly Mother was associated with women's rights and enfranchisement for women in Utah and also with what appeared to be a longing for a maternal presence in the universe; the 1920s and 1930s when the idea was associated with "eternal" motherhood; and the 1960s and 1970s when the concept was used by the General Authorities to broaden images of deity and to tie the idea of a Heavenly Mother with the affirmation of woman's "call" to motherhood and the care of children.

Wilcox identifies grass roots efforts during the last decade to reconceptualize Heavenly Mother as a more feminist deity. Nineteen eighty was the first year in which there were poems about Heavenly Mother submitted to the Eliza R. Snow poetry contest sponsored by the Relief Society (the primary LDS women's organization). The poems offered speculations about Heavenly Mother's characteristics and her roles, but they revealed "a vague sense of not really knowing enough to feel as close as one would like to the Heavenly Mother—wondering about her name and how we might react to it if we were to know it, transferring the Father's attributes to her, yet realizing that she can only be apprehended 'darkly' with a resultant feeling of unease and incompletion."[16] If the poems do not yield a satisfying picture of Heavenly Mother, they point to a growing interest in the concept.

Wilcox also refers to poetry taken from less mainstream sources in Mormonism, poems that express longing for the kind of model that Heavenly Mother might provide and that also try to expand her image from that of a nurturing to a more creative presence. "Why are you silent, Mother," says one poet. "How can I become a goddess when the patterns here are those of gods?" This sentiment points to the constructive task that confronts Mormon women in their imaging of a female deity: to suggest attributes of both nurturance and spiritual power, as Wilcox puts it; to offer as a model a female deity who affirms childbearing and child rearing without also intimating and even insisting that they are the only aspects of women's lives that have true spiritual worth; to conceptualize a partner for Heavenly Father who reflects "strength, sexuality, and mutuality," attributes that Wilcox acknowledges are still rare."[17]

The women I have cited are women who remain within the LDS Church. Jan Shipps describes them as asking their questions and making their statements *in faith*.[18] They might well echo the feelings of Mary Lythgoe Bradford, a woman who is candid about her experiences of sexism within the church but who chooses to remain: "The Mormon religion is an undeniable part of my being. I have accepted the fact that the church is part of my body, and I am part of the church body. I feel that the church belongs as much to me as to anyone."[19]

These Mormon women are asking hard questions, exploring the Bible and the LDS Scriptures for positive and negative references to women and their own history and theology to see why their roles have been so limited within the church. They are refuting the assumption that something about women's makeup keeps them from priesthood by pointing to it as a historical construction and a construction of Mormon theology rather than a divinely ordained precept. They are beginning to recognize and make use of the advantages that their own tradition offers to women. There is the possibility of greatly expanding the "goddess" image of Heavenly Mother in a tradition that has always told women that to become goddesses is their natural heritage. There is potential in Mormon theology for lifting the curse of Eve from women. There is a relatively short, well documented history that is being reclaimed to show that women's roles have not always been so limited. There is the foundation of continuing revelation on which Mormonism rests with its potential for new revelations about women and priesthood. And, in a tradition that has tightly regulated sexuality because of its emphasis on family and repro-duction, there is nonetheless an affirmation of the physical body that may soon stand Mormon women in good stead as they continue to reflect upon their connections with the workings of the universe.

Roman Catholicism

Like Mormonism, Roman Catholicism does not ordain women. The hierarchy of the church continues to offer reasons from Scripture and historical tradition which Mary Jo Weaver sums up succinctly in *New Catholic Women:* "The church has always opposed it; Jesus did not do it [ordain women]; no one has a 'right' to it; the priest, acting in the name of Christ, must represent him physically; and whether or not there were deaconesses in early Christianity has no bearing on ordination as such."[20]

The responses of American Catholic women to the church's refusal to ordain women have been numerous and varied over the last twenty years. They have included exploration of the Scriptures; a critique of the past as well as an attempt to recover a usable history; new images for God and new interpretations of central doctrines of the church; movements, both formal and informal, like Women-Church, which question whether women want any part of ordained priesthood and whether there is even any need for it. In addition, Roman Catholic women are asking radical questions about connections between their experiences, their bodies, and the cen-tral mysteries of the Christian story as they have been articulated by the church.

Much of this work has been done by Roman Catholic women who have emerged as prominent academic theologians in American culture. Among the best known are Anne Carr, Mary Daly, Elizabeth Schüssler Fiorenza, and Rosemary Radford Ruether. Mary Jo Weaver describes these women as engaged in enlarging the discipline of theology.[21]

As instructive as it is to encounter the writings of these four women and others, such as Joann Wolski Conn, Margaret Farley, Monika Helwig, Mary E. Hunt, and Sandra Schneiders, much can be learned, also, about the creativity of Roman Catholic feminist theology from women who are social activists, artists, and spiritual directors. Catholic women express themselves theologically in the mission statements of religious orders, in alternative liturgies, and in the newsletters of shelters for battered women.

These are women who claim and interpret the traditions out of their own particular experiences and who define their relationship to it on their own terms. They describe the work they do as an attempt to fathom the imaginative depths of the tradition in order to see whether it has the power to yield insights about women's experiences. And they claim, in the words of Christin Lore Weber, that if the tradition is "patriarchal and dualistic;" that is, if it excludes the God-experiences of women, "it is not Christian."[22]

Fran Ferder, a member of the Franciscan Sisters of Perpetual Adoration, belongs to a religious community that devotes much of its energy to spiritual direction and to work in Central America. In a reflection she wrote for her order entitled "Emerging Wisdom," she depicts "Wisdom" as a woman seeking a relationship with the tradition beyond that of either obedient daughter or oppressed daughter. For her, Wisdom looks like a "releasing woman":

> A woman with one hand behind her
> in one great gesture of letting go. . . .
> Letting go of all the traditions that no longer fit in her
> hand,
>   that limit her dance.
> Wisdom doesn't scorn the traditions of yesterday,
>   she releases them.
> Once outside her grasp, they are free to float to the
> place
> where memories link the best of what was
>   to all the energies of tomorrow.[23]

As an artist, Meinrad Craighead joins Ferder in claiming for herself what has been nurturing in the Roman Catholic tradition and letting the rest go. Craighead grew up in Chicago and Arkansas and lived for many years in Italy and Spain. She spent fourteen years in an English monastery and since 1983 has lived in New Mexico. She speaks of herself as having internalized the structure of the Roman Catholic tradition. "The structure is inside me," she says. She does not see herself as a part of the Catholic institution, but neither does she see herself as having left the church. "I haven't left the church; it would be like leaving my family. You might have all sorts of arguments. You might not fit in, you might outgrow them, but your family's still your family. My original soil, going back countless generations, is the Catholic Church, and I honor it."[24]

Craighead would not describe herself as honoring the doctrine or orthodoxy of Catholicism. Her debts as an artist are more primal; her paintings, as she describes them, emerge from body memories of her connections with her grandmother and mother and with the liturgies of Catholicism. She draws and paints from what she calls, "my own myth of personal origin."[25]

In *The Mother's Songs: Images of God the Mother,* a book of paintings and accompanying texts, Craighead speaks of having had in childhood a "natural religious instinct for my Mothergod." She kept this image secret but she describes it as giving her "a profound sense of security and stability. She was the sure ground I grew in, the groundsill of my spirituality."[26] In a painting titled "Milk" that is filled with breasts and images of animal and human babies nursing, milk pours from a central figure whose arms look like breasts. The milk flows into a jar and out again from two openings into a stream. Craighead interprets the painting as a celebration of all the life-sustaining body fluids of the Mother, human and divine. "I am born connected," she says. "I am born remembering rivers flowing from my mother's body into my body. I pray at her Fountain of life, saturated in her milk and blood, water and honey. She passes on to me the meaning of religion because she links me to our origin in God the Mother."[27] In "Wind," a large figure with four hands pulls spun yarn from her mouth. Ovarian spheres extend from her third and fourth hands and rest on golden fallopian-shaped spirals. "The dark wind of my Mother," says Craighead, "spirals, uncoiling and recoiling, leaving and returning to her source; her spirit evolving, involving the entire universe."[28] It is the Mothergod she says, who inspires these paintings, and it is the Mothergod, in turn, whose images are multiplied in them.

In *The Litany of the Great River,* Craighead recalls the mesmerizing power of the processions and litanies of her childhood: "The very monotony shifted us into a different mood. The rhythmical flow and the precise syllables of the sacred language got inside our bodies; the step-pause-recite-pause response movements were as regular and drumlike as our heartbeats. All the spirits and holy ancestors we were invoking seemed to walk along with us, our remembering them made them present."[29] The titles of the paintings in this book are phrased as intercessions from traditional litanies—"O Heart of the Fire, *sear us we beseech Thee.*" "O Holy Mountain, *bear us we beseech Thee.*" O Rain from Heaven, *temper us, we beseech Thee.*" Many of the images in the paintings come from Craighead's dreams, from her past, from the New Mexico landscape in which she lives, and from her connections with animals. All of them are tied to her ongoing search for ways to image the divine. In the painting entitled "O Rosa Mystica, *enclose us, we beseech Thee,*" the mountains of New Mexico at sunset are the backdrop for a cave with an arched entrance made of stone. Wings extend from the top of the arch, and a figure with a four-winged bird at its throat sits in the entrance. The bird

holds a vessel in its talons and pours milk into the mouth of a head—a
baby's head it appears—centered in a many-petaled rose. God speaks in
these warmed caves, says Craighead: "God says, Come into my lap and sit
in the center of your soul. Drink the living waters of memory and give
birth to yourself. What you unearth will stun you. You will paint the walls
of this cave in thanksgiving."[30]

This is not traditional Catholic theology. And yet, says Craighead,
what she paints and what she says emerge from Catholicism as she
experienced it—in Catholic schools, in her family, in a monastery, within
her own psyche—and from which she draws for her multiple images of
God the Mother. In that claim she is joined by Christin Lore Weber.
Weber is a Roman Catholic woman, a former member of a religious
order, a spiritual director, and an author. She has been a teacher and a
chaplain at a home for emotionally disturbed children. She has experienced marriage, widowhood, and remarriage. Weber chooses to remain
within the Christian tradition, because, as she says, "its images and
mysteries are rooted deep in my soul." But, she is not willing to make this
choice at the expense of "other natural energies constellated in my
psychic depths." Her theological work, as she describes it, is to take
her place "in the movement of creation that Jesus revealed and attempt
from the perspective of my experience and the experiences of the women
who surround me to re-vision and reconstruct a Christian spirituality
of women's mysteries."[31] She speaks in terms of a "WomanChrist
spirituality," one that "brings together and reconciles the most fundamental opposites known to traditional patriarchal Christianity: Woman and
the Christ."[32]

Weber has set herself the task of constructing a feminist spirituality in a
tradition that has made of Jesus, a male, the human model for women and
men. For Weber, the journey that will yield a radical revisioning of the
tradition and its central figures—Jesus and Mary—is the descent into
womanbody. In this interpretation of the Christian story, the experiences
of women and the goals of their experiences must necessarily be different
from acknowledging one's sinfulness, hoping to achieve salvation or
perfection vicariously through Jesus's death and resurrection, and, finally,
bursting the bonds of the body and of the earthly life.

Weber implies that it is just this understanding of woman's spiritual
task that has deprived her of self-knowledge and of the creative power of
the feminine. For women, the journey must be one of descent rather than
ascent, descent into womanbody, into the earth, into the underworld and
the dwelling place of the Great Goddess. The goals of the journey are not
perfection or disembodiment. The journey, according to Weber, has to do
with the stripping away of lies, the clearing of blocked passageways of

creativity, the claiming of the body and its connections with earth and death, and the restoration of wholeness.

The journey of descent, according to Weber, is dangerous. It asks women to let go of past images of God: "What was once an image powerful enough to connect me to all being with a cosmic consciousness now is revealed as an idol."[33] It asks, also, that women accept the very bodyself that has been feared and reviled by men and women alike, because it is connected with earth and with death. Finally, it asks of women that they accept what they find in the journey of descent: that in their wholeness they are not necessarily perfect. Sylvia Brinton Perea describes it this way in *Descent to the Goddess:* "She is not a beautiful maid, daughter of the fathers, but ugly, selfish, ruthless, willing to be very negative, willing not to care."[34]

Even though she is interpreting the Christian tradition, Weber does not hesitate to use the goddess Inanna as a model for women on the journey of descent.[35] In the Babylonian traditional story, Inanna, queen of heaven and earth, journeys to the underworld where she meets Ereshkigal, queen of the underworld. Ereshkigal turns Inanna into a corpse and hangs her from a hook on the wall. She is restored to life by Enki, god of wisdom and water, who makes two creatures out of dirt and gives them the food and water of life. These creatures journey to the underworld, retrieve the corpse of Inanna from Ereshkigal, and restore her to life with food and water. Weber sees Inanna as a metaphor of survival for women who are brave enough to make the descent to self-knowledge. She sees her also as "a promise that the pain we experience during the transformation process will not last forever. Instead, the food and water of life will be given to us freely. We will break through the pain and apparent certain death to greater being."[36]

What will the journey of descent yield by way of insight for women into the central figures of Catholicism—Jesus and Mary in particular? Much more, says Weber, than the literal interpretations to which Catholicism has tied itself. She does not choose to repudiate Jesus and grounds her revisioning in "my belief in his continuing life, my fascination with the manner in which he broke open the human to reveal our power of life, my love for and sense of connectedness with the women who have seen through to the truth of his messages."[37] Her wish is to broaden the interpretation of Jesus and the meaning of incarnation. Jesus's significance, according to Weber, lies in his embodiedness, not in his maleness: "It is because Jesus *realizes* his radical Incarnation," Weber says, "through his conscious descent into embodiedness, that he is able to say, 'Before Abraham ever was, I Am' (John 8:58 JB). Jesus knew who he was: "He was God's Word; that is not to say the rest of us are not."[38]

222 Contemporary Women as Creators of Religion

What does Jesus' incarnation—and his death and resurrection—have to do with women? Weber insists that women are not bystanders in this central mystery of Christianity deriving some kind of vicarious spiritual benefit and meaning from Jesus. "The dying of Jesus," says Weber, "happened in womanspace, as did his birth and rising." Woman does not derive her meaning from Jesus: "Rather she is a source of meaning in herself, as woman. She is, with him, the original priest: there can be no priesthood when they are separate, one from the other. She is ultimate. She contains the emptiness from which he springs forth. Out of her he lives, and into her he dies. Together they are the process of creation, the ebb and the flow."[39]

Weber also uses the Virgin Mary as a model for women as they learn to accept the many facets of themselves that they will encounter in the journey of descent. Like Jesus, Weber contends, Mary has been interpreted by the church in reductionistic and limiting ways that have little use for the contemporary woman. Weber identifies Mary as the embodiment of Wisdom, the reconciler of opposites, who is active and present "whenever what is below is drawn together with what is above, when the shadow is united with the image of light."[40] Mary is the original WomanChrist. In her roles as both virgin and mother, she becomes a particularly powerful model for the reconciliation of opposites. Too much energy, says Weber, has gone into pondering how Mary could have conceived a child without experiencing sexual intercourse. Such speculation has tended to diminish emphasis on Mary's bodiliness. "Instead of literalizing," says Weber, "we could have been wondering all these years about the mystery of one woman becoming, in a single image, the representation of archetypal opposites—the virgin and the mother."[41] As virgin, Mary is whole in herself. As mother, she lives for another; she personifies Gaia, the mother goddess, and "earth and body are her manifestations. She is birthing power."[42]

Mary is not only virgin and mother according to Weber; she is also bride and widow. She argues that the image of Mary will have strength and power for women only if we "admit into it all of those aspects of womanhood so long buried. Some of those aspects severely frighten men and women both. Our ability to see Mary-full-of-grace depends on our willingness to assume into ourselves the fullness of womannature." The Prayer of Mary, as Weber has fashioned it, begins thus: "Abba, I will stand before you whole or not at all."[43]

Like Craighead, Weber makes use of the traditional form of the litany to offer new titles for Mary, titles that are meant to expand radically the traditional understanding of her nature beyond that of obedient and passive servant. "Fear Woman," Weber calls Mary. "Woman Without

Edges." "Haunted Woman." "Witch Woman." For each of these titles and others, Weber constructs a lengthy string of descriptive phrases—"Woman who hides indoors. Woman burning a light through the night. Woman who looks under the bed"—and a prayer of recognition and praise: "Fear woman, you are myself. I take you to my heart. I assume you into my soul. I honor you. I rename you vigilance."[44]

Craighead's and Weber's revisionings of Catholicism and its central symbols in light of feminist spirituality go far beyond the issue of ordained priesthood in the Roman Catholic church. Any priesthood they have in mind is more cosmic and archetypal in nature than the institutionalized priesthood of Catholicism. But they are nonetheless addressing those broad issues that the controversy over priesthood has raised in Catholicism. What is the nature of woman? What do her particular experiences of the divine have to say to the rest of the tradition? How is her body connected with the creative powers of the universe? What role does she play in the wielding of those powers? Craighead paints her answers to these questions, and Weber fashions them into stories and litanies and contemporary versions of ancient mysteries.

Theosophy

Mormon women and Catholic women engage in theological reflection within the worldview of a particular tradition. No matter how hard they push at the boundaries and no matter with what creativity they probe the imaginative depths of that tradition, they choose, finally, to be grounded in its central stories and theological concepts. Their understandings of woman's nature and her connection to the universe reflect this reality. A great deal of feminist theology is emerging, however, from outside established religious traditions, and it is instructive to look at prominent themes and their sources.

One particularly interesting category of women working on feminist spirituality is comprised of those who have been influenced by the worldview of Theosophy. I have looked before at the writings of women in the Theosophical movement in the nineteenth and early twentieth centuries. For the purposes of this essay, I am interested in writings that have been published within the last decade. In terms of the broader continuum of feminist spirituality in the United States, Theosophy presents a kind of metaphysical middle ground between the totally earth-centered spirituality of some feminists and the body-denying worldviews of others such as healer Louise L. Hay.[45]

Theosophy has a history of women leaders and a long-standing interest in the feminine principle or the eternal feminine. At the same time,

Theosophy has in its history a kind of antifeminism that emerges from an occult worldview. In 1920 Charles W. Leadbeater, a Theosophist and a bishop in the Liberal Catholic Church,[46] published *The Science of the Sacraments,* an occult interpretation of the seven sacraments of the Roman Catholic church. In this volume he addresses the issue of women's ordination. "The forces now arranged for distribution through the priesthood," he says, "would not work efficiently through a feminine body." Leadbeater speculates that God might alter the present nature of things and either "revive some form of the old religions in which the feminine Aspect of the Deity was served by priestesses, or so to modify the physics of the Catholic scheme of forces that a feminine body could be satisfactorily employed in the work. Meantime we have no choice but to administer His Church along the lines laid down for us."[47]

It is the matter-of-factness that is so striking about Leadbeater's statement, particularly since it issues from one who participated extensively in a religious movement with a woman founder and strong women leaders. Even his willingness to accept the possibility of change seems to reinforce the inevitability of the way things are now rather than to call them into question. As he understands it, there is something about the very makeup of a woman's body as it is related to the nature of the universe that keeps her from summoning or ordering or celebrating or distributing those spiritual powers that the sacraments bestow on humankind.

Women Theosophists early in the twentieth century refuted Leadbeater directly and by implication, drawing from what Madame Helena Blavatsky said and wrote about the feminine principle in the universe. But they did not move far beyond interpretations of the feminine principle that served to intensify cultural stereotypes of woman—that she is more nurturing, more emotional, more passive and receptive, more spiritual, than man—even though they insisted that these qualities were necessary not only in individual and family life but in politics as well.[48]

In response to the contemporary women's movement, women influenced by the Theosophical worldview are beginning to move in new directions. They have begun to speculate about the divine feminine and to connect this concept in Theosophy with the interest in the Goddess in feminist spirituality. The women writing today agree that the presence of the Mother or the Goddess is necessary if human persons are to prosper and the planet is to survive, but they do not confine her activities to nurturing. Instead, the emphasis is on the divine feminine as healer, as reconciler of heaven and earth, spirit and matter, as maker of connections.

In an article in *The Quest,* a journal of philosophy, science, religion, and the arts published by the Theosophical Society in America, Corinne McLaughlin writes of "The Mystery of the Veiled Mother of the World" and speculates that the absence of any strong sense of her identity is responsible for the ecological crisis and the alienation of both men and women from their earthly roots. McLaughlin sees the remedy for this alienation in the reawakening of the goddess: "Reawakening to the Goddess helps us to honor the inherent sacredness of the physical life—in ourselves and our world."[49] McLaughlin acknowledges the many faces of the Goddess—as Isis who is concerned with the unity of all life, as Sophia, who fosters the development of intuition and psychic abilities, as Aphrodite, who gives permission for freer sexual expression. She sees Goddess consciousness emerging in both men and women, a consciousness that "always sees the connections between things, no matter how disparate, and works to restore wholeness everywhere."

McLaughlin explores the teachings about the Divine Mother as they have appeared in the writings of women from the beginning of the Theosophical movement—Helena Blavatsky, Helen Roerich, Alice Bailey, and Dion Fortune. "Each of them," she says, "embodied the wisdom and compassion of the feminine principle, and they were 'liberated women' more than sixty years before it became popular."[50] It is in her reliance on these writers and on the Theosophical worldview that McLaughlin departs from the earth-centered feminists and advocates of goddess spirituality who, she says, see the Divine Mother as solely an Earth Goddess.

As McLaughlin interprets the Divine Mother, she must be honored as both Queen of Heaven and Queen of Earth, if we are to make contact with the spiritual reality that Theosophy holds is hidden in matter: "Besides the earthly side of the Great Mother, there is also a cosmic and celestial aspect that is essential for us to connect with."[51] In this sense the Divine Mother is goddess of the whole universe and devotion to her keeps us from the bondage of a distorting materialism. It is in this dual honoring of the Divine Mother that human persons are able to act out their central task of bringing heaven down to earth. McLaughlin is quite clear that this is not a process of "de-materializing," for she provides a rather homespun example: "When we put vibrations of love and caring into a physical object by cleaning, beautifying, or refining it, we help to release its inner beauty and light. . . . When we lovingly cut and sand a piece of wood to make a piece of furniture we are bringing forth Spirit within matter."[52]

McLaughlin suggests meditations to honor the Divine Mother as Queen of heaven and earth and to add "a dimension that is often left out by those who see the Divine Mother as purely an Earth Mother." In one meditation the exercise is to visualize the energy of the Earth Mother moving up through feet and body to the heart center and then to visualize the energy of the Queen of Heaven moving down through the head and throat to heart to meet the energy coming from below. In so doing, "we visualize the earth being made sacred and blessed by us, and we circulate the energy down to the earth and up to the heavens, feeling ourselves in perfect harmony with both." In another meditation, there is a descent—a journey into the earth in order to embrace the veiled Isis and to honor the "mysteries of deep earth and so redeeming matter."[53]

McLaughlin ties what she sees as growing devotion to the Virgin Mary and some of her recent appearances and emerging interest in the Goddess to the "feminine awakening" and the need for a cosmic function of the feminine principle described by Helena Roerich sixty years ago. In this she is joined by another woman, Carol Parrish-Harra, a former Roman Catholic and founder of the Light of Christ Community Church, a New Age religious movement that owes much of its worldview to Theosophy. Parrish-Harra is very specific in her delineation of a time period in the history of the planet when the influence of the divine feminine is particularly needed: from August 17, 1987, the date of the Harmonic Convergence celebrated by its participants as a particularly efficacious time for the coming together of higher forces in the universe, until December 21, 2012. She sees these years as "a period of transition, a cleansing, " and she ties the transition to ecological concerns about the survival of the planet: "We, as a body of cellular life, have to be able to live together as interlocking cells at the human level. All life on the planet has to participate in the experience of preserving the planetary body."[54] This is the time, according to Parrish-Harra, that the planet needs to extend particular devotion to the Cosmic Mother, the Divine Feminine Principle.

It is Parrish-Harra's understanding that humanity needs the help of rituals in this work of saving the planet. These must be rituals of "great love and spiritual power which can be easily used with large numbers of people." They must have the capacity to stabilize during the unrest caused by transformation. As an example of a ritual that meets all these requirements, Parrish-Harra offers the Aquarian Rosary as a vehicle for summoning the healing power of the Divine Feminine Principle. She suggests that the saying of the rosary is similar to mantra yoga in that both are designed "to create union (yoga) between levels of self: spirit and matter, or lesser self and high self."[55]

Parrish-Harra details the esoteric effects of chanting the rosary, its ability to pull together the right and left hemispheres of the brain, for example, and to open the human brain to revelation. But it is the rosary's capacity to summon the aid of the Divine Feminine for the individual and the planet that makes the ritual so powerful. "In performing the ritual of the rosary," says Parrish-Harra, "we are consciously seeking to heal our separation from the Divine Feminine that nurtures and protects. We are strengthening the relationship between humanity, nature, the planet and the Mother principle; and we are invoking from the great wholeness a positive memory of humanity in right-relationship to the All."[56]

Neither McLaughlin nor Parrish-Harra has much to say about the nature of woman. Those connections are meant to be implicit, perhaps, in their discussions of the healing, connecting powers of the Divine Feminine. It is in Diane Stein's book, *The Women's Book of Healing,* that one encounters in detail Theosophy's understanding of the complexities of human nature as they are related to women's nature and the ways in which women's nature, in turn, is related to the workings of the universe.

Stein's book is a call to women to reclaim their right to heal and be healed. In the spirit of Theosophy and of contemporary feminist spirituality, she looks back to ancient times when healing was in the hands of women who "respected the wholeness of body, emotions, mind and spirit, saw the goddess within all Be-ing, and treated their patients with respect and caring."[57] For Stein, healing—of the individual and of the planet—is women's work, and healing is a power that proceeds from woman's very nature and her ability to call upon the power of the Goddess-within. Women have the power to heal, according to Stein, and they have the right to be healed: "Women need to know that they deserve wellness, and that well-being is their natural, positive state."[58]

Stein contrasts women's healing with allopathic medicine, that which is practiced by established medicine. Allopathic healing, she says, treats only the body, and "there is little or no re-cognition of woman (or man) as a unified combination of body, emotions, mind and spirit, or that treating dis-ease means treating the whole person on all of her levels."[59] Allopathic healing is in the hands of professionals. Psychic healing can be done by anyone, a secret that Stein claims has been kept by practitioners of allopathic medicine.

Stein sees women's reclaiming of health as a rediscovering of the goodness of woman's body and a respect for its functions. These functions—menstruation, sexuality, birth, breast-feeding, menopause—are not disgusting or base; they are reflections of the power of goddess-creation. "Women contain the powers of life and healing in their own goddess-Being," says Stein. "Women *are* this healing power, and women and men once knew it planetwide in the ancient goddess matriarchies of early civilizations."[60]

Up to this point Stein's interpretation of woman's body and its healing power coincides in great part with that of many other women who are engaged in formulating feminist spiritualities. But Stein draws upon the Theosophical understanding of the body for her healing techniques, and, like McLaughlin, holds that the seen conceals within itself the unseen. Healing, then, must involve a connecting of the seen with the unseen.

What is "seen" in Theosophy is the physical body. What remains "unseen" are the emotional, mental, and spiritual aspects of the human person. A woman's aura made up of layers of energy surrounds her dense physical body. The first layer, the etheric double, is a key to well-being: "Health begins here, is mirrored here, and this is where dis-ease manifests first before it reaches the physical flesh."[61] In the next three layers, the emotional, mental, and spiritual bodies with their various auras, are a woman's connection with feeling, with rational and intuitive thought, and the goddess and the universe. Any healing system that ignores these realities, says Stein, will fail to heal except in a fragmentary and temporary manner.

Women's healing cannot involve only medicine for the physical body. It makes use of visualization and meditation, psychic healing, the laying on of hands, crystals, and gemstones. All of these are designed to help the unseen layers of healing affect the physical body. These methods work, says Stein, "with free will, with the goddess and natural law, with the aura, the dense physical body and power-within to achieve cell-source healing in harmony with all the levels."[62]

Stein does not confine women's healing simply to restoring health to individuals. She assumes that healing has a much broader context and purpose. When women realize that they have the power to heal by going within, when they discover the power of the goddess at the core of their own being, she says, they will eventually turn outward. They will acquire the strength and the self-determination to broaden the arena in which they work, because "Attunement to the self leads to attunement with others, leads to attunement with the universe/goddess/Earth, and attunement means health and well-being."[63] Thus, in her insistence that women's healing is done "for the benefit of women and men, children, animals, and the planet alike"[64] Stein provides a refutation of Leadbeater's statement about woman's physical body and its capacity for wielding spiritual powers. Ironically, her refutation arises out of a radically different interpretation of the same occult worldview that undergirded Leadbeater's statement. At the end of the twentieth century women are more and more assertively claiming their roles as theologians—as shapers of a chosen tradition rather than simply recipients of it. As they do so, even so small a sampling of women's voices as can be found in this essay points to the emergence of some common themes in their work. There is apparent a growing preference for Goddess(es) rather than God; an emphasis on divine immanence rather than transcendence; affirmation of the body in addition to spirit as the source of both spiritual and earthly wisdom; descent as the prototypical spiritual journey rather than ascent; community and interconnectedness over—or at least in addition to—individualism; relationship as an organizational principle rather than hierarchy; self-knowledge or transformation as the worthy goal rather than perfection; sin as self-denigration rather than pride.

All of these themes must be qualified in terms of the ways they are manifested in particular traditions. To widen the banks of the theological mainstream of a tradition is necessarily to draw from its own stories, symbols, and rituals. Thus, each religion—in this case, Mormonism, Roman Catholicism, and Theosophy—is its own case. But the women in these traditions are participating, also, in the wider cultural phenomenon of the contemporary women's movement and its efforts to find the hidden voices of women of the past, to urge women of the present to speak out, and to point to a future in which an absence of women's voices is unimaginable.

NOTES

1. Gordon D. Kaufman, *Theology for a Nuclear Age* (Manchester, UK: Manchester University Press and The Westminster Press, 1985), 19.

2. Jan Shipps, "Foreword," *Sisters in Spirit: Mormon Women in Cultural and Historical Perspective,* ed. Maureen Ursenbach Beecher and Lavina Fielding Anderson (Urbana: University of Illinois Press, 1987), xii.

3. Elder Robert L. Backman, "Women and the Priesthood" in *Priesthood,* ed. Spencer W. Kimball et al. (Salt Lake City: Deseret Books, 1981), 152.

4. Ibid., 148.

5. Oscar W. McConkie, *She Shall Be Called Woman* (Salt Lake City: Bookcraft, 1979), 1.

6. Backman, "Women and the Priesthood," 149.

7. Ibid., 152.

8. Grethe Ballif Peterson, "Priesthood and Latter-day Saint Women: Eight Contemporary Definitions," in *Sisters in Spirit,* 260.

9. Ibid., 261.

10. Meg Wheatley-Pesci, "An Expanded Definition of Priesthood? Some Present and Future Consequences," *Dialogue* 18, no. 3 (Fall, 1985): 33.

11. Ibid., 41.

12. Linda P. Wilcox, "Mormon Motherhood: Official Images," in *Sisters in Spirit,* 141. See also Linda King Newell, "The Historical Relation of Mormon Women and Priesthood," *Dialogue* 18, no. 3 (Fall, 1985): 21–42.

13. Linda King Newell, "Gifts of the Spirit: Women's Share," in *Sisters in Spirit,* 125, 141.

14. Linda P. Wilcox, "The Mormon Concept of a Mother in Heaven," in *Sisters in Spirit,* 65. See also Catherine L. Albanese, "Mormonism and the Male-Female God: An Exploration in Active Mysticism," *Sunstone* 6, no. 2 (Mar.-Apr. 1981): 52–58.

15. Ibid., 67.

16. Ibid., 71.

17. Ibid., 73–74.

18. Jan Shipps, Foreword, *Sisters in Spirit,* xii. Italics Shipps's.

19. Mary Lythgoe Bradford, " 'They Also Serve' . . . (Who Only Sit and Write)," in *A Time To Weep, A Time To Sing,* ed. Mary Jo Meadow and Carole A. Rayburn (Minneapolis: Winston Press, 1985), 80, 92.

20. Mary Jo Weaver, *New Catholic Women: A Contemporary Challenge to Traditional Religious Authority* (San Francisco: Harper and Row, 1986), 114.

21. Ibid., 145. See chapter 5 in which Weaver outlines the theologies of these four women.

22. Christin Lore Weber, *Blessings: A WomanChrist Reflection on the Beatitudes* (San Francisco: Harper and Row, 1989), 198.

23. Fran Ferder, FSPA, *Emerging Wisdom,* (La Crosse, Wisconsin: Franciscan Sisters of Perpetual Adoration, 1990), 15.

24. Pythia Peay, "Making the Invisible Visible," in *Common Boundary* (Nov./Dec. 1990), 20. This article is an interview with Craighead.

25. Meinrad Craighead, *The Mother's Songs: Images of the Mother* (New York: Paulist Press, 1986), Introduction, n.p.

26. Ibid.

27. Ibid., 29.

28. Ibid., 65.

29. Meinrad Craighead, *The Litany of the Great River* (New York: Paulist Press, 1991), 9. Craighead's paintings appear as illustrations in the works of other feminist theologians, for example Miriam Therese Winter, *WomanWord: A Feminist Lectionary and Psalter, Women, Women of the New Testament* (New York: Crossroad, 1990).

30. Ibid., 53–54.

31. Christin Lore Weber, *WomanChrist: A New Vision of Feminist Spirituality* (San Francisco: Harper and Row, 1987), ix.

32. Christin Lore Weber, *Blessings,* 2.

33. Ibid., 37.

34. Sylvia Brinton Perera, *Descent to the Goddess: A Way of Initiation for Women* (Toronto: Inner City Books, 1981), 78.

35. For another version of the descent of Inanna as a model for woman's spiritual journey, see Starkhawk, *Truth or Dare: Encounters with Power, Authority, and Mystery* (San Francisco: Harper and Row, 1987).

36. Weber, *WomanChrist,* 25. Weber is by no means the only Roman Catholic woman who sees connections between goddess stories and Christian stories. In *Emerging Wisdom* Fran Ferder connects the voice of Wisdom with both Isis and Jesus: "I am ISIS, the goddess, whose tender words: 'Come to me, all you who labor and are burdened and I will give you rest,' were heard by Jesus, long after I first spoke them" (p. 25).

37. Ibid

38. Ibid., 43.

39. Ibid., 20.

40. Ibid., 152

41. Ibid., 156

42. Ibid., 162.

43. Christin Lore Weber,"Aspects of Womanhood," in *St. Joseph's House News* 4, no. 9 (Sept. 1990), 4. This newsletter is published by the staff of a shelter for battered women and their children in Minneapolis, Minnesota.

44. Ibid.

45. This is, perhaps, too simplified an assessment of the worldview of Hay, but her understanding of the nature of reality comes in part from the teachings of Religious Science. Although she treats the body, her metaphysical contention is that "thought" is the ultimate reality: illness is caused by thoughts and thoughts can be changed. For an elaboration, see Louise L. Hay, *You Can Heal Your Life* (Santa Monica, Calif.: Hay House, 1984).

46. The Liberal Catholic Church, founded in England in 1916, is independent of the Roman Catholic church. It describes itself as a ceremonial church that celebrates the seven sacraments of Roman Catholicism and interprets them from within an occult worldview; but it also understands itself as a noncreedal church that offers freedom from dogma. A small denomination, that does not ordain women, its provincial office in the United States is in Ojai, California. Theosophists were involved with the founding of the church and many Theosophists to this day are members, but there is no connection between the church and various Theosophical societies.

47. The Reverend C. W. Leadbeater, *The Science of the Sacraments* (Adyar, India: Theosophical Publishing House, 1920), 391.

48. See Mary Farrell Bednarowski, "Women in Occult America," in *The Occult in America: New Historical Perspectives,* ed. Howard Kerr and Charles L. Crow (Urbana: University of Illinois Press, 1983), 175–95.

49. Corinne McLaughlin, "The Mystery of the Veiled Mother of the World," *The Quest* 3, no. 2 (Summer, 1990): 56.

50. Ibid., 59–60.

51. Ibid., 62.

52. Ibid., 63.

53. Ibid.

54. Carol W. Parrish-Harra, *The Aquarian Rosary: Reviving the Art of Mantra Yoga* (Tahlequah, Okla.: Sparrow Hawk Press, 1988), xvii.

55. Ibid., 6

56. Ibid., 21.

57. Diane Stein, *The Women's Book of Healing* (St. Paul, Minn.: Llewellyn Publications, 1988) n.p.

58. Ibid., 102

59. Ibid., xxi-xxii.

60. Ibid., xvii.

61. Ibid., 3

62. Ibid., 6.

63. Ibid., xxiii

64. Ibid., n.p.

Contributors

MARY FARRELL BEDNAROWSKI is professor of religious studies at United Theological Seminary of the Twin Cities. She is the author of *American Religion: A Cultural Perspective* (Prentice Hall, 1984) and *New Religions and the Theological Imagination in America* (Indiana University Press, 1989) as well as articles on women and religion and theology and culture. Her work in progress is a book on women's religion in American culture.

ANN BRAUDE is associate professor of religion at Carleton College. She is author of *Radical Spirits: Spiritualism and Women's Rights in Nineteenth-Century America* (Beacon, 1989), and "The Jewish Woman's Encounter with American Culture" in vol. 1 and "Jewish Women in the Twentieth Century: Building a Life in America" in vol. 3 of *Women and Religion in America,* ed. Ruether and Keller (Harper and Row, 1981, 1986), as well as other articles on gender and ethnicity in American religion and culture.

DELL DECHANT is an ordained Unity minister serving as associate minister at Unity-Clearwater Church. He has an M.A. in religious studies from the University of South Florida. He teaches at the Unity-Progressive Theological Seminary and the University of South Florida. He is currently acting dean of the Unity-Progressive Theological Seminary. He has published *Unity and History* (Unity-Progressive Press, 1991), *Libertas et Veritas* (Unity-Progressive Press, 1990), and articles in *The Dictionary of Christianity in America* (InterVarsity Press, 1990), *The New Age Encyclopedia* (Gale, 1989), *American National Biography* (Oxford, forthcoming), and *The New Thought Quarterly,* and *The Quest.* He is currently editing a collection of interpretative essays, *Renaissance and Regeneration: New and Renewed Visions of the Unity Movement.*

CYNTHIA ELLER is the author of *Living in the Lap of the Goddess: The Feminist Spirituality Movement in America* (Crossroad, 1993), a sociological study of the feminist spirituality movement. She received her Ph.D. in religion and social ethics from the University of Southern California and spent two years at Yale Divinity School as a Henry R. Luce Postdoctoral Fellow.

ROBERT ELLWOOD is professor of religion at the University of Southern California, with a Ph.D. in the history of religions from the University of Chicago. He is author of several books, including *Alternative Altars: Unconventional and Eastern Spirituality in America* (University of Chicago Press, 1979), *Eastern Spirituality in America: Selected Readings* (Paulist, 1987), with coauthor Harry Partin, *Religious and Spiritual Groups in Modern America,* 2d ed. (Prentice Hall, 1988), and *Many Peoples, Many Faiths: An Introduction to the Religious Life of Human Kind,* 4th ed. (Prentice Hall, 1992).

DAVID C. ESTES is associate professor of English at Loyola University, New Orleans. His articles on literature and folklore have appeared in *Contemporary Literature, Cultural Perspectives on the American South, Southern Folklore,* and *Southern Quarterly.*

ELAINE J. LAWLESS is professor of English/folklore and women's studies at the University of Missouri. She holds an M.A. in English from the University of Illinois and a Ph.D. in folklore from Indiana University. In addition to numerous articles on women and religion, she is the author of three books: *God's Peculiar People: Women's Voices and Folk Tradition in a Pentecostal Church* (University of Kentucky, 1988); *Handmaidens of the Lord: Pentecostal Women Preachers and Traditional Religion* (University of Pennsylvania, 1988); and *Holy Women, Wholly Women: Sharing Ministries through Life Stories and Reciprocal Ethnography,* (University of Pennsylvania Press and Publications of the American Folklore Society, 1993).

J. GORDON MELTON is director of the Institute for the Study of American Religion and is research specialist with the department of religious studies, University of California, Santa Barbara. He is the author of *The Encyclopedia of American Religions* (Gale), editor of *Islam in North America: A Sourcebook* (Garland, 1992), coauthor of *Encyclopedia of African-American Religion* (Garland, 1992), among many other publications.

MARJORIE PROCTER–SMITH is associate professor of worship at Perkins School of Theology, Southern Methodist University. She is author of *Women in Shaker Community and Worship* (Edwin Mellen Press, 1985), and *In Her Own Rite: Constructing Feminist Liturgical Traditions* (Abingdon, 1990).

ROSEMARY RADFORD RUETHER is the Georgia Harkness Professor of Applied Theology at the Garrett-Evangelical Theological Seminary in Evanston, Illinois. She received her Master's and Doctoral degrees at the Claremont Graduate School in Claremont, California. She is the author or editor of twenty-three books and numerous articles on religion and social justice issues. Her most recent book, published by Harper San Francisco in 1992, is *Gaia and God: An Ecofeminist Theology of Earth-healing.*

CATHERINE WESSINGER is associate professor of the history of religions and women's studies at Loyola University, New Orleans. She holds a Ph.D. in the history of religions from the University of Iowa. She is the author of *Annie Besant and Progressive Messianism* (Edwin Mellen Press, 1988) and is currently editing a book on women's ministries and leadership in American denominations and writing a textbook on women in religions and cultures.

Index

Abbenhouse, Dorothy, 80
Abolition, 89
Acts 2:17–18, 16–17*n10*, 90
Adam: in Mormonism, 212; in Unity, 109
Adams, Bishop Inez, 152, 157, 158, 159, 160, 161, 162, 163, 164, 165, 168
Affirmations, 103
Age of Aquarius, 80
Ahlstrom, Sydney, 75, 85*n12*
All India Women's Conference, 80
American Indians: as spirit guides, 154
American Woman's Suffrage Association, 91–92
Ananda, 137
Ancient Wisdom, 70, 73, 74, 76, 79, 82
Anderson, Mother Leafy, 150, 151, 152, 153, 154, 156, 157–60, 161, 166, 168, 170*n19*
Animal magnetism, 63, 64
Animism: in metaphysical movement, 8
Anthony, Susan B., 59
Anticlericalism, 13, 65; in Spiritualism, 59; in Women-Church, 196
Antimaterialism, 188–89, 190–91
Aphrodite, 225
Apple: meaning of, in Women-Church, 208
Aquarian Rosary, 226
Arcane School, 80
Artemis, 182
Ashram, 126, 127, 133–34, 143*n34*
Asian Women's Resource Center for Culture and Theology, 200
Assemblies of God, 41, 44
Association of Unity Churches (AUC), 96, 104, 105, 106, 113, 114–20

Aura: Theosophy, 228
Authoritarianism, 135, 139, 140, 146*n62*

Backman, Elder Robert L., 213
Baer, Hans, 149, 150, 153
Bailey, Alice, 80, 97, 225
Baptism: Pentecostal, 41, 44
Baptists: black, 151, 152
Base community, 197
Bassett, Peggy, 96
Baum, Frank L., 74, 84*n10*
Beaty, Louise C., 112
Beauchesne, Richard, 16*n9*
Beck, Joko, 139
Bednarowski, Mary Farrell: characteristics supporting women's religious leadership, 2–4, 7, 9, 10–15, 24, 34, 50–51, 55–56, 66*n3*, 81–82, 120–21, 151, 187–88, 190, 196, 200, 210
Besant, Annie, 68, 76–78, 79, 80–81, 82, 83, 86*n24*, 188
Bhaktivedanta, 135
Biblical passages: and women, 16*n10*
Bingham, Kate, 95
Birth control, 189, 191
Bishops: Roman Catholic, 202
Black Hawk, 160
Blackwell, Antoinette Brown. *See* Brown, Antoinette
Blavatsky, Helena P., 1, 9, 68, 69, 70, 71, 72–75, 76, 77, 79, 84*n9*, 91, 97, 212, 224, 225
Blavatsky, Nikifor, 73, 84*n8*
Body: affirming, 14; in Christian Science, 60,